Frederick Denison Maurice

The Doctrine of Sacrifice Deduced from the Scriptures

A Series of Sermons

Frederick Denison Maurice

The Doctrine of Sacrifice Deduced from the Scriptures
A Series of Sermons

ISBN/EAN: 9783744742771

Printed in Europe, USA, Canada, Australia, Japan

Cover: Foto ©Lupo / pixelio.de

More available books at **www.hansebooks.com**

THE

DOCTRINE OF SACRIFICE

DEDUCED FROM THE SCRIPTURES

A Series of Sermons

BY

FREDERICK DENISON MAURICE, M.A.

CHAPLAIN OF LINCOLN'S INN

London

MACMILLAN AND CO.

AND NEW YORK

1893

First Edition, printed 1854.
Second Edition, printed 1879.
Reprinted, 1893.

Dedicatory Letter.

TO THE MEMBERS
OF THE
YOUNG MEN'S CHRISTIAN ASSOCIATION.

My Friends,

According to the maxims of the world, I have no right to address you so familiarly; for as individuals and as a body you are unknown to me; and till last February, I suspect that a majority of you had scarcely heard of my existence. The information which you received about me, at that time, is not likely to make you desirous of my friendship, probably will make you zealous to repudiate it. Nevertheless, I thrust it upon you in this rude manner, because all that I have been told of you, and of the motives which have led you to form yourselves into an association, inspires me with an esteem and affection which the absence of any corresponding feelings on your side cannot extinguish.

Though you may think me bold in speaking of you as friends, you will not, I think, dispute my claim to be heard by you in my own defence. An eminent divine of the Free Church of Scotland selected you, last winter, as persons who were fit judges of a book which I had published a few months before. To all intents and purposes, he impanelled you as a jury to try my treasons against a higher authority than that of our Sovereign Lady the Queen. By accepting him as a lecturer on the subject of my Essays, you took upon yourselves the office which he had assigned you. I need not tell you, that I had no power of challenging my jurors. Each one of them was to decide in his own conscience whether he was in possession of such evidence as would enable him to pronounce a just verdict. I hope none of you think that the charges were less serious, than those which are brought against any criminal at the Old Bailey. To me they seem immeasurably more serious. They affect my moral character infinitely more than a charge of some fraudulent transaction in relation to money could affect it. I was distinctly accused before you, of professing to believe, of professing to preach, that which in fact I deny. Ask yourselves what guilt is comparable to this? If you refuse to hold intercourse with a man who has committed a forgery,—even with one who has stolen a loaf, perhaps, under the strong temptation of poverty,—how must you regard a man who has been for years lying to God, and forging His name in support of the frauds which he has practised upon His creatures? This charge, and nothing less than this, was brought against me by Dr. Candlish. You were constituted as judges to examine it. I venture to think, that as Englishmen, you will hold, that I am entitled to tell you why I say 'not guilty' to it.

But this is not my chief reason for writing to you. I do not consider you my judges, though Dr. Candlish does. I can leave my own cause and my own character to that day in which he says I do not believe. The craving to justify one's self is, I know well, a very strong one. How strongly it has been working in me for the last six months, I might find it difficult to explain to you. But I have resisted it, for many reasons. I have felt that it was very dangerous, to mix up petty questions concerning myself with the solemnest and deepest questions concerning man and God. I have been reminded by Dr. Candlish's book of the infirmities of my temper. He has discovered in almost every line I have written, some proof of personal irritation. He has even supposed that I quoted the awful words which our Lord spoke to the Pharisees, respecting the damnation of hell, for the sake of gratifying my spite against some who had found fault with me. My conscience acquits me of that enormous wickedness. If I had committed it, I ought never to write another line, nor to speak another word. But I must have given some excuse for so dreadful a suspicion, or it is hardly possible that a man of ordinary candour would have indulged it. I felt, therefore, that I was bound to be on my guard, and rather to omit any opportunity of self-defence, to let any persons who would suppose that I admitted the accusations against me to be true, than incur the risk of mixing private passions with what I believe to be the cause of God, and of His Church. And most people, I should suppose, at this time have some intimations, that their tongues and their pens were given them for other purposes than those of controversy; and that they had better let judgment go by default against them, than disturb with miserable personal apologies the sorrows of mourners, and the words of Christian consolation. I have, therefore, allowed you to fancy till now, that I have cared nothing for your good opinion, or that I was totally unable to refute the charges which may have robbed me of it. And I should not have broken silence now, if an opportunity had not been afforded me of showing you, without reference to anything that has been said by Dr. Candlish, what kind of teaching I give my ordinary hearers on the subject upon which I am accused of being most heretical; and if I did not think that I might use that opportunity, to remove impressions from your minds, which will hinder you from understanding, not me, but your own selves and the word of God.

I believe that it will be the fairest and best course, not to go through Dr. Candlish's lecture (for how could I hope to do justice to so elaborate a discourse in a short preface ?), but to select some one passage of it, in which he has condensed his complaints against me,—and which, at the same time, touches upon topics of so general a character, that I may make the vindication of myself entirely subordinate to the purpose which I have in view—that of explaining to you the principles, which in other books, and especially in this book, I have been endeavouring to assert. I take the following, because it contains some most true assertions respecting me ; because it is evidently intended to wound my vanity more severely than any other in the lecture ; and because it sums up the imputations to which I have already referred, those imputations which, if they are well founded, ought to exclude me from my function as a Clergyman—from the Church of Christ—from the society of all honest men.

"I had intended to trace slightly the author's views, as developed in this book, to some of the sources whence they might have been, if they have not been derived. There is little or nothing that is really new in them. Mr. Maurice cannot be called an original writer as to matter, though his manner and style are fresh. He is not probably much acquainted with the literature of Protestant theology. If he is, it is the worse for his candour, for in that case his misrepresentations are inexcusable. He writes as if the field had never been gone over before, and as if he was making discoveries; never indicating any knowledge of the fact, that all his reasonings against the current orthodox and evangelical doctrines have been anticipated and answered over and over again. I might show the coincidence of his views, as to the inward light, with those of Barclay and the Friends; the extent of his obligation to Edward Irving and Thomas Erskine for his ideas of the Incarnation and Atonement; and the agreement of his opinions on all the leading points of Christian doctrine, with those of ordinary Unitarians: with these two exceptions, that under whatever limitations, they admit a resurrection, a judgment, and a future state of rewards and punishments; whilst on the other hand, with whatever explanations, he asserts strongly the doctrine of the Trinity."—Pp. 483, 484.

How thankfully do I accept the testimony of Dr. Candlish to the fact, 'that there is little or nothing that is really new' in my writings! It is the point which I have been labouring to establish in every one of them. If he can point out even 'the little' which he has found new in any part of them, I shall at once begin to suspect it; nay, I shall cheerfully give it up to his mercy. I have affirmed continually—I have affirmed again in this book,—that I have discovered nothing; that what I am saying is to be found in every creed of the Catholic Church; in the Prayers and Articles of the Church to which I belong; most emphatically in the Bible, from which they derive their authority, and to which they refer as their ultimate standard. But while I utterly disclaim *novelty*, which, I suppose, is what Dr. Candlish means by *originality in matter*, there is a sense in which I earnestly desire to be original myself; and in which I desire that you, and all the young men of England, should be so likewise. An original man is not one who invents —not one who refuses to learn from others. I say, boldly, no original man ever did that. But he is one who does not take words and phrases at second hand; who asks what they signify; who does not feel that they are his, or that he has a right to use them till he knows what they signify. The original man is fighting for his life; he must know whether he has any ground to stand upon; he must ask God to tell him, because man cannot. I have met some of these original men in all classes of society, in all religious schools. Wherever I have found them, I have felt that I could not copy them, but that I could sympathise with them; that they did me good when I differed with them most; that they instructed me, though they might scarcely know their letters. All men are capable of this originality; it is not a special talent; it comes from that earnestness of purpose, that longing to find what is not dependent on ourselves or on human caprice which, I believe, is awakened in us by the Spirit of Truth, and by Him only. If I have not this originality, may that Spirit impart it to me, for to be without it is death. If I have it in any measure, I shall not make anyone who receives any influence from me the retailer of my opinions; I shall help to put him in a position in which he can unfold my imperfect perceptions and correct my errors—because I shall point him to the true Teacher of him, of me, of every man.

I am, therefore, most anxious to confess what I owe not only to the Creeds and to the Bible, but to those men of different communions—from every one from whom Dr. Candlish thinks he has caught me robbing. I cannot give him credit for any particular sagacity in this instance. The robbery was done in broad daylight. I confessed it instantly. Seventeen years ago I declared in print, how thoroughly I sympathised with Barclay and the Friends, in what is called their main doctrine. All that Dr. Candlish knows of my debts—ever increasing debts—to my honoured friend, Mr. Erskine, he learnt from a dedication which I prefixed to a volume of Sermons on the Prophets and Kings of the Old Testament. He did not guess from my Theological Essays that I was under obligations to the Unitarians; I said so in plain terms, and that I felt bound to return the obligation, by showing them how dear those doctrines were to me which they rejected. He has, however, mentioned one name, which I have never uttered, publicly nor privately, without honour and admiration, but to which I have not done the same justice in print as to the others. I will repair the fault by putting that name first in my confessions here. I do it the more gladly, because it is the name of a Scotchman and a Presbyterian.

(1.) I had no personal intercourse with the late Mr. Irving, and I heard him preach very rarely. Though I know a few members of that Church, which is, wrongly, connected with his name, and respect them highly, I have no special sympathy with their modes of thinking and acting. But I learnt lessons from some of Mr. Irving's books, which I hope I shall never forget. I recollect with gratitude portions of his sermons on the Incarnation of our Lord ;—by some portions of them I was grieved. What peculiar views he had on the subject of the Atonement I do not know; if he had any, I never entered into them. What he taught me was to reverence the education he had received in the John Knox school, and the fathers who had imparted it to him. I had not that reverence before ; I had shrunk from what I believed to be hard, narrow, and inhuman. He showed me, that the old patriarchs of Scotland had a belief in GOD, as a Living Being, as the Ruler of the earth, as the Standard of Righteousness, as the Orderer of men's acts in all the common relations of life, which was the most precious of all possessions to them, the want of which is the cause of all feebleness and immorality in our age. He made me perceive how entirely different their *godliness* was from the *sentimental religion*, which consists in feelings about God ; or from the *systematic religion,* which consists of notions about Him. He led me to see, that unless we begin from God —unless we start from the conviction, that *the thing which is done upon earth He doeth it Himself*—the belief in Christ will pass into a belief in a mere Saviour for us—the belief in a Spirit will be at first a mere recognition of certain influences acting upon us, and will evaporate at last into Pantheism.

I perceived, clearly, that Mr. Irving had not acquired *these* convictions in England. He acknowledged—brave man as he was—his obligations to Coleridge as a teacher, at a time when such an acknowledgment was perilous, almost fatal, to his reputation with the circle which then paid homage to the young Scotch preacher. It is no courage for any man—above all, it would be no courage in me who have no reputation to lose, who cannot be in worse plight with the religious world than I am—to express the utmost depth of gratitude to that benefactor; still I am sure that what Irving owed to him, though it was *theological* lore in the strictest sense, was not this *theocratic* faith. That he brought with him; it was part of his covenanting, Calvinistical culture. As such I paid it, and still pay it, the profoundest homage. I have learnt since to honour the teaching of the English Church. I have to bless God for teaching which belongs to what calls itself the Catholic Church. But I have found nothing in either to supersede this. I have found nothing in either which is good without this. I reverence it as Protestant theology in the highest, purest meaning of that word, and as the very ground of all theology.

Dr. Candlish has told you, that I am 'not 'probably much acquainted with the literature of 'Protestant theology; if I am, it is the worse for 'my candour; for, in that case, my misrepre- 'sentations are inexcusable.' I am much less acquainted with the literature of Protestant theology, and with all literature and all theology, than I wish to be; if Dr. Candlish will put me in the way of improving my knowledge, I shall be most thankful to him. But when he spoke of my misrepresentations of this theology, he was bound, I think, to point them out. I have gone, at some length, in my 'Kingdom of Christ,' into a consideration of the services which Luther, Calvin, and Zuinglius, have rendered to the Church and to mankind. If he finds there any disposition to undervalue the work which they accomplished, or the principles which they brought to light, I hope he will expose me. He *will* find there very deep regrets expressed,—in which, I suppose, every Protestant shares,—that they were not able to agree among themselves; very deep regrets for the divisions which have been perpetuated and multiplied by men who have inherited from them the negative opinions that kept them apart, but who have—if we believe the statements of the different reformers, such as Spener and Francke, that have risen up in their communities—speedily forgotten the truths to which these opinions attached themselves. I have endeavoured to trace the causes of these failures, and to remove the excessive despair which they commonly occasion to the student of history, by showing that their *principles*, though buried under notions and negations, are still vital, and will rise again, and will become united whenever Protestants shall once more feel that they have a Gospel from God, and a Gospel concerning God,—not *a scheme of religion* to be set up against *the scheme of religion* which Romanists maintain. The Protestant of old, as I conceive, shook the vast fabric of Romish despotism, because he proclaimed that God Himself was justifying, and calling, and redeeming His creatures; because he threw down the ladder by which men hoped to climb to heaven with the proclamation,—asserted in every Romish creed, denied in a thousand Romish practices,—that heaven had stooped to earth. Protestants are now trembling, and with good reason, lest that despotism should utterly vanquish them; because they have a number of theories about justification, election, redemption; because they have *their* ladders which are much more awkwardly constructed, and are made of more flexible materials than the Romish: because they deny in fact what they declare in words,— that God has reconciled the world to Himself. I thank Mr. Irving for showing me that this must needs be; that if Protestantism is only a religious machinery, it must be a very bad religious machinery; that if it assumes its higher, diviner right, it will be stronger than ever it was—just because it cannot stand alone, but will demand a humanity as wide as its theology, and grounded upon that.

(2.) Mr. Irving did not, however, show where I might find this humanity, or how I might connect it with God. He *did* make me feel, by his own—commonly, desperate and abortive—attempts to bridge over the chasm, that there was something wanting in the teachers of his country. By observing the incapacity of the great Genevan and German theologians, from whom they had learnt, to establish peace among themselves, I was led to perceive more clearly where, and what this deficiency was. God was the absolutely good and righteous Will. To proclaim Him as the source of all good and righteousness to men, as the only mover of their wills to good, was to preach the Gospel, the doctrines of grace. But how had this good and righteous Will manifested itself as such? How had it proved its might against that which opposed it? I found most various answers to these questions, given by those who were called orthodox and evangelical divines. They were perpetually engaged in answering objections to their doctrines. As Dr. Candlish says, with melancholy truth—though it

A*

is a truth of which he proclaims me to be ignorant—they were 'answering these objections over and over again.' That seemed to be especially their function; not to preach a Gospel or good news to men, but to answer 'over and over again' the doubts and difficulties that arose in human hearts respecting their views of the character of God and of His relation to His creatures. The doubts and difficulties were not satisfied; they were not even quelled. And of what kind were they? They were doubts whether what was preached was a Gospel at all, whether it was not a message of curses rather than blessings; they were difficulties whether God's righteousness was asserted in *this* Gospel, whether it was not utterly denied, whether He was not represented as doing acts which He forbad men to do, as having feelings, which men, according to Christ's teaching, ought not to have. These mighty questions were at issue. Dr. Candlish says, they have been answered 'over and over again.' If they had been answered once, it would have been enough. That is what men demand; that is the demand which must be met. You divines can justify God 'over and over again;' but has He, as your fathers said, justified Himself? Has He made His own righteousness clear? Has He removed the blackness and darkness which are over it? I do confess my obligations to that other Scotchman of whom Dr. Candlish has spoken, and to his friend Mr. Campbell, for making me see, as I had never seen before, that the death of Christ was the answer, given once in the end of the world, to that demand; that in it God did fully manifest His own character; that when a man accepts that death as the revelation of God, he owns Him as altogether righteous, as altogether hating sin; sees that His will is that all should be saved from sin; sees that when righteousness and evil were brought into the most tremendous of all conflicts, righteousness prevailed, and evil was discomfited.

(3.) But it is evident from Mr. Erskine's book on Election, that he has perceived more to be involved in this belief than he, perhaps, at first, was aware of. 'God,' it is said, 'was in Christ reconciling the world to Himself.' 'It pleased God,' says St. Paul, 'to reveal His Son *in me*, that I might preach Him among the Gentiles.' Was man, then, according to his original constitution related to Christ? Was the reconciliation of the world to God, the restoration of it to its proper condition in the well-beloved Son? Was that Son really in Saul of Tarsus, and did he only become Paul the converted when that Son was *revealed* in him? Could he preach to the Gentiles, who were bowing to gods of wood and stone, Christ is in you? So, 'Barclay and the Friends' had said. It was very shocking to agree with Barclay and the Friends; but I saw no help for it. They said what I found St. Paul and St. John saying. They said what Philo the Jew, and a number of the Christian fathers had perceived that all the prophets of the Old Testament were saying; what they perceived was implied in the true words and acts of every heathen. They said what I found enabled me to read the Bible with open eyes; to accept its words literally; to feel their connexion with each other. They said what enabled me to understand the contradictions in myself; to feel how the light had always struggled with the darkness; how the darkness had tried to comprehend it and could not. They said what enabled me, when I grasped it and believed it, to feel that I was in union with every man, however he might differ from me; and that I had nothing good in me but what belongs equally to him. They said what cleared up to me difficulties in the Evangelical divines, and showed me the deep foundation of those doctrines which the early Quakers scorned; for the sake of which some of the latter were disposed to abandon the teaching of their ancestors. What they said discovered to me the spiritual, eternal ground of those sacraments which the Quakers cast aside as material and earthly. It could not signify whether Barclay the Quaker, or Philo the Jew, or Socrates the Heathen, had had apprehensions of this truth; if it were a truth, God had given it to them, and I could ask Him to give me strength to hold it fast, and to declare it to my fellows.

(4.) In doing so, words which I had always known, but which had not the same traditional hold upon me as upon many of my countrymen, presented themselves to me, with a power which I had never dreamed was in them. I mean the words of our Articles, of our Catechism, of our Prayers. I was conscious of very radical differences between us and the Scotch people, for whom I had begun to feel so much respect; I had felt that there had been, on the whole, a larger and freer humanity in this country than in theirs, with probably a greater tendency to secularity and State churchmanship. I had been taught that Scotchmen were less bound by forms than we were;—and I thought that they had maintained a very brave fight against our prelacy, when Charles and Laud would have forced it on them. I tell you this, that you may not fancy I had any strong prejudices which inclined me to see a meaning in our services that was not in them. But when I began to study the Articles, for the purpose of discovering their theological method, I perceived one characteristic contrast between them and the Confession that was drawn up by Knox for the Kirk; a contrast which, it seemed to me, had been unaccountably overlooked. The second article in Knox's Confession is on the Fall of Man. The second article in our Thirty-nine is on Christ the God-Man. Not till the ninth article, do we speak of the Fall; and then not historically, as if it explained the condition of mankind, but morally, as accounting for 'an infection and corruption of nature which exists in every man of the progeny of Adam, even in the regenerate.' The importance of this diversity could scarcely be overrated. I was sure that it could not be confined to a learned and formal exposition of doctrine; I was sure there must be some practical and general expression of it. That expression was not far to seek. The Catechism, which we teach to all children who have been baptized, tells them that they are members of Christ, children of God, inheritors of the kingdom of Heaven. The Prayers framed for all the motley body which frequents our Churches, assume that all may call upon God as a reconciled Father. Here was the article translated into life. Human beings were treated as redeemed,—not in consequence of any act they had done, of any faith they had exercised; their faith was to be grounded on a foregone conclusion; their acts were to be the fruits of a state they already possessed.

The more I became acquainted with the parties in the English Church, the more I felt the necessity of standing upon this principle, that *Christ is in every man*, if I was to use our formularies in the plain literal sense. I found that literal sense evaded or denied by some of the most devout men among us,—because they could not reconcile it with their strong conviction, derived from the express assertions of

Scripture, that in us, that is in our flesh, dwelleth
no good thing; with their equally strong and
reasonable conviction, that we cannot be made
spiritual by a few drops of water, or by certain
words acting as a charm. I found other excellent men as zealous for the literal sense of the
words,—because they had believed, also on the
testimony of Scripture, that God has called us in
Christ to be sons, in a sense in which men did
not and could not claim that title under the
earlier dispensation. I had no dream that I
could reconcile these parties. I knew from
history and a little experience, that I should be
denounced as a silly coxcomb by both, if I made
the experiment. But for myself here was the
reconciliation. I needed it for my own life,
whether others saw any sense in it or not. I felt
that it enabled me to love and learn from the
Prayers; which, if I adopted either of the
opposing hypotheses, would have tormented me
continually, and have forced me at once to become a Protestant Dissenter, or a Romanist.
Whereas while I clung to it, these Prayers,
instead of separating me from either of the
classes which repudiate and despise us, gave me
the power, if I would avail myself of it, of claiming unity and fellowship with both. I could feel
the Protestant Dissenter had done a good work,
in *asserting* Protestantism to have a positive
worth of its own, distinct from our Anglicanism,
—though it seemed to me that he had failed to

realize its worth. I could see that the Romanist was bearing witness for an Universal Church, governed and filled by the Spirit of God,—though I thought that he had enfeebled and destroyed that witness, had changed his Church into a sect, had made that which was spiritual, mundane and material, by representing the belief in God as dependent on the belief in the Church, and not the belief in the Church as dependent (according to the Creed) on the belief in God.

(5.) I have now given you a glimpse, my friends, into a part of the history of my own 'Christian instruction.' I have shown you how a foolish young man was led by his folly to seek for a wisdom, which the arguments that have been repeated 'over and over again' by Dr. Candlish and his friends could not supply. And now I come to that part of his accusation which concerns the Unitarians. I will repeat his words, that there may be no mistake about them. 'I 'might show . . . the agreement of his opinions 'on all the leading points of Christian doctrine 'with those of ordinary Unitarians: with these 'two exceptions, that under whatever limitations, 'they admit a resurrection, a judgment, and a 'future state of rewards and punishments; whilst 'on the other hand, with whatever explanations, 'he asserts strongly the doctrine of the Trinity.' That is to say, Dr. Candlish told you (the 3,000 in Exeter Hall, who knew next to nothing about me but what he chose to tell you), that he could show that I, being under the most solemn pledge when I took orders to teach doctrines which the Unitarians reject, and having renewed, year by year, and day by day, my protestation of adherence to these doctrines, am, nevertheless, in agreement with those who say they are false; with these exceptions, that they admit, under some modification, a resurrection and a judgment, —whereas I, who repeat daily the words, 'I 'believe that Jesus Christ shall come again to 'judge the quick and dead; I believe in the 'resurrection of the body,' admit them under no modification whatever. This is literally the statement which he made to you, and which he deliberately printed, after he had made it. And it is respecting that statement that I affirmed before, and I affirm now again. It is an immeasurably more horrible libel,—more destructive of my moral character,—than if he had said, that on a certain day, I committed a forgery on the Bank of England, or that I had, in some court of justice, been guilty of a wilful and corrupt perjury. That is my fixed, considerate opinion. I shall be grieved, if you who are, as I trust, honest men, do not share it with me. I shall fear that your moral standard is not what the standard of Christian young men ought to be. I shall begin to think, that you judge of the magnitude of crimes by the amount of the external and visible penalties to which they subject those who commit them. I shall suspect that you have fallen into that incredulity respecting a day in which the secrets of all hearts shall be made known, and acts seen as they really are, which Dr. Candlish attributes to me.

I must do Dr. Candlish the justice to say, that he does wish that I might be brought before another tribunal than yours. The main object, I suspect, of his coming to England was, not to arraign an individual whom he knew to be insignificant, but to arraign the English Church for not treating me as his Church would have treated me, if I had belonged to it. He explained to you how, if I had been subject to that jurisdiction, I should have been convened, not before a college tribunal for corrupting the minds of young men about the one point of everlasting punishment, but before an ecclesiastical tribunal for my whole scheme of doctrine, that I might show cause why I should not be silenced as a Minister, and excommunicated from the body of the faithful. I am perfectly aware that I should have experienced that difference of treatment if my lot had been cast among Presbyterians, or among English Dissenters. And if that difference had involved a more full and thorough examination into all my words and acts,—if it had led to a trial according to the evidence, and to a decision such as would be given in Westminster Hall, or in the Court of Session upon any ordinary case, between man and man, or between the Queen and her subjects,—no one could have rejoiced more than I should have done. But Dr. Candlish must permit me to doubt, whether I or any man brought before one of *his* tribunals would have experienced this kind of justice. I must suppose that he is a fair, an advantageous, specimen of the temper which would prevail in them. And I do say, that I should use the old formula, *God give thee a good deliverance,* with a very solemn and a very melancholy feeling to any accused man having a righteous cause, who had this representative of the Scotch Free Church to conduct his trial, and to pronounce his judgment. For I cannot pretend to regard that man as having in him the conditions of a *righteous* judge—(I ask for no mercy or courtesy) who took advantage of a moment when he knew that I was under a stigma from a learned body in my own country, and that the religious press of Great Britain was almost without exception[1] denouncing

[1] I am bound to name the only exceptions which I know; and I do it with the greatest pleasure, for reasons which will be immediately apparent. The *Nonconformist* newspaper had every reason to dislike me, as one who had defended publicly, not only the formularies of my Church, but the union of Church and State. The writers in it seized the moment when they might have had a triumph over me, to treat me with peculiar consideration and kindness. The *Guardian* newspaper had generally expressed for me and my writings suspicion and aversion. Instead of manifesting these feelings more strongly, when I lost my respectability with the class for which it was written, and which it represents, that was the time in which it showed me an indulgence and courtesy which was the more honourable and grateful, because the Editor thoroughly disapproved of my opinions, and approved of my expulsion. Instances of generosity so rare—as far as I know, so unprecedented—in the history of religious periodicals, ought to be recorded.

me, to appeal to your passions and your ignorance, and to the passions and ignorance of the clergymen and Dissenting ministers who were countenancing him on the platform of Exeter Hall, in support of a charge which I solemnly declare (and I call upon the authorities of the College which has condemned me, upon the Bishops of my Church who suspect me, upon all who have impugned my preaching and my manner of life, and who personally dislike me,— to say if they know, to examine if they do not know, whether I am speaking truly or falsely), is belied by all that I have written or preached, by every line of the book upon which he professed to rest it.

Did I not then say, in that book, that I had learnt much from Unitarians, and that what I had learnt from them were truths—essential truths—the very staff of my being? Have I not confessed as much in this Letter? Most assuredly. I said there—I say here—that just as I accepted the positive teaching of Mr. Irving, and of his Calvinistical Scotch forefathers, respecting God and His righteous government, and His war against evil, and did *not* accept that negative teaching which seemed to me to weaken and darken His righteousness, to contract His power, to make His war with evil ineffectual;— just as I accepted the positive teaching of Barclay and the Friends, respecting the Inward Light, and rejected that negative teaching which made the manifestation of this Light in the acts of the Son of God on earth and in heaven, of such small significance;—just so I testified the most entire and cordial sympathy with the declaration of the Unitarians, that God is pure and absolute Love—that God is a Father; and therefore expressed the most thorough dissent from *every one* of those negative doctrines of theirs, which, as I affirmed, and in my book endeavoured to prove, turn the love of God into an unreality; into an indifference to evil; into a tolerance of the sins and miseries which are destroying God's creation. This language I used at the outset of that book which called forth Dr. Candlish's lecture; this language the whole of it is written to explain and illustrate. I have maintained that the Unitarian denial of the fact, that the Son of God—being of one substance with the Father, being the Eternal Word of God, the express Image of God, the only Lord, and Teacher, and Guide of Man—took human flesh and died man's death, and that by these acts God reconciled man to Himself, justifying us in Christ from all things from which we could not be justified by the Law of Moses, glorifying our Nature at the right hand of God, is, *ipso facto*, a denial that God loves man, and has interfered to rescue our race from the misery and curse, which all history shows that mankind has felt and groaned under, which each one of us groans under. I have said that the denial, by the old or 'ordinary' Unitarians (to use Dr. Candlish's word), of a Spirit, or personal Comforter, and the substitution for that denial, by some modern Unitarians, of a vague belief in Influences or a pervading universal Spirit, empties God of His fatherly character, and robs us of the privileges of sons. I have further contended with great— some of the orthodox journals seem to think with excessive—vehemence, that the denial of an Evil Spirit, of a Devil, confuses the facts of the universe, our own inmost experience, and the divine witness concerning God's victory over evil. It is in this way, members of the Young Men's Christian Instruction Society! that I have shown *the agreement of my opinions on all the leading points of Christian doctrine with the ordinary Unitarians.*

But there are exceptions. '*The Unitarians believe in a resurrection under certain modifications.*' There, says your lecturer, I am *not* in agreement with them. Will you listen for a moment to the ground upon which this charge stands? I found the ordinary Unitarian acknowledging, as Dr. Candlish says, *a* resurrection. The Resurrection of Christ from the dead seemed to him a proof, which he could not obtain elsewhere, that men are immortal, that they do not perish altogether, when the breath leaves their bodies. I rejoiced, I said, that any had that faith, because more was implied in it than those who held it knew. But I contended that this was not the meaning of Christ's Resurrection, as St. Paul sets it forth to us. According to him, *Christ died for our sins* and *rose again for our justification.* If He did rise to prove that we were immortal, He would have proved what the conscience of men confessed, with trembling and horror. To deliver us from that horror, to show us that God claimed us as His sons and daughters, was surely a nobler result of so transcendent a work. It was the foundation of a Gospel; the other could never be. But I contended as earnestly, that this emancipation of men's *spirits* was not the only or final effort of Christ's Resurrection. The redemption of the *body* was quite as much a part of His work for man; its redemption from death, the grave, and hell. What I believed that orthodox Christians, being in this respect 'in entire agreement with the ordinary Unitarians,' had done, was to exhaust the belief of the resurrection of the body of all its force, its meaning, its consolation, by substituting for the resurrection of the living powers and principles of which our bodies consist, the renovation of those elements which were the signs of its decay, its curse, its death. By substituting a gathering together, at some distant day, of *them*, for that gathering together of all Christ's members in Him, which the Apostle spoke of, they have destroyed the connexion between our resurrection and Christ's; they have justified the Romish worship of relics; they have made the reunion of the soul with the corruption, which we desire to be rid of, the very object of our hopes. Because I have asserted in this full manner the resurrection of both spirit and body as the fruit of the Resurrection of Christ, I am said to be far worse than the Unitarians, in that they *do*, with some modifications, admit a resurrection![1]

But they differ from me again, because 'under whatever modification, they admit a 'Judgment.' I acknowledge that they admit it, much in the same way, so far as I can gather from his lecture and his book on my Essays, as Dr. Candlish admits it. That is to say, they

---

[1] A writer in the *Christian Observer* for February, who has accused me of philosophical cowardice, of literary dishonesty, of preaching another Gospel than that which the Apostles preached,— in other words, has pronounced me ACCURSED of God and man (for who can doubt that he recollected himself, and intended his readers to recollect, the words in the first chapter of the Epistle to the Galatians?),—this writer has charged me with holding the doctrine of Hymenæus and Philetus, that the Resurrection has passed already, that is to say, the doctrine that there is no resurrection of the body, but only of the spirit; since if men *have* bodies which are not risen, and they are to rise, that resurrection must be future. May God help him to a clearer judgment, if he wrote down the charge believing it to be true! May God forgive him, if he threw it out in mere recklessness! How one rejoices that these prophets wear veils when they curse; so that we may merely regard them as representing the habit of mind in what is called the religious world, not as actual living men. Very probably, when the mask is off, they may not only be capable of ordinary humanity, but may follow some of the precepts of the Sermon on the Mount, which in their official character they are obliged to repudiate. I ought to say, that this writer has understood better than any I have met with, the real issue upon which the dispute between his school and me turns. It is the question whether the Fall or the Redemption is the ground on which humanity rests.

admit that God will hereafter pronounce a certain sentence upon good acts, and upon bad acts; the sentence upon one to be followed by certain rewards; the sentence on the other by certain punishments. There is to be a great trial day of the universe, they think, when these sentences will go forth, and when the rewards and the punishments will begin. I say, I apprehend this is both the old Unitarian idea of a judgment, and Dr. Candlish's. If it was not his, he would not have joined the word 'Judgment,' which occurs in almost every book and every page of the Bible, to the phrase 'Future state of rewards and punishments,' which is to be found in no book or page of Scripture, which belongs peculiarly to the age that all Evangelical writers have described as the Unitarian age — the eighteenth century. What I have tried is to recover for the Scriptural word the sense in which Scripture employs it; a sense immeasurably deeper and more comprehensive than any conveyed by the eighteenth century phrase; a sense often in direct moral contradiction to that. A judgment of the heart and reins, a judgment of the man, a judgment of the principles from which acts flow—this is what the Scripture teaches me to believe in here, to expect hereafter. Under the sense of this judgment—in the confidence that the Judge is always at the door—it desires that I should live every day and every hour; it teaches me also to look for a complete day of revelation, when everything that has been hidden shall come forth; when every creature shall be made manifest in God's sight. This is that day of Christ to which I desire that I myself, and that every one of you should look forward; and which I am sure will come to me and to you, because Christ is the King and Lord of our hearts now,—and because the word which He has spoken will judge us then. And, therefore, you are told that I do not admit a judgment, which the Unitarians, under whatever modification, do admit.

But Dr. Candlish makes a concession, which he felt to be singularly liberal. He acknowledges—reluctantly, but still he acknowledges—that I do, *with whatever explanations,* assert strongly the doctrine of the Trinity. This is the conclusion of the passage I am now commenting upon. I shall speak of it for a moment, since there is none which more curiously illustrates the mind of the author, or throws more light upon his theology. He regards the Christian faith as made up of a certain set of opinions—an opinion about the resurrection, an opinion about the judgment, an opinion about sacrifice, an opinion about the Trinity. He finds me wanting in the proper opinions about some of these subjects; he finds that I entertain something like what he has been used to hold about another, though with explanations which puzzle him. Shall I tell you what these explanations are? I affirm that when I believe in God the Father, in God the Son, and in God the Holy Ghost,— when I give glory to the Father, and to the Son, and to the Holy Ghost,—I am escaping from opinions. I believe that I am at the centre of God's revelations of Himself; I believe that He has led us out of our crude and miserable opinions about Him, to that Name which expresses what He is in Himself, what He is in relation to me, and to all the universe. And, therefore, believing in the Trinity,—or if you must put Him, in whom you live and move and have your being, at a greater distance from you—in the *doctrine* of the Trinity—I am at the point whence all other truths radiate, and to which they converge. I cannot separate the belief in Christ's incarnation, or death, or resurrection, or in the death and resurrection of myself, or any human being, from this Name. It is the only explanation of them all; it is that which reconciles and harmonizes all the brighter thoughts of God, that men have been cherishing in all ages; it is that which scatters their darkness, it is that which declares to them, that there is an Absolute Root of truth and good at the foundation of all things, —the Eternal Father; that there is a perfect Utterer and Revealer of that truth and good,—the Eternal Word, the only-begotten Son; that there is a Living Person, who carries out that truth and good, and makes it effectual and triumphant over rebellious wills,—the Spirit that proceedeth from the Father and the Son, and with the Father and the Son together, is worshipped and glorified for ever.

These 'explanations' of mine make Dr. Candlish feel that our faith in the Trinity, though it may be expressed in the same words, is substantially different. I am most unwilling to think so. I trust and believe that the 'explanations' of the doctrine, which I have read with exceeding pain in his book, do not express his inward mind; but only show what a hard, intellectual, logical crust has formed about it. If I had not that confidence, I should tremble indeed for Scotland. I will tell you why. Nothing has seemed to me more beautiful than the pictures of patriarchal life, which have been drawn from the homes of the old Scotch Calvinists; that life of which Burns, with all his hatred of some of their opinions and habits, has spoken as the very bulwark of his land. Now this domestic life, grounded first on the authority of the father, and the example of righteousness which he afforded to his children, had its ultimate root in the belief that God was the righteous Father, and that each head of a household was to present Him in that character through his own acts. But I have now heard a Scotch preacher, the very head of the body in Scotland which boasts that it preserves most of the old faith, actually complaining of that idea of the Trinity which makes it the ground of human relations; and insisting that the idea of Persons who perform certain acts of creation, redemption, sanctification (which, subject to the other, I accept also), is the only orthodox one. I am certain that every early Church father, every sixteenth century reformer, would have seen in this complaint that which threatens all orthodoxy and all faith. And I beseech you, young men desirous of Christian instruction, if you care to restore the old domestic morality, which is so fast deserting us,—if you care to leave to your sons a belief which they shall feel is really the ground of their life,—not to admit into your minds these dead, official explanations of a mystery, which God, in His Bible, has revealed to us through our actual relations; which He would have us accept as the great instrument of exalting and transfiguring them.

There is another particular, in which I have found Dr. Candlish strangely at variance—so far, at least, as his language goes—with the maxims of his forefathers. His objections to my mode of speaking against 'current' notions and habits, strike at the root, it appears to me, of the office of a minister of God. If he is not to be a reprover in the gate, he is nothing ; if he is to confine his reproofs to those with whom he is scarcely ever brought into contact—to Romanists, for instance—he is making his work an easy and popular one enough ; but he is not imitating those who denounced Popery in other ages, for they did it at the risk of their reputations and their lives. If he talks against the world—meaning thereby the gay or fashionable world—and sympathizes with what is called the religious world, he may again get great credit to himself, and contemplate his own position with much contentment; but he will find, by degrees, that the world which flatters him, and which he flatters, is that very one whereof St. James spoke, when he said, 'To be in friendship with it, is to be at enmity with God.' So the prophets of old found; so the apostles found; so the reformers found; so it was in the days when our Lord walked on earth. All had to contend with the religious world of their day—He most of all. What were the Scribes and the Pharisees but the most respected, and most exclusive, portion of that world?

This is a most serious question for a disciple of John Knox to consider. Dr. Candlish has appeared among you, not so much to denounce me, as to represent and advocate the 'current' religious notions of the day, which he supposes I have impugned. He has had no excuse for saying that I have denounced any individual teacher; if I had, I should have escaped many of his censures which turn upon my vague use of the words 'divines' and 'religious teachers.' I was aware of the vagueness. I was tempted to remove it, by quoting instances, and producing authorities. I resisted the inclination. I would not imitate the religious periodicals, by denouncing men instead of systems;—men, who may be blessing God in their hearts, and teaching others to bless Him, while they use language which seems to me utterly inconsistent with all that His word declares respecting Him. While, therefore, in my *Theological Essays*, I often spoke by name of the great Evangelical teachers of the last century, because I never felt disposed to mention *them* without honour, I alluded only to maxims and habits, when I referred to my contemporaries. I had no need to prove that the opinions and maxims exist; the groans of thousands in religious families testify to that fact. I knew very well that they might be explained away—as all the most idolatrous practices, and all the most subtle outrages upon Scripture and morality, in Romish countries, have been explained away—'over and over again;' but I knew that they remained, in spite of the explanations,—and I believed that they were destroying the Christianity of our land. Dr. Candlish has come to England to convince the religious world, that it is in a very right and satisfactory state. Who can doubt that he will succeed? Who can wonder that the religious periodicals which embody all the tempers and inclinations of that which he has defended, should hail such a champion? But is he doing you good by his apologies? Are they such as would have been heard from one of the old men whom he reveres? Would not they have appeared as witnesses of God, to show the people of Israel their sins? Would they not have called those false prophets, who said, 'Peace, peace'?

I would say again, that I do not take Dr.

Candlish's lecture, or his book, as evidence of what he himself is. I know nothing of him personally; but I know enough of his history to be aware that he has not lived to make his own countrymen content with the notions, at least on the subject of church government, which he supposed were 'current' among them. I know that he has made sacrifices to what he holds to be a neglected principle. I would ask of God, that we may imitate his faith, and apply it in the way that it is wanted in our country. I do not think, if we cherish it, we shall cause any disruption in the church of our fathers. I do think that we shall be continually at war with the religious world, which is the counterfeit of the Church, and which is trying to reduce all Churches into a Babel of sects.

I have now said all I intend ever to say on the subject of Dr. Candlish, his lecture, and his book. I have to thank him for some passages in both, which I had not the least reason to expect. Once or twice, he has spoken of me, almost as if he thought I might be a believer in Christ; he has even expressed something like a sympathy with some words I have written; he has half admitted that I may not be merely throwing out mystical or 'misty' phrases, when I have discoursed of the divine Word as the great Teacher of mankind. I see that some of his reviewers, in his own country, are scandalized and alarmed at these expressions; they earnestly beg him to cancel them in a future edition. So far as consistency goes, I believe they are right. He should not lead you, or any, to milder thoughts of one whom he has pronounced a deliberately and habitually dishonest man. I value the words, however, not for my sake, but for his; or for mine only, because they enable me to separate, as I always desire to do, the man from the apologist and the controversialist, and make me ashamed of myself, whenever, for a moment, I confound them.

Having taken leave of my accuser, I wish to explain, as shortly as I can, how the work, which I now present to you, is connected with the subjects which he has brought under your notice, and of which I have been speaking in this letter. My desire is to ground all theology upon the Name of God the Father, the Son, and the Holy Ghost; not to begin from ourselves and our sins; not to measure the straight line by the crooked one. This is the method which I have learnt from the Bible. There everything proceeds from God; He is revealing Himself, He is acting, speaking, ruling. Next, my desire is to ground all human morality upon the relation in which man stands to God; to exhibit whatever is right and true in man, as only the image and reflex of the original Righteousness and Truth. I cannot base this morality upon the dread of some future punishments, upon the expectation of some future rewards. I believe the attempts to make men moral by such means have failed always; are never more egregiously and monstrously failing than now. I believe that they fail because they are in conformity with our notions, and not with God's purpose, as set forth in Holy Scripture. There I find God using punishments, to make men sensible of the great misery of being at war with His will; showing them the blessed results to their spirits, to their bodies, to nations, to families, to individuals, to the father and the child, the master and the workman, to the persons who subdue the earth, and to the earth which they subdue, from conformity to His will. There I find the kingdom of Heaven set forth as the kingdom of righteousness, and peace, and joy in the Holy Ghost, which Christ, the only-begotten of the Father, came to reveal; the kingdom over our spirits, the kingdom into which the poor in spirit, who renounce themselves and trust in God, enter. There I find Hell set before me, as the loss of this state, as separation from God, as the darkness into which those fall who love darkness rather than the light which has come into the world, and is shining into their hearts. There I am taught, that God by all His discipline and government here, is leading men to fly from the darkness and turn to the light; and that they are resisting His will when they prefer Hell to Heaven. There I learn to look upon the future state, as even a divine of the eighteenth century represented it to be, not as the commencement of a new state of things,—but as the carrying out and consummation of all God's plans and government,—as the state in which the victory of good over evil is no longer a question of doubt or uncertainty.

Now this theology and this morality are all, I think, involved in, and tested by, the doctrine of Sacrifice. That doctrine I hold, as our forefathers held it, to be *the* doctrine of the Bible, *the* doctrine of the Gospel. The Bible is, from first to last, setting forth to us the meaning of Sacrifice. If we cannot preach that that meaning has been accomplished, that the perfect Sacrifice has been made for the sins of the whole world, that God has made peace with us by the death of His Son, I do not see that we have any gospel from God to men. As little do I see what ground there is for human morality; since that morality consists, as I believe, in the giving up of ourselves. All immorality consists in self-seeking, self-pleasing, self-glorifying. But I find from the history of the world expounded by the Bible, that there has been always a tendency in the corrupt heart of man to make Sacrifice itself the minister of man's self-will, self-indulgence, self-glorification. Instead of giving himself up to God, man seeks to make his God, or his gods, give up to him; he offers sacrifices, that he may persuade the power which he thinks he has wronged, to exempt him from the punishment of his wrong. This is man's theology; this is what has produced all the hateful superstitions under which the world groans. If I say that the seeds of this theology, of these superstitions, are not in your hearts and in mine, I contradict the Bible, I contradict the witness of my conscience. If I suppose that there is any heathen tendency to which a Christian man is not liable, I deny the fact of the corruption in the heart of every man of the progeny of Adam, or I suppose that, by some marvellous accident, we are exempted from the operation of it. I must, therefore, ask the Bible, the book of God, to explain to me in what form that evil is likely to appear in my age and in me; I must ask God Himself to tell me how I may be delivered from it,—how I may receive the true sacrifice which taketh away the sins of the world,—and so be prevented from accepting notions of sacrifice which increase and deepen the sin of the world, which suggest thoughts of God that destroy His righteousness, and make Him after the image of my unrighteousness, which lead men to practices that are hateful to Him, and destructive of themselves.

In these Sermons I have compared these two sacrifices; the sacrifice which manifests the mind of God,—which proceeds from God, which accomplishes the purposes of God in the redemption and reconciliation of His creatures, which enables those creatures to become like their Father in Heaven by offering up themselves;—and the sacrifices which men have dreamed of in one country or another, as means of changing the purposes of God, of converting Him to their mind, of procuring deliverance from the punishment of evil, while the evil still exists. If you like to read what I have written, you will see whether, as you have been told upon authority which you are not likely to dispute, I do reject the faith of our forefathers in the might and efficacy of Christ's Cross; whether I disbelieve in His advocacy, and intercession, and eternal priesthood; whether I measure the glory and the end of His Sacrifice by some paltry notions of my own; whether I ask the Bible to confirm those notions, or to deliver me from them; whether I am introducing a 'cowardly philosophy' which shrinks from the thought of God as a punisher and as a judge; whether I am guilty of 'dishonesty' in using words in some sense of my own, not in the sense in which God's word and His Church have used them; whether I am one of those accursed men who rob the world of the Gospel which God has sent them to proclaim in it, and substitute another of their own.

I have tried to speak of Sacrifice under every aspect in which the Bible presents it. If I have not connected it with the adjective *Vicarious*, which is so favourite a one in modern theology, the reason is that I did not find that word in the Bible. Nor does it occur once in our Thirty-nine Articles. Nevertheless, I do not object to the word. It may have, I conceive, an excellent meaning. If, when we call Christ a Vicar, we understand what the Scripture understands when it calls Him a Redeemer, a Reconciler, an Advocate, a Priest, a Mediator, a Son; if when we call His Sacrifice a vicarious one, we understand what the Scripture understands when it says that He was set forth as a propitiation, that He bore the sins of the world, that He was made a curse, that He was made sin; then I hold that He is a Vicar, and that His sacrifice is vicarious in the fullest sense; for I only complain of those who would evade or dilute the force of these expressions. But if a meaning is attached to Vicar or vicarious, which is *not* in harmony with this language, most assuredly I reject that meaning, and have taken some pains to show how mischievous it has been.

I preached these Sermons with an oppressive feeling that a crisis may be at hand which will try us all of what sort we are: which will show whether we believe in God or are Atheists; whether we worship Him or the devil. But I preached them also with a strong and ever growing conviction, that if some of the notions of sacrifice which prevail among us are doing more than anything else to separate us from God and from each other, the true Sacrifice, which was made once for all, will be found to be a bond of peace between God and man, and between all the different tribes, races, and sects of men. In that bond may you and I be united for ever.

Your Friend and Well-wisher,
F. D. Maurice.

CONTENTS.

		PAGE
SERMON I.—THE SACRIFICES OF CAIN AND ABEL	. . .	1
,, II.—NOAH'S SACRIFICE	. . . . . .	18
,, III.—THE SACRIFICE OF ABRAHAM	. . . .	33
,, IV.—SACRIFICE OF THE PASSOVER	. . . .	49
,, V.—THE LEGAL SACRIFICES	. . . . .	67
,, VI.—DAVID'S SACRIFICE	. . . . . .	85
,, VII.—THE LAMB BEFORE THE FOUNDATION OF THE WORLD	. . . .	99
,, VIII.—CHRIST'S SACRIFICE A REDEMPTION	. . .	114
,, IX.—CHRIST'S SACRIFICE A DELIVERANCE FROM THE CURSE OF THE LAW	. . . . .	130
,, X.—THE SACRIFICE OF CHRIST A PROPITIATION	.	144
,, XI.—THE SACRIFICE OF CHRIST THE PURIFICATION OF THE CONSCIENCE	. . . . .	161

		PAGE
SERMON XII.—CHRIST MADE SIN FOR US	. . . .	179
,, XIII.—CHRIST'S SACRIFICE THE PEACE-OFFERING FOR MANKIND	. . . .	195
,, XIV.—CHRIST'S SACRIFICE A POWER TO FORM US AFTER HIS LIKENESS	. . . . .	212
,, XV.—CHRIST'S DEATH A VICTORY OVER THE DEVIL		227
,, XVI.—CHRIST THE ADVOCATE .	. . . .	242
,, XVII.—CHRIST THE HIGH-PRIEST	. . . .	260
,, XVIII.—THE ADORATION OF THE LAMB	. . .	276
,, XIX.—THE WORD OF GOD CONQUERING BY SACRIFICE		294

THE

DOCTRINE OF SACRIFICE.

SERMON I.

THE SACRIFICES OF CAIN AND ABEL.

(Lincoln's Inn, Quinquagesima Sunday, Feb. 26, 1854.)

' And in process of time it came to pass, that Cain brought of the fruit of the ground an offering unto the Lord. And Abel, he also brought of the firstlings of his flock, and of the fat thereof. And the Lord had respect unto Abel and to his offering: but unto Cain and to his offering he had not respect. And Cain was very wroth, and his countenance fell. And the Lord said unto Cain, why art thou wroth? and why is thy countenance fallen? If thou doest well, shalt thou not be accepted? and if thou doest not well, sin lieth at the door.'—GENESIS iv. 3-7.

I BELIEVE the teaching of the Bible on the subject of Sacrifice is very methodical. By mixing together texts concerning it, which are taken at random from any book between Genesis and the Apocalypse, we confuse our minds, and often end with holding the notions which we should have held if no such words had been written. Perhaps, if we have sufficient reverence for the book to follow in the steps which it marks out for us, we may learn something from it. We shall not learn, even then, if we forget that all true words—the truest most of all—only speak *to* us when they speak *in* us, when they awaken us to thought, self-questioning, wonder, hope. It is not, therefore, an idle form which preachers use—if it is, it must be a blasphemous form —when they ask that the Spirit of God may quicken and raise the hearts which the word of God is sent to illuminate. To imagine that any book or any living voice can give, if there is not a receiver, or that it can give, except according to the measure of the receiver, is to contradict all experience and all reason.

The passage I have read to you is the first in the Bible which refers to a sacrifice. It has stirred up a number of doubts in the minds of men. I will refer to a few of them, and I will say how far I think this story will resolve them, how far it obliges us to seek for further light, which it does not impart, and which it ought not to impart.

(1.) The first question is this: What did Cain and Abel know about sacrifice? Were they told by a special revelation that they were to offer *something*, and *what* they were to offer? or had that revelation been made to Adam, and did they receive the knowledge by transmission? You say, 'It may be very well to form 'guesses upon this point, but who can give us any 'satisfaction? The Scriptures are silent; what can we 'do but set up one speculation against another?' The objection is a plausible one, to a great extent a substantial one, confirmed by the experience of those who

have travelled this road. But yet men will ask themselves again and again, 'How did this knowledge re-
'specting the way of approaching God reach men in
'early days?' They will feel that this demand has
very much to do with another: 'How do we become
'possessed of it now? Can we have that knowledge?
'Is it not all a dream?' The most practical issues
appear to be involved in some way with this inquiry;
however we may wish to avoid it, we find it continually
coming round to us and confronting us.

We are bound, I conceive, never to assume the
existence of a *decree* which is not expressly announced
to us. A decree is an open, explicit, formal thing; if it
is to be obeyed, it must be set forth in intelligible terms.
The book of Genesis has already recognised that principle. The command not to eat of the fruit of the tree
in the midst of the garden, is strict and definite. It is
proclaimed as the precept which the parents of the race
were to recollect and follow; the one which they could
not disobey without bringing death upon themselves.
If another precept of wider range and greater permanence, as definite and positive, was made either then or
speedily afterwards, would the historian have left those
whom he wrote to instruct, to guess or divine it?

But is it at variance with his principle, or with the
style of his narrative, to assume that a *revelation* of
God had preceded any acts of theirs, and was the
cause of them? I am most anxious to lead you to
notice this distinction; it is so important for the

understanding of this subject, and of the whole doctrine of Scripture. I think you will find that throughout the Scriptures, an announcement about this or that act which it behoves a man to do or to leave undone, is called a *statute* or an *ordinance*. It is said to proceed from the Lord; He makes it, He enforces it. But a *revelation* is a discovery of Himself to a creature whom He has formed to know Him. Such revelations, when they mark out great epochs in the history, as that to Moses in the bush did, may be recorded with especial solemnity; but they are implied in every part of the narrative. It is constructed upon the assumption that they occur continually. The postulate of the Bible is, that man could not be what he is, if God did not hold converse with him; that this is his distinction from other creatures; that this is the root of all that he knows, the ground of what is right and reasonable in him. You cannot read the Bible narratives simply without perceiving that this is the maxim from which they start; people who will not acknowledge it as a true maxim, talk of the language they find in the sacred writings as characteristic of a Semitic people, or of the infancy of civilisation; but they cannot help perceiving that it is there, and that the essence, as well as the outward form, of the history depends upon it.

Although, then, we should certainly have expected Moses to inform us plainly if there had been a direct ordinance to Adam, or his sons, concerning the offering of fruits or animals, we have no right to expect that he should say more than he has said, to make us understand that they received this much more deep and awful kind of communication. If he has laid it down that man is made in the image of God—if he has illustrated that principle after the fall, by showing how God met Adam in the garden in the cool of the day, and awakened him to a sense of his disobedience—we do not want any further assurance that the children whom he begat would be born and would grow up under the same law. We *should* want a very distinct assurance, and we should have reason to be very much startled and perplexed if we received it, that this was *not* the case. Certainly, we have no such intimation. The history of Cain, as I shall show you presently, affirms in the most simple and distinct manner, that he as well as his brother was under the divine teaching, that he knew he was, and that he did not lose that knowledge till he had brought himself into an utterly inhuman condition.

Do not, I beseech you, try to realise this conviction, by imagining these two men to be different from others of their kind. Conceive of them just as the Scripture represents them—one as the tiller of the ground, the other as a keeper of sheep. They are working just as men have worked in all countries and in all generations since. They look now and then to the sky over their heads; generally they are busy with the stubborn earth, which they are weeding of its thorns and thistles, or with the animals they are watching and folding, and following when they wander. To such men there come thoughts of One who is ruling them as they rule the sheep, who in some strange way makes the seeds grow which they put in the ground. These thoughts are altogether wonderful; they cannot weigh them nor measure them; at times they are crushed by them; at times they are lifted up by them. No doubt their parents have told them that they have a Lord, and that He sees them, and that he is ordering their ways. Surely it is He who is making them feel His presence, urging them to confess Him. How shall they confess Him? What is the simplest of all possible methods, in which they can manifest their subjection? Ask yourselves: Is it speech? Is it some vehement phrase of thanksgiving, some passionate petition? These may come in time, but they cannot come first; they are not the most childlike way of testifying homage, not the one which ordinary human experience would lead us to look for, when One has revealed Himself to us whom we perceive but dimly, yet with whom we feel we have to do. Acts go before words. The shepherd takes the sheep; he desires to present it to this Ruler, who must be near him, whom he must find some way of acknowledging. The tiller of the ground takes the fruits of the earth; he would present these. You ask why one mode of presenting them occurs to him rather than another? I cannot tell, any more than I can tell you why one mode of tillage, or one mode of folding the sheep, occurs to him rather than another. There is no doubt one mode which is better than another; it may be shown him in due time, if he has not found it. Whatever he discovers on that subject, or any other, he receives. It is wisdom which is imparted to him, light which comes to him from the Source of light. I do not see what one can say different, or more, in the other case. There, too, the suggestion of the mode in which the service is to be performed is welcomed as divine; yet it is felt to be natural and reasonable. When once it has been practised, it seems as if there could scarcely be another mode. The historian, however, does not tell us in what way Abel or Cain offered their gifts; he merely says that they *did* offer them. Everything is done to make us feel that we are not reading of a time when laws have been established which prescribe the nature and method of sacrifice,—that we are in a much more elementary stage of culture; but that the Teacher in each stage is the same, and that we shall recognise Him in more advanced periods, if we understand His lessons in this.

(2.) It has been asked again, 'Was not Abel right 'in presenting the animal, and Cain wrong in presenting 'the fruits of the earth? Must not the first have been 'obeying a precept, and the second transgressing one?' I must apply the same rule as before. We are not told this; we may not put a notion of ours into the text. Moses does not inform us that Cain's was an illegitimate kind of offering. It would have been strange if he had; for the fruits of the earth were offerings which the law that was given to the children of Israel required, as well as those of sheep and oxen. The latter may have had a deeper significance; I shall hope to consider that significance on some future occasion. But the former had certainly their own honour, and the notice of them here is not a disparaging one. It would appear from the narrative, as if each brother brought the gift which most suited his occupation. The pastoral occupation may suggest more living and human thoughts than that of the mere husbandman. The care of animals, with their caprices and their affections, may call forth a patience and a sympathy which are rarely found in him who is only busy with the inanimate clods. But our Lord revealed divine analogies in the sower and the seed, as well as in the shepherd and the sheep. It is not safe to disparage any work, or not to own it as pregnant with wisdom and mystery. God is surely present in all. It cannot be that he who in dependence and submission offers Him of the fruits of the ground, which it is his calling to rear, is therefore rejected, or will not be taught a deeper lore by other means, if at present he lacks it.

(3.) In saying this, I have anticipated a third, and still more serious question, which is raised by the words, *And the Lord had respect unto Abel and to his offering: but unto Cain and to his offering he had not respect.* In their haste to determine why this difference was made between two brothers, many have resorted to the notion of some disobedience or ignorance on the part of Cain, in the choice of his gift. I have tried to show you that this opinion is not sanctioned by the passage in which we should have looked for some confirmation of it. The words of *this* clause are still more repugnant to it. When it is said, *unto Abel and to his offering, unto Cain and to his offering,* we are led to think that, at all events, the distinction is to be first sought in the *persons*; that the *things* which they bring are quite secondary.

It is needful to clear our minds of *this* confusion, though I am well aware that, when it is removed, the difficulty acquires a more terrible character than it had before. 'These brothers, then,' we say to ourselves, ' without having done good or evil, each testifying his ' gratitude in his own way, in the way which was most ' natural to him, are said to be respectively accepted and ' rejected, merely because it pleased God to accept one ' and reject one. Are we not then met at the very thres- ' hold of the Bible—in the very infancy of our race—with ' that tremendous assertion of arbitrary power, of simple ' sovereignty, at the root of all things, which has driven, ' and is driving, its thousands to despair, its tens of thou- ' sands to Atheism ? Are not the foundations of moral ' order and distinction sapped at the very opening of the ' records from which we derive our belief in righteous- ' ness and evil ?' I do not suppress the statement of this doubt, because I know how many are racked by it, and how many merely escape the torment by assuming that the subject is one which has nothing to do with them, and which it is safer not to think about. Would to God we all felt how much it has to do with us; how unsafe it is to put such a subject at a distance from us; how impossible it is for us to see into the nature of it, till it is brought near to us, close to our inmost being! There was never a more faithful description than that which Milton gives of the way in which evil spirits discuss such arguments:

> 'Others apart, sat on a hill retired,
> In thoughts more elevate, and reasoned high
> Of Providence, Foreknowledge, Will and Fate;
> Fixed Fate, Free Will, Foreknowledge absolute,
> And found no end, in wandering mazes lost.'

All 'who sit apart upon a hill retired' to amuse themselves with such reasonings, supposing that they have no concern with the crowds who are wandering below—supposing that these are topics for the wise to speculate about, not realities for living and suffering men—enter upon them in the same temper as those of whom our poet writes, and, whether their starting-point is a philosophical or a theological one, arrive at the same result. Only it is much more frightful when they talk their cruel metaphysics in the name of God; when they put him in place of the Fate which others more reverently speak of; when they pretend to build up a *faith* on the assumption that He is a being whom men generally cannot and should not trust.

Brethren, the Bible does not lead us in this way! It shows us how we may find another and more excellent way. Cain and Abel, in this early portion of it, are brought before us as both presenting their offerings to God. But the effect is different. They feel it to be different. We are not told how they came to feel it; whether any outward sign or token satisfied the one, and left the other discontented. The historian has not time to speak of such trifles. He only makes us understand that they *did* know it, and that *Cain was very wroth, and his countenance fell.* Thereby he at once connects the story with human experience,—with the experience of each human being. It is a fact which we cannot dispute, which all the world's history confirms, that some have been the better for their prayers, and some very much the worse; that some have brought sacrifices and have gone away with their countenances shining as they had been angels, full of affection to their fellow-men, ready to do them all good,—that others have gone away with their countenances moody, discontented, wrathful, ready to wreak their vengeance on the first creature they met. There are these extreme differences,—there may be many degrees between each extreme—denoting that a blessing or a curse has followed the offering. It is so in what we call, formally, religious services; it is so with every ordinary work and service among our fellow-creatures. The Bible would not be a true book, if it did not exhibit this difference to us. We should look to see it exhibited early in such a record; for it must be one of those primary characteristics of human beings which will go through all periods, but which, by some means, make themselves manifest from the first. Having set it before us, we are left to find out much of the explanation from its own after-revelations. It does not anticipate the discovery which it is to make to us, by degrees, of the nature of Him who was governing both the shepherd and the tiller of the ground. It does not anticipate the discovery it will make to us of the mystery of evil, and of the sense of righteousness and good, which lay in the hearts of both—because they were not shepherds and tillers of the ground only, but men. It does, however, hasten at once to remove that which would make all these after-revelations incredible and self-contradictory. It does say, that God spake to Cain, and said, '*Why art thou wroth? and why is thy countenance fallen? If thou doest well, shalt thou not be accepted? and if thou doest not well, sin lieth at the door.*' It does denounce at the very outset, the notion of a self-willed arbitrary being, who is making decrees for men, what they shall be, or what they shall not be; who of his pleasure is choosing one and rejecting another. It does set before us a *righteous* Being, who holds discourse with His creature, who treats him as a being made for right, and capable of following right; as only following wrong when he yields to *the sin which lieth at the door*, and not to that righteous Guide who is close to the same door, urging him to take the true and upward path. It does make us perceive that Cain defied that righteous Being and chose the evil guide, when he denied that he was his brother's keeper, and became his murderer. It does show us that the issue of this *crime*, not of some fatal necessity, was, that he went out of the presence of God; that he became shut up in his atheism.

And thus, my brethren, the Bible brings this history to a test which we may all use, if we will; by which we may prove whether it is true or not; by which we may rid ourselves of hard and artificial interpretations of it. We know—we positively know—what the Cain offering is, because we have presented the like ourselves. We have prayed; and then have complained, just as the Jews did, that it has all been in vain, that no good has come of it. We have made sacrifices, and we have wondered that we got no reward for them. Perhaps we have been angry that, being so good, we have not been more favoured by fortune and circumstances. Perhaps we have been angry that, trying so hard to make ourselves good, we have succeeded so little. Perhaps we have had a general notion that God could not be persuaded to be gracious to us and to forgive us, in spite of all the sacrifices we have offered, and that we must try others which are more costly. In all cases, *the countenance has fallen*; in all cases, we have gone forth with thoughts that were anything but gracious and brotherly to our fellow-men. We have thought of them as more in the favour of Heaven, on one ground or another, than we were; we have felt envious and spiteful to them, if we have done them no actual mischief. Assuredly, this is the Cain spirit in us all; assuredly, we have often been led by it; and, if so, have we not had a proof, the clearest which could be given, that it was not an arbitrary Being we were opposing, but a righteous and gracious Being? Was not our sin that we *supposed* Him to be an arbitrary Being, whom we, by our sacrifices and prayers, were to conciliate? Was not this *the* false notion which lay at the root of all our discontent, of all the evil thoughts and acts which sprung out of it? We did not begin with trust, but with distrust; we did not worship God because we believed in Him, but because we dreaded Him—because we desired His presence, but because we wished to persuade Him not to come near us.

And does not this experience, brethren, enable us to understand the nature of that true and better sacrifice which Abel offered? Must not all its worth have arisen from this, that he was weak, and that he cast himself upon One whom he knew to be strong; that he was ignorant, and that he trusted in One, who he was sure must be wise; that he had the sense of death, and that he turned to One whence life must have come; that he had the sense of wrong, and that he fled to One who must be right? Was not his sacrifice the mute expression of this helplessness, dependence, confidence? And was not the acceptance of it, the pledge that the Creator is goodness and truth, and that all creatures have goodness and truth, so far as they disclaim them in themselves and seek them in Him?

If this be the case, we have had a glimpse into the

nature of sacrifice, and into its connection with the nature of every human creature, which we may hope will expand into clearer and brighter vision.

We have seen that sacrifice has its ground in something deeper than legal enactments. We may have to consider how such enactments affect it; how they may strengthen or weaken the principle which is implied in it. We have seen that sacrifice infers more than the giving up of a *thing*. We shall have to ask how the *person* who presents it may be enabled to give up himself, and into what errors he may fall in his effort to do that. We have seen that sacrifice has something to do with sin, something to do with thanksgiving. We must ask the Bible to tell us what it has to do with each, and how, in its application to each of these purposes, it may be perverted. We have contemplated it in the case of two individuals. We ought to inquire whether the principle of it belongs to society, and how the social and the individual sacrifice are connected, how they may be separated to the peril of the community and its members. We have seen that sacrifice is offered by man, and yet that the sacrifice becomes evil and immoral, when the man attaches any value to his own act, and does not attribute the whole worth of it to God. It will be our duty to ask, how it is possible that man should present the sacrifice, of which God is at once the Author and the Acceptor. These are questions which the history we have considered to-day suggests, but does not answer. We shall have reason enough to be thankful for it, if it has discovered to us a principle which can never forsake us, or be contradicted, at any step of our future progress; which will receive illustration as much from our own lives as from the word of God; which we deny whenever we try to interpret the one without the aid of the other.

My brethren, we are told, in the Gospel for to-day, that '*as Jesus was going up with His twelve Apostles to Jerusalem, He said to them, The Son of Man shall be delivered to the Gentiles, and shall be mocked and spitefully entreated, and spitted on: and they shall scourge Him, and put Him to death; and the third day He shall rise again.*' The twelve Apostles, says the Evangelist, '*understood none of these things, and this saying was hid from them, neither understood they the things which were spoken.*' Those who were to be teachers of the world had not yet learnt the mystery of sacrifice. They heard of it from the lips of Him whom they called Lord and Master. His words at present fell dead upon their ears. But the story goes on: '*And it came to pass, that as He was come nigh unto Jericho, a certain blind man sat by the wayside begging: and hearing the multitude pass by, he asked what it meant. And they told him, that Jesus of Nazareth passeth by. And he cried, saying, Jesus, thou Son of David, have mercy on me. And they which went before rebuked him, that he should hold his peace. But he cried so much the more, Thou Son of David, have mercy on me. And Jesus stood and commanded him to be brought unto Him; and when he was come near, He asked him, saying, What wilt thou that I should do unto thee? And he said, Lord, that I may receive my sight. And Jesus said unto Him, Receive thy sight; thy faith hath saved thee.'*

That blind man entered into the meaning of sacrifice, into which the Apostles had not yet entered. He felt his blindness. He trusted in a Deliverer. He could believe that that Deliverer had given himself up to bear his infirmities and carry his sicknesses. He could expect that there were wonders of His mercy, which a still more complete sacrifice would be needed to reveal.

SERMON II.

NOAH'S SACRIFICE.

(Lincoln's Inn, 1st Sunday in Lent, March 5, 1854.)

' And Noah builded an altar unto the Lord; and took of every clean beast, and of every clean fowl, and offered burnt-offerings on the altar. And the Lord smelled a sweet savour; and the Lord said in his heart, I will not again curse the ground any more for man's sake; for the imagination of man's heart is evil from his youth; neither will I again smite any more everything living, as I have done. While the earth remaineth, seed-time and harvest, and cold and heat, and summer and winter, and day and night shall not cease.'—GENESIS viii. 20-22.

AFTER the story of Cain and Abel, there is no further allusion to sacrifice in the records of the world before the flood. But the meaning of these two sacrifices goes through the history. The confession of dependence and trust on a righteous Being, from whom life came, which made Abel's offering an acceptable one; the proud feeling of Cain, that he had something to give, which led to discontent when he received nothing in return for his gift—which led to murder when he had someone upon whom he could put forth his power,—

these are the characteristics of the period, because that period exhibits the characteristics of human beings in the simplest and earliest stage of their development. The faith of the patriarchs who called on the name of the Lord,—who walked with God,—who begat sons and daughters, and died,—who looked *for someone to comfort them concerning the work and toil of their hands because of the ground which the Lord had cursed*, was merely an expansion of that faith which had been the blessing of Abel and the cause of his death. The violence and corruption with which the earth is said to have been filled, were merely the natural outcomings of that unbelief in right, that confidence in might, of which Cain had been the first example. Do not let us say, as some have said, that Abel was a *religious* man, and Cain an irreligious man; that is not the Bible language, either concerning them or their successors. The acts of Cain are just as religious as those of his brother; one brought a sacrifice just as well as the other. We have no reason to suppose, that there may not have been abundance of religion among those upon whom the flood came. The old words are the true words. Abel was a *righteous* man; his sacrifice was offered to a righteous Being: it expressed faith in *such* a Being. Cain was unrighteous; he believed in power, and nothing else. His sacrifice was presented to a power, and was designed to win its favour. It was not presented to God; it was no worship of Him; it could not be acknowledged by Him. It was the same afterwards. *Noah, we are told, was a just man and perfect in his generations, and he walked with God.* This language is in strict harmony with all that we read afterwards in the Old Testament Scriptures; it is carried out and interpreted in the New. Noah reverenced right and justice; he ordered his family well; he lived in the presence of an unseen Being who is right and true, and who had appointed him to be the head of a family. These are the best modern equivalents we can find for the older and nobler phraseology. They make the rest of his life intelligible to us. Such a man, seeing violence, tyranny, ill-doing, brutality all around him, knew assuredly that this was not meant to be; that God had not made the world for this. He was sure it could not last; no matter how many were taking part in the evil, and were sanctioning it in their neighbours; no matter whether the race of Seth was defiled with it as well as the race of Cain; no matter whether the whole scheme of men's lives, aye, and the scheme of their religion, was framed on the notion that wrong was tolerable or inevitable, and that the powers above might be bribed to overlook it. Such a state of things had a curse upon it; God's own curse. He knew it; for he walked with God. A Teacher, whom he could not see with his eyes, but who was with him, opened his heart to know that every injustice and every lie is contrary to his nature,—contrary to the order He has established; that He is actually fighting against injustice and lies in His universe, and in every being upon it; that He will prevail. This Noah learnt, not by any sagacity of his, not because he was in different circumstances from the men about him, or had a finer temperament than theirs; but because he confessed the Voice of God who was speaking to him, warning him, judging him; because he feared to disobey that Voice. It was the God of his fathers, who made him understand this,—the God to whom they had listened, and whom they had worshipped. He had not ceased to be; He would not cease to be. With that knowledge of the past and present comes also knowledge of the future. One is as hard for man to read as the other. God interprets each to him by the other. Noah was verily certain that there was an end designed for the wickedness of men. When it would come he might not know; but it would come;—the day and the hour were determined though they might not concern him. Such faith, once cherished, is fed day by day; it grows stronger through the very sight of the evils which are so appalling; it becomes deeper as they become deeper; it becomes also more distinct and definite. The man who holds it, acts upon it; he goes on in a plain, simple course, dwells with his family, begets sons and daughters. By the orderliness and quietness of his life, he becomes a witness against the turbulent, self-willed world, in the midst of which he is dwelling. By degrees he receives light respecting the nature of the punishment which will overtake that world. He is taught by God how to act as a provident man should act when a danger is impending: how to warn his neighbours of it, that they may escape it too. There is called forth in him, through his faith, the foresight and wisdom, which are every day departing from the heartless, anxious self-seekers, who are in continual dread of danger, and are continually hunting after safety and comfort. But there is called forth in him also, by this same faith, an earnest interest in his fellow-men. He separates from them, only that he may be a witness to them of the good which they are flying from, and which he claims for himself and his family, because he believes that God designs it for the creatures He has formed.

If we give any different explanation from this of the act of Noah in preparing the ark, we contradict the words of the New Testament as well as the Old; we take the sense and moral out of the story; we make it immoral and selfish. And by doing so, we make the sacrifice which Noah offered when the flood had subsided, and he came forth into the restored world, a Cain sacrifice; we do not find in the narrative of it— what is assuredly there—a beautiful and consistent exposition of the reason why the Lord had respect to Abel's offering, and not to his brother's.

There is an evident difference between this history and the one of which I spoke last Sunday. There were no particulars given us respecting the form and method of Abel's or Cain's sacrifice. It was merely said, that one brought of the firstlings of his flock, the other of the fruits of the ground. Now we are told of an *altar* which Noah *builded,* of *his choosing out clean beasts and clean fowls,* of *his offering a burnt-offering on the altar.* You may have observed how accurately the form of the ark is described in the previous chapter, and how all the arrangements of it are referred to the divine Teacher. It is assumed that a stage has come in the life of the world, when the working in wood and iron is no longer the fruit of men's eagerness to put forth powers which they are not fit to exercise; that these powers can now be used and cultivated for the worthiest ends under the highest guidance. Here, under the same inward guidance, the mound of turf gives place to the altar which is built; an order is discovered in the dignity of the inferior creatures; the worthiest are selected for an oblation to God; the fire which consumes, the flame which ascends, are used to express the intention of him who presents the victim. If you asked him to tell you *what* these visible things signified to him, he could have given you no answer. At a later time men might have muttered one which would have a certain sense, but not a very clear sense; now they would simply act on their intuition, and let it justify itself as it could. Noah would be sure that it had not come from himself; that God had awakened it in him; if He had something different to teach other men elsewhere, so let it be. All he had to do, was to follow where a light, which had not deceived him hitherto, was pointing the way.

And, I think, we must all feel that there was an inward progress in the heart of the man, corresponding to this progress in his method of uttering his submission and his aspirations. There was a certain solitude in the condition of the patriarchs of the old world—not an absolute solitude, for that can never be where there are husbands and wives, fathers and children, where they look upon the graves of those who have gone before them, and upon the faces which are beginning to express wonder and hope—but still the solitude of men who feel that they have little to do with the greatest portion of the earth, inhabited or uninhabited; who think of what lies beyond their own homes only as full of crime.

But the man who came out of the ark, and builded an altar to the Lord, must have felt that he was representing all human beings; that he was not speaking what was in himself so much as offering the homage of the restored universe. He *had prepared an ark for the saving of his house*; but that ark had been for the saving of the race which God had made in His own image, of all the races which He had made subject to that. The simple mind of a patriarch could not take in so vast a thought as this; what need that he should take it in? It was true; if he could not comprehend it, he yet could speak out the marvel and the awe of his heart to Him who knew all.

What was Noah's sacrifice but this? As childlike as that of the man who first gazed on the strange world, and could not interpret it; who first saw death, and wanted to be told what it signified; who first felt sin, and would fly from it. As childlike as his; perhaps more childlike, because the oppression of ages and of the sin which had been done in them, of the deaths which had been died in them, was greater than that which the other could experience—and therefore the need of casting it on someone who could bear it was greater; and because the sense of deliverance and redemption and restoration—the assurance that the righteous God was a deliverer, redeemer, restorer—must have been such as none could have had who had not seen how all the powers of the world were used for the punishment of those who had braved Him instead of believing in Him; and how, nevertheless, the order stood fast, and came forth fresher and fairer out of the ruin. In what words was it possible to express a sense of man's greatness—the king over the mightiest animals—and of man's littleness in the presence of the elements which had been let loose upon him; of the intimate, inseparable union between man and man; of the bitter strifes which tore them asunder; of the awful nearness of men to their Maker; of their estrangement from Him? How could he and his sons say: 'We confess that Thou hast made 'us rulers; help us to govern; we know that the world 'can crush us; help us not to fear it, but Thee. We 'are sure that we have rebelled against Thee; we bless 'thee that Thou upholdest us and unitest us to Thee?' The altar, the clean beasts, the fire, and the man presenting the animals to Him whom he cannot see, in the fire as one of the mightiest ministers of His will, these were the signs which supplied the want of language, or translated the language of earth into that of Heaven.

If that translation is possible, the converse is possible also. The next clause of our text is an example of the way in which the mysteries of Heaven may be presented in the forms of earth: '*And the Lord smelled a sweet savour; and the Lord said in his heart, I will not again curse the ground any more for man's sake; for the imagination of man's heart is evil from his youth; neither will I again smite any more everything living, as I have done.*' 'How gross,' exclaims the critic of our day, 'this 'phraseology is! *Smelled a sweet savour!* How can we 'tolerate such modes of speaking when they are applied 'to the Divine Majesty?' Have you ever thought what *other* modes of speech you would use as a substitute for these? Have you ever considered whether *abstract* modes of speech would convey the same truth, half so effectually, half so reverently, as those which are drawn from the wonderful senses with which God has endowed us? If these senses seem to you vulgar, not full of meaning and mystery, it is a pity; there is much in what is nearest you which you have not reflected on; you had better dwell for awhile on the acts with which you are most familiar, before you travel round earth and to the stars. If expressions that have no sensible correspondents please you better, at least try to give yourselves some account of *them*; if they are more intellectual, be sure that you understand them; if you can ascend on these wings more rapidly into the empyrean, be sure that you do ascend, and that you bring some authentic and credible reports of what you find there. Take care that you do not come back with the blank and melancholy tidings—the most dismal which human beings can hear—that there is an abstraction there, and not a Father; a negation of all that we possess and admire below, not one in whom is the fullness of light and glory, of which all things here serve as faint hints and likenesses. Perhaps, after some experience of what a phantom you have created for yourselves, by merely emptying Him whom you profess to adore of all that connects Him with human beings, you may begin better to appreciate the book which teaches us to see everywhere in the world of sense the tokens of that connexion; which shows us everywhere some steps of the ladder which is set upon the ground we tread, and which reaches to the throne of God. *The smelling the sweet savour* of a sacrifice imports, I think, more vividly, more truly, than almost any image could, the complacency and satisfaction of the God who had desired men to obey Him, to confide in Him, to seek Him, with acts which testified their submission, their trust, their craving for more perfect communion. And the words which follow as clearly intimate the progressive, and yet the permanent, character of the divine education and government. The flood was necessary in one period of man's discipline and growth; it would not need to be repeated in another. It had not taken, and could not take away sin; that was not its object— *the imaginations of man's heart remained evil continually*, as they were before. But it had declared the unchangeableness of God's righteous order; that that would bend to no transgression; that that would overcome all who set up mere power and disorder against it. And now the same order would assert itself by the regular succession of seed-time and harvest, of day and night, of summer and winter. Apparent breaches in the regular course of events, surprising visitations, prove at times what the evenness and persistency of nature proves habitually—that the just God, of whom man is the image, against whose laws he is so continually striving, is the Author and Ruler of all things.

The foundation of sacrifice, as we find it set forth in these early records of the Bible, is laid in this fixed will of God; in His fixed purpose to assert righteousness; in the wisdom which adapts its means to the condition of the creature for whose sake they are used; in the graciousness which seeks by all these means to bring man out of a wrong state, to establish him in his true state. The sacrifice assumes eternal right to be in the Ruler of the universe, all the caprice to have come from man, from his struggle to be an independent being, from his habit of distrust. When the sense of dependence is restored to man by the discovery of his own impotence—when trust is restored by the discovery that the Lord of all seeks his good—he comes to make surrender, he brings the sacrifice which is the expression of his surrender. If he is maintaining a struggle with his own tendency to self-will and disobedience, if he is striving to submit, then the sacrifice is the regular expression of the purpose of his life; he is learning every day that the imagination of the thoughts of his heart is evil continually; therefore, he has more necessity every day of escaping from himself—of escaping to God. And in doing so, he is confessing the government of God over the world, of which he is but one inhabitant; the ordinance of *seed-time and harvest, summer and winter, day and night*, in which every man around him is as much concerned as he is. He is confessing the government of God over himself, because he is a man formed in His image; capable of being right only so far as He reflects that image; capable of doing right only so far as he is the instrument of fulfilling God's will. And that also is equally true of all about him. He desires to be delivered from the darkness which hinders him from entering into God's light that is shining so clearly and gloriously, if there were eyes to behold it, upon his whole race. I wish you to see how everlasting and universal that principle is, which we have discovered in the act of Noah, when he came forth from the ark and saw that the world which had been covered with waters was the same goodly world still; when he felt that he and his wife and his sons and his daughters had been more the objects of the care

and watchfulness of God than any of the things which
He had created, though all these had been dear to
Him; when he received the sure witness that the same
God would be with his sons and his sons' sons to what-
ever part of the earth they might travel—that He would
never forget the works of His own hands.

And have we not an equal right to say that the
principle, which is expressed in the words that declare
the complacency of God in the burnt-offering which
Noah offered upon the altar, is everlasting and universal? Have we the least ground for thinking that
He accepts coldly and distantly the homage of men's
hearts, and acts, and words; that He is not well pleased
with it? Is not the joy with which any parent receives
the free habitual service of a child striving to be
dutiful, and the submission of one who has been un-
dutiful, the faint image of the joy with which the
Father of lights receives him who wishes to dwell at
home, as well as the prodigal who has just recollected
that he has a home to which he may return? If,
indeed, the thought intrudes itself into the elder
brother's heart; 'I have earned a right to my father's
'favour by my daily offerings; who is he that comes
'from dwelling with harlots to eat the fatted calf?'—if
the thought intrudes itself into the younger brother's
heart; 'By some sacrifices of mine I may purchase
'again that which I had lost—I may persuade my
'father to overlook my wanderings and to free me from
'the punishments which they deserve at his hands,'—

the sacrifice of each becomes a Cain sacrifice; there is no submission in it, no trust in it; there can be no sweetness in the savour of it, for there is that in it which is not of God, which has no fellowship with God, which is hateful to God—pride, malice, envy. These habits haunt every man; none can say, I am free from them. But if he comes to offer sacrifice to God, he comes to confess and seek deliverance from them as from the greatest and most direful curses that can rest upon him in this world or in the world to come.

These principles, seeing that they are involved in the relation of man to God—in his eternal order—were the same in Noah's days as in ours, the same in Abel's as in Noah's. But we have learnt something from Noah's sacrifice which we could not learn from Abel's; something more of the social nature of these offerings; something more of their meaning, as following after long centuries of evil, and after a wonderful redemption; something more of the intercourse and sympathy which exist between him who sacrifices and Him to whom the sacrifice is made. Noah, we felt, was representing the race in his sacrifice; he was confessing the evil in him, and in his fellows, which had brought ruin upon the world, and was confessing the wisdom which had preserved it. These are great steps onward in the history.

But, after all, are we not conscious that they are mere hints of truths which must be unfolded, as they could not be in Abel's sacrifice or in Noah's? The representative of humanity after the flood lived his nine hundred years, and died. Has humanity no continual representative? The imagination of men's thoughts remained evil continually after the fire had ascended from the altar. Is there no offering which has power to reach the heart and to purge it? That sweet sacrifice was presented, the flame went out, the incense evaporated, and foul pestilent vapours rose from the earth and grew thicker with each generation. Is there no altar from which the flame is ever ascending, no sweet savour, of which God may say always: ' With this I am 'well pleased. For the sake of this *I will dwell with* '*men and walk with them, and they shall be my people,* '*and I will be their God: and their sins and iniquities* '*I will remember no more*'?

SERMON III.

THE SACRIFICE OF ABRAHAM.

(Lincoln's Inn, 3rd Sunday in Lent, March 19, 1854.)

And it came to pass after these things, that God did tempt Abraham, and said unto him, Abraham: and he said, Behold, here I am. And he said, Take now thy son, thine only son Isaac, whom thou lovest, and get thee into the land of Moriah; and 'offer him there for a burnt-offering upon one of the mountains which I will tell thee of.'—GENESIS xxii. 1, 2.

I SAID some Sundays ago, that the offering of Abel did not imply a precept enjoining sacrifice, but that it *did* imply a revelation from God. That revelation was not an exceptional, or anomalous accident. It was just as much presumed in the ordinary tillage of the ground as in the most awful worship. The doctrine of the Bible, as it comes out to us in the book of Genesis,—as it is consistently evolved in every subsequent book—is, that man would not be a thinking, reasonable, moral being, if there were not an intercourse between him and his Creator,—if God were not awakening him continually to a sense of that which he has to do, and of the principles upon which he is to do it.

If Revelations of this kind are not strange and irregular, but orderly, the sacrifice which responded to them seemed to be of the same character. It was the most simple way,—more simple and primitive than words,—in which a man could confess that there was a higher Being, whom his eye could not see, who was near him, acting upon him, ruling him, causing the seeds which he had sown to bring forth, giving life to those creatures which were His servants and which were also subject to death. The wonder, awe and mystery of the universe, and of that creature who alone was capable of feeling awe and wonder, and of being perplexed by a mystery, came forth in that offering. It explained him, though he was not able to explain it.

But it was intimated to us in this first story, that sacrifice may be the expression of the two most contrary feelings and states of mind;—the most contrary, and yet lying so close to each other in every man that only the eye of God can distinguish them, till they distinguish themselves by the acts which they generate. Sacrifice may import the confession of a child, who feels that he has nothing, and is a mere receiver. It may import the sense in a man that he has something to offer which his Maker ought to accept. It may import the trust of a child depending on One from whom it believes all good comes, aware that what is not good is its own. It may import the hope of a man—an uncertain sullen hope—that he may persuade the power he supposes is ruling, to give him some benefit,—to avert from him some danger. It may be an act of simple giving up, of surrender; it may be an act of barter,— a bargain to relinquish a less good on the chance of obtaining a greater. These different tempers are indicated in Scripture, by the effects which follow the offering of the fruits and of the animal. It ends with Abel becoming himself the sacrifice, Cain the murderer.

The sacrifice of Noah led us on to another stage in the development of the idea of sacrifice. Trust in a righteous and life-giving Being was, in his case, as much as in that of Abel, the meaning of his offering. The disorder and unrighteousness of the world had destroyed it; its order had been preserved; God had upholden it and would uphold it; Noah represented his own race and all the creatures that bowed to that race, when he took of the clean beasts and offered them to the Lord. The delight which the Lord is said to have taken in that act, is the testimony that He sympathises with His creatures; that He recognises them as meant for fellowship with him; that He is leading them on, by all His secret government, to know that that fellowship is the foundation of their intercourse with each other.

The passage I have read to you, this afternoon, implies what we have learnt from both the others; but it leads us much farther into the heart of the subject. It is very needful to remark, that we are not *yet* come to the period of decrees and regulations concerning worship or anything else. The book of Genesis becomes absolutely unintelligible—its distinction from the one which follows is altogether lost—if we suppose the patriarchs to be living under a code, or under any of the conditions which belong to an organised nation. They are simply men on a plain, taking care of flocks and herds, dwelling in tents. Their *apparent* difference from those who surround them is, that they have made less progress in social arts and social government. The *real* difference is, that they believe and that they hope. They believe in a righteous Lord, who has given them their flocks, and their man-servants and maid-servants. They hope for a Seed in which all the families of the earth are to be blessed. Those who dwell in the cities of the plain have had their kings and armies for one knows not how long. Abraham is just at the beginning of the political life, which is nearly at an end with them. In Egypt there are priests and sacrifices; a hierarchy; a kingdom. In Assyria there are already the rudiments of an empire, and probably works of art indicating a knowledge of animal forms and a singular power of representing them. Abraham has to learn the very elements of worship, what a priesthood exist for, how man comes to have that dominion over animals which the monuments of Nineveh express; how he is liable to abuse that dominion till it turns into slavery. I have endeavoured to point out these facts to you before, and to show how the discoveries which prove the might and wisdom and antiquity of Asiatic or African empires, prove also the necessity of a society so entirely elementary, so purely pastoral, as that which the first book of the Bible presents to us ; in order that the whole civilisation of the world might not turn out to be its curse and its ruin, by proceeding on principles utterly inverted, inhuman, false. I am now desirous to apply this observation to the particular case before us, to consider by what process the father of the faithful was instructed in the doctrine of sacrifice, while so many people around him were practising sacrificial rites, and were connecting them with the outward and inward economy of their lives.

A man who has been what is called lucky or fortunate in all his enterprises, may feel as if he had no one to thank but himself for what he possesses, or if anything but himself, some power which does not especially want his thanks, and will not set any store by them. A man who has failed in whatever he has undertaken, may look upon earth and heaven as if they were conspiring against him. But a man who has waited long for some good, which has seemed to him more blessed each day that has *not* brought it to him, and yet has also seemed each day more improbable—who has been sure from the first that, if it ever came, it must be a gift from one who watched over him and cared for him, and who, for that very reason, has gone on trusting that he shall receive it—yes, growing in trust as the natural difficulties looked more insurmountable,—such a man, when the dream of his heart becomes a substantial reality, has a sense of grateful joy, which turns to pain, which is actually oppressive, till it can find some outlet. Yet what outlet can it find? what can he do for the giver more than rejoice and wonder at the gift; more than say, 'It is thine?' Nothing, perhaps; but how can he say *that?* how can he utter what he means to one who, he knows, is the source of all he has, and can need nothing from him? What can he offer?—a mere sign or symbol?—a sheep which he would slay for his own food, and which he would not miss out of his flock?—a miserable sample of the fruits which the earth is pouring out to him? It must surely be something better, more precious than any of these. His own heart seems to scorn such presents: must not the heart of Him to whom he brings them?

The description I have given is precisely the description which, in simpler, truer language, the book of Genesis gives us of Abraham. He has waited, longed, feared, trusted, received. The child has come to him in his old age,—a child to whom blessings are attached, which he cannot measure, which stretch into the farthest future. From him are to come as many as the stars or as the sands. It is indeed a child of laughter and joy. He has lived for this; as he looks upon it, it appears to him the pledge and witness of an infinite, inexhaustible life. The child has brought him nearer to God; though he has believed in him so long, it is as if he now believed in Him for the first time,—so much is he carried out of himself, such a vision has he of One who orders ages past and to come, and yet is interested for him, is interested for the feeblest of those whom He has made. Out of such feelings comes the craving for the power to make some sacrifice, to find a sacrifice which shall be not nominal but real.

Many strange and perplexing thoughts invaded men's minds in past times, as they invade men's minds now. When they became very tormenting, then, as now, people betook themselves to some wise man. They asked, What do these thoughts mean? whence do they come? what are we to do in consequence of them? They got various answers. The answers, in different places, shaped themselves into different rules and maxims; forms of service and devotion were grounded upon them; above all, sacrifices were suggested, which might satisfy the desires of the creature, perhaps might satisfy the demands of his ruler. The book of Genesis says, '*GOD did tempt Abraham.*' It leads us back to the source from which the thoughts that were working in him were derived. It says broadly and distinctly, This seed did not drop by accident into the patriarch's mind; it was not self-sown; it was not put into him by the suggestion of some of his fellows. It was part of the discipline to which he was subjected that these questions should be excited in him. It was his divine Teacher who led him on to the terrible conclusion : 'The sacri-
'fice that I must offer is that very gift which has caused
'me all my joy. That belongs to God. I can only ex-
'press my dependence upon God, my thankfulness to

'Him, by laying my son upon the altar.' If it was true that he had been called out by the living and true God to serve Him and trust Him and be a witness for Him— if it was true that he had received his child from God— it was true also, he could not doubt it, that this was a command, that it was a command directly addressed to him; that he was to obey it.

'But is it not very frightful to think that such an
'impression as this could be made on the heart of a good
'man?—should become a fixed purpose in him?—that he
'should passively surrender himself to it? If the case
'was peculiar, if Abraham's experience was to be no pre-
'cedent for other men, what is the history of the Bible
'worth, what does it teach, whom is it to guide? If it
'was a precedent, then have not the followers of it been
'the fanatics, whose opinions we consider signs of mad-
'ness; whose open acts, being outrages upon society, states
'are obliged to restrain and punish?' I answer, Before you determine whether Abraham's history is an example or a beacon, try to understand what it is. You say that it is ignominious for a man to be the victim of an impression. This history says the same. It does not represent Abraham as feeling an impulse to slay his son, and as surrendering himself to that impulse; still less does it represent God as designing that the man should commit that enormity. But it tells us that a man who thoroughly trusted God,—thoroughly believed Him to be a righteous Being,—was thoroughly persuaded that he cared for him, and had proved that He

did by giving him a son—became convinced that this
God, for some reason which he could not interpret,
claimed his child of him again. It was a horrible
thought that this was the only victim with which God
could be content, a more horrible thought still that
he was to slay the victim. Do you suppose that it
was less horrible to Abraham than it would have been
to a man of less faith? I believe it was horrible
precisely in proportion to his faith. For it was all in all
to him to think that he was serving a true God, a Judge
who must do right. And here something seemed to be
demanded of him which was not right—which was
wrong. And yet who made the demand? Whence but
from God had the deep conviction proceeded, that he
was to offer this sacrifice, and no other? An Assyrian
or Egyptian might have shrunk from such a deed through
a paternal instinct; but there could have been nothing
very tremendous to him in supposing that a god had
decreed it. If the soothsayer or priest told him so, he
could have little doubt that to obey would be the safer
course, though he might not have courage to follow it.
But with Abraham, that which was almost nothing to
them, was everything. To give up his confidence in
God, to regard Him as a man who did what He liked
to do, was to give up his calling, his covenant, all that
made existence a blessing and not a curse. Therefore,
he must know what this contradiction signified. He
could not quench the thought if he tried. And what
comfort would there have been in such a trial? How

can a man who has reposed in the justice and affection of a fellow-man, entertain a suspicion that he is requiring something of him which is inconsistent with both, and merely let that suspicion dwell as one of the citizens of his heart? Will it not cause a revolt among all the rest? He can have no peace till he sees through his doubt, till it is cleared entirely away. And if he has perfectly trusted in his friend, if he is one to whom he has always bowed in submission, who has taught him all that he knows of what is right and true, he will say: 'I do 'not understand this suggestion of yours. If you mean 'by it what I mean, all is over with me,—my faith is 'gone. But that cannot be. I will leave nothing 'undone that will help me to find out what it is you 'really wish of me; at all events, I will give *myself* into 'your hands.'

Conceive such a trust as never can be put in the righteousness of any human creature, and this is Abraham's story. He *must* know what God's meaning is; he is certain that in some way it will be proved that He has not designed His creature to do a wicked and monstrous thing, and yet that there is a purpose in the revelation that has been made to him; that a submission and a sacrifice, such as he had never made yet, were called for now. He takes his son; he goes three days' journey to Mount Moriah; he prepares the altar, and the wood, and the knife; his son is with him; but he has already offered up *himself*. And now he is taught that this is the offering which God was seeking for; that when he had presented that, he had given the real thing for which he had perceived no sacrifice of a lamb or an ox could be exchanged; that when the *real* victim had been slain, the ram caught in the thicket was all that was needed for the *symbolical* expression of that inward oblation.

And what was the reward? '*In blessing*' (said the divine voice) '*I will bless thee, in multiplying I will multiply thee.*' When this secret had been learnt,—learnt in this plain manner through an act,—when he had done God's will, and been so taught of His doctrine,—every blessing became an actual, vital blessing; every gift that might have been only an outside possession, was changed into a spiritual treasure. He had become free of God's universe; for he had begun to understand the principle upon which God rules it, and the law of man's position in it. He had found sacrifice to be no one solitary act, no sudden expression of joy, no violent effort to make a return for blessings which we can only return by accepting; but that it lies at the very root of our being; that our lives stand upon it; that society is held together by it; that all power to be right, and to do right, begins with the offering up of ourselves, because it is thus that the righteous Lord makes us like Himself.

Yes, like Himself! There was a mystery in this, which Abraham could dimly and awfully look into, which ages to come must unfold. I do not anticipate any of the deeper truths respecting the nature of sacrifice, which were hidden in this act, and which God in His own method would bring to light. I only wish you to perceive how perfectly adapted this teaching was to remove those falsehoods which we know beset and tormented the hearts of men in the old world, and which we still find are besetting and tormenting men in the nineteenth century.

The tradition in old Greece respecting the sacrifice which the god demanded before the fleet could sail for Troy, took possession of the minds of her greatest thinkers. The tragic poet, as he recorded with such tenderness the conflict in the heart of the father, and the preparation for slaying the victim, evidently felt in his devout and earnest spirit, that he was celebrating a victory of patriotic over paternal feeling, as well as a sublime though tremendous act of homage to the rulers of nature and of man. On the other hand, the Roman Epicurean poet, translating the description of Æschylus in language and in a spirit worthy of his model, expressed the most intense disgust and loathing for the whole narrative; it embodied to him all the crimes of which a belief in divinities interested in human affairs had been the origin. I think that the conscience of mankind has responded to the sympathy of one poet and the indignant denunciation of the other; that it has recognised a positive truth in each, however little it may have been able to bring them into accordance. In our days, we rather value ourselves upon the equity and tolerance with which we can admit that there is *something* in these opposing statements; the misfortune is, that in general we care but little about either. We are impartial critics; the fear is, that we shall cease to be men, really understanding that those whom we criticise had the same flesh and blood with ourselves; that there is no infirmity of theirs to which we are not subject, no right and high conviction which we do not want as much as they did. Depend upon it, brethren, we shall be reminded by very decisive evidence of that truth, if we have been shutting our eyes to it. We have not got rid, any of us, of these old dreams about sacrifices; we cannot get rid of them; they haunt us in innumerable ways; no man, or woman, or child, is unaffected by them: no theory, religious or philosophical, dispossesses the heart of them. The Atheist has his own notion and method of immolation—his own victims; you cannot exorcise a fellow-creature of the most radical part of his being by your incantations; they will prove very ineffectual for yourselves. Soft, silken phrases about the superstitions of old times and the enlightenment and benevolence of the present serve well, when men have enough to eat and drink and little to disturb them in themselves or in their fortunes. Try them in any dark hour of individual experience, in any 'popular convulsions, with men who toil and suffer, and they are found empty and hollow. But if instead of pretending to disbelieve facts which the history of the world and of yourselves establishes, you will look these facts in the face—if you will ask why this notion of sacrifice has been so mighty and so mischievous? why you must act upon it? why you feel often as if you could not act upon it without doing evil?—then, as you are in earnest, as you are seeking, not for the satisfaction of your curiosity, but for the satisfaction of your consciences—these old records of the world will, I am sure, point your path through the mists by which you are encircled, into the clear sunlight. Perhaps you fancied it was a book which tolerated no difficulties, which merely pronounced authoritative sentences. You will find it exhibiting to you men who were beset by the very perplexities which beset you; unable to find any road through them till they confessed a guide, of whom they lived to testify that He would be ours as much as he was theirs. Perhaps you will suppose that, as it professes to contain divine revelations, it can take no account of those speculations of heathens, to which I have alluded; that it must treat them as profane, or else pass them by altogether. You will here find the practical reconciliation of those speculations,—the only reconciliation which is not worse than either of them separately. For it shows you why sacrifice must be precious and dear in the eyes of Him who governs the spirits of men; why He cannot ask for any sacrifice which a loving father would not make and a loving child would not offer. And you will find in this story of the method by which Abraham came to knowledge and to peace, what must be your course too. You cannot trust God too much. You cannot be too confident that He himself is guiding you, and that every embarrassment in your thoughts, every complication in your circumstances, is known by Him, is intended by Him as a means to enable you to understand wisdom secretly, that you may show forth the fruits of it openly. The rashness that leads you to act at once upon some impression, to make some apparently great sacrifice which will startle and astonish other men, is a sign of distrust and of pride. The cowardice that makes you wish to stifle the suggestions of your hearts, the witness of your consciences, has the same origin. Faith in the righteousness of God gives that prudence or providence which will make you wary of your footsteps, suspicious of yourselves. Faith in the righteousness of God gives you that courage which will enable you to move on steadily, calmly, resolutely, certain that you will have light to see what you ought to do, and that in doing it you will know more of the just and gracious mind of God towards all men as well as towards yourselves.

If we follow this teaching, we shall learn that we must be ready to present our souls and bodies, and all that is dear to us, every day as sacrifices to God. And then we may leave it to Him how and when it shall please Him to take these souls and bodies for other services than those to which He has appointed them here. It may be in the battle-field; it may be on the judgment-seat, like him whom many of you here knew as the accomplished scholar and cordial friend, and whose dying words of wisdom all of us should earnestly lay to heart.[1] At sunset or at cock-crowing, on the sick-bed, or in the midst of work, the voice may reach any of us. It is enough for us to know whose voice it is, and to what it is summoning us. It is the voice of Him who made a covenant with Abraham; who has made a better covenant with us. It is calling us to make a real sacrifice, to present ourselves to God. Then we shall see in the thicket the Lamb that has been already slain; we shall see in that Lamb a Son whom the Father has offered up, and who has gone together with Him in a voluntary and perfect self-oblation.

[1] Mr. Justice Talfourd died the Monday before this Sermon was preached.

SERMON IV.

SACRIFICE OF THE PASSOVER.

(Lincoln's Inn, 4th Sunday in Lent, March 26, 1854.)

'And it shall be when thy son asketh thee in time to come, saying, What is this? that thou shalt say unto him, By strength of hand the Lord brought us out from Egypt, from the house of bondage: and it came to pass, when Pharaoh would hardly let us go, that the Lord slew all the firstborn in the land of Egypt, both the firstborn of man, and the firstborn of beast: therefore I sacrifice to the Lord all that openeth the matrix, being males; but all the firstborn of my children I redeem. And it shall be for a token upon thine hand, and for frontlets between thine eyes: for by strength of hand the Lord brought us forth out of Egypt.'— EXODUS xiii. 14–17.

THE book of Exodus, as I intimated last Sunday, introduces that new epoch in the scriptural history of sacrifices, when they begin to be regulated by fixed laws, to be part of a national economy. I say the book of Exodus, for I am anxious that you should distinguish between that and the following book, which is expressly devoted to the subject of sacrifices, and of the tribe which offered them. If we hurried on to the lessons which are contained in Leviticus, we should miss a link in the chain of instruction which is quite indispensable. Before we study the institutions of a nation, we ought to know what the nation itself is, upon what foundation its order stands. The second book in the Bible contains the answer to that question, as far as the Jewish nation is concerned. I do not know where we can find the principle of it more accurately, or livingly, set forth than in the verses I have just read to you. Moses supposes a son to be asking a father, in some distant time, about the Passover, which he and his family are keeping. The answer is simple and historical, adapted to the comprehension of a child. But the most learned Israelite would have made it far less satisfactory, would have well-nigh destroyed the meaning of it, if he had tried to give it a more profound and abstract character.

You must consider what the most ignorant of the Israelites who had dwelt in Egypt had seen,—what their descendants in Canaan were likely to see,—before you can appreciate the force, either of the question or of the answer. An organised hierarchy, as I said last Sunday, most probably existed in Egypt in the time of Abraham. The Scripture notices it in the time of Joseph. It must have grown stronger, and have introduced more complicated forms of worship before the time of Moses. The wisdom of the Egyptians may have concerned itself with things in heaven above or in the earth beneath, with the motions of the stars and the processes of agriculture, with nature and art; but we may be sure that notions respecting the objects of worship and the means of propitiating them, were worked into every part of it, and that this was *the* part of it which would present the most glaring and obvious effects to the looker-on. Sacrifices of various kinds, sacrifices to various divinities, sacrifices to procure the removal of particular local evils or of recurring general evils, sacrifices to avert the wrath of the gods for transgressions that had been undoubtedly committed, sacrifices for transgressions that were suspected to have been committed, sacrifices regular and habitual, sacrifices new and unwonted for strange emergencies, all these would have been seen or heard of by the slaves in Goshen as well as by the native subjects of the Pharaohs. Much might be hidden from both; much might be done to impress both with the feeling that the priest or the magician had a lore which he could not communicate: but the material part of the worship would be patent; the very object would be to force *that* upon the attention of the most vulgar.

Therefore any Israelitish child in the Wilderness who pointed to the paschal lamb and asked, '*What is this?*' may have been supposed to mean, 'Is this like one of 'the sacrifices which you have told me the Egyptians 'offered? Is this feast like one of the feasts they make 'at their sacrifices? If it is not so, what is the differ- 'ence?' And any child who said to his father in the land of Canaan, '*What is this?*' would mean in like manner, 'Is this such a sacrifice as the Canaanites or 'the Phœnicians are offering to their Baal and Astoreth?

'If not, tell us what the difference is. Why are we not
'like them? Why do you bid us keep aloof from their
'worship and their offerings?' Consider what would have
been the natural and expected reply to such a question,
supposing the principle upon which the Israelites offered
sacrifices had been the same with that on which the
Egyptians or the Phœnicians offered them. The child
would have heard of some great advantage which this
sacrifice was to buy,—of some threatened peril which it
was to keep off. It would have been told that the Lord
God of the Hebrews was mightier and more terrible
than the gods of On or of Ekron; and, therefore, that,
if it was thought necessary to offer them sacrifices with
which they would be pleased, it must be far more prudent
and necessary to offer them to Him. The consequences
of neglecting them would have been pointed out from
past experience. 'What might not He who ruled the
'winds and the waves be contriving against them? How
'likely was it, that He who had favoured their fathers
'might desert them, and choose some more devout
'suppliants if they neglected Him!'

Perhaps more refined arguments than these might
have been adapted to people with devout spiritual
tastes and instincts; but would not you have thought
these, or such as these, exceedingly suitable to the condition of the uninformed man or boy who is supposed
to be taking part in the dialogue? Would not they be
just such as religious teachers, in all countries and ages,
have thought were desirable to impress people, not

capable of understanding high truths, or being influenced by nobler motives, with a salutary fear of omitting duties which it was needful that they should perform? There can be no doubt that the legislator desired fathers to give their children a deep sense of the sacredness of the national service in which they were engaged, of the exceeding evil that might come from indifference to it. For such a purpose, what course could be so obvious as the one I have pointed out; what other can we think of that must not be less effectual?

It is *not* the course, you perceive, which Moses prescribes. We can scarcely conceive of one more opposed to it than his. Instead of beginning with saying what was to be gained for those who should perform this service at any given time, he speaks of it as commemorating an act which was done already, which might have been done ages before the conversation occurred. '*By strength of hand the Lord brought us out from Egypt.*' 'We are recollecting an event which 'happened to our fathers' fathers, to men who were 'suffering from evils which we are not suffering from, 'who were bondsmen in a land which we have not seen, 'and are never likely to see.' But again, 'This sacrifice 'which we are offering never did purchase the good- 'will of Him to whom it was presented—was *not* the 'influence by which in past days, any more than in these 'days, He was moved to look favourably upon our race. 'He Himself chose our fathers; He Himself wrought

'out their deliverance. The origin of it, the whole con-
'duct of it, was in Him. He claimed us for his people:
'by this act our fathers declared, and we declare, that
'He is our King. Do you think that we want to
'persuade Him to deliver us from certain mischiefs
'and evils which He has brought upon us? Why! we
'know Him only by that name of *Deliverer.* We were
'in bondage to a tyrant; He broke our chains. Pharaoh
'was grinding down our fathers with hard tasks, He
'said that He had seen their affliction and pitied them.
'Pharaoh would hardly let us go out of our bondage;
'by fire and by blood, and by the slaughter of the first-
'born, He obliged him to let us go.'

Still the child or the inquiring man might answer,
'This does not explain the sacrifice; that has surely
'something to do with punishment and vengeance; that
'must be intended to avert punishment and vengeance
'from those who present it. You spoke of a slaughter
'of the firstborn in Egypt, both of man and beast; you
'spoke of the firstborn of the Israelites being passed
'over; you spoke of their offering a lamb, and marking
'the door-posts of their houses with the blood of it. If
'God is the Deliverer of some, He surely executes wrath
'upon others. Do you not offer the lamb and keep this
'feast, that you may be the objects of His mercy, not of
'His wrath?' 'Most assuredly,' the answer would be,
if it was framed in the spirit of the one which Moses
gives us, 'most assuredly we do believe in a God of
'wrath and vengeance—in One who executes wrath and

'vengeance upon the oppressor, and this without respect
' of persons. His anger may descend upon the king or
' the subject, upon the Israelite as well as upon the
' Egyptian. It not only *may*, but we know assuredly
' that it *will*. His government is not one of accident or
' caprice, but of fixed eternal law. He is the God of
' righteousness, and without iniquity; whatever is un-
' righteous, iniquitous, sets itself at war against Him;
' He is pledged to destroy it. Pharaoh was self-willed;
' he believed in might, not in right; he became an
' oppressor, and his people became oppressors of others,
' while they suffered from his wrong. Therefore, the
' righteous God smote them. Because He was the Deli-
' verer of the poor, and of them that had no helper, He
' manifested His strength against those who trampled
' upon them, against the proud man of the earth. The
' slaughter of the firstborn tells us what it is that
' causes the great visitations upon the world—what
' overthrows families and kingdoms. Looked at on one
' side, it is their own tyranny, and brutality, and hatred;
' looked at from the other side, it is the righteousness
' and truth upon which the world stands, which the
' powers in heaven obey, which none can transgress
' without encountering that which is mightier. You are
' right, that our sacrifice has to do with the slaughter of
' the firstborn. It is *therefore* that we sacrifice the
' firstborn of every beast being male. This is the witness
' we bear, that we hold everything of the righteous Lord,
' the Redeemer; thus we declare that we look upon the

'life of every animal as given by Him; thus we declare 'that we do not worship this animal life in any creature, 'or in ourselves; thus we affirm that we have dominion 'over it, and that we are to devote it to the use of that 'which is higher than itself. *But all the firstborn of my 'children I redeem.* I dare not treat them as I treat the 'animals; I know that they are made in God's image; 'I know that to slay them upon an altar would not be 'to sacrifice them to God; He wants them for other 'services than that. But He *does* want them, and I 'devote them to Him. I declare that they belong to 'Him as much as any beast belongs to Him; I offer 'them up as sacrifices to Him who has redeemed them; 'I declare that every day and hour they live, they are 'to bear witness of the redemption He has made for 'them—to prove, by their words and acts, that they are 'servants of One who cares for them and whom they 'can trust, not of a tyrant who uses them as his tools, 'and whom they hate.'

This offering of the firstborn, then,—of the firstborn of the animals as dead sacrifices, of the firstborn of men as living sacrifices,—was the dedication and consecration of the whole Jewish nation. The firstborn represented its strength, its vitality, its endurance. This act signified that its strength lay only in its dependence on God's strength; that its vitality came from the life which is in Him; that it would endure from generation to generation, because He is the same, and His years fail not. By this earliest token,

God signified that He had constituted a society upon this divine basis; a society which would stand so long as it confessed this basis—which would fall as soon as it tried to establish itself upon any other. What was true of the nation as a body, was true of each member of it. He was at once adopted into the covenant; he came in under this law of sacrifice. Before he could understand anything of its meaning, the devotion and consecration were made on his behalf; he was put into his right and reasonable position; he was claimed as a holy thing, separated to the Lord. His parents were bound to assert this privilege for him; it was the pledge that they looked upon him as their true child; it was the pledge that they did not look upon him only as their child, but as the child of Abraham; it was the pledge that they regarded the child of Abraham as united by a living bond to the God of Abraham. To fail in the act which denoted the sacrifice of the individual infant, was to show that they thought nothing of the privilege of being God's servants and witnesses; that they did not hold that to be the inheritance of their sons; that they did not send them forth as the soldiers of the Invisible King. To omit the general annual service which attested the redemption and sacrifice of the whole nation—which affirmed that it was a holy nation, separated for holy uses and services—was to show that they were indifferent to their standing as Israelites, and were choosing out some new ground for themselves. To choose that new ground was, in fact, to choose a new God. Their calling, as Israelites, was the calling to confess a Redeemer of Israel, a righteous Being who had brought out their fathers from the house of bondage. It was certain that whenever they forgot this confession,—whenever they became careless about the appointed means of expressing it,—they would cease to believe in a Redeemer at all. That name would not be their high tower, their refuge from all enemies. Gradually, if not at once, it would be changed for other names, indicating the most opposite convictions, involving the most opposite kinds of devotion and sacrifice; and out of that new name, that new worship, would proceed moral and political plagues and curses, which nothing would avert but a national repentance and a return to the faith which they had cast off.

I wish you to think of these plagues and curses as they are presented to us in the books of the Old Testament, that you may judge how truly human as well as divine the constitution of the Jewish nation was; how necessarily it was the one because it was the other; how exactly the Passover sacrifice and the dedication of the firstborn expressed the union. To say that belief in God as a Redeemer and a Deliverer is easy and natural for men, that it is their tendency to accept and retain this belief, is to contradict the evidence of all history. Egypt, Assyria, Phœnicia, every country with which the Jews came in contact, disproved such a dream. No doubt the belief was latent in every one of them; the more light one has upon their mythology, the more one sees that it is—the more one feels that it was—the truth which lay beneath the existence of every nation and sustained it. This undoubted fact is not at variance with the facts which show that there was a perpetual tendency in the popular mind to let go this truth, to substitute for it the worship of a tyrant—whom they could rarely, through God's mercy, contemplate in one concentrated form—whom they were *obliged* to see in a multitude of broken inconsistent forms. The two parts of the evidence illustrate and confirm each other. These popular tendencies, which became moulded into a system by the priests who had first yielded to them, were the causes of a continually increasing superstition, division, brutality, cowardice; can there be a greater proof that in that which they were resisting and subverting we are to seek for the unity of every people, for the secret of the powers which it put forth? The Bible, instead of urging any claim of special virtue for the chosen people, is careful, as I have so often remarked, to point out how liable they were to every corruption of other people; how every element of superstition and division was lying secretly in their hearts; how it did actually manifest itself at every new opportunity, under any fresh provocation from without. The consistency of this testimony throughout all the books of their History and Prophecy, is one of the most curious signs of their unity, a sign which the most areless reader cannot help noticing, but which becomes more striking the more we reflect upon it. The plague and curse of the Israelites, as it is represented to us, not in one but in all of these books, was their falling into the acknowledgment of tyrant gods—of brute gods—their losing their faith in the High God, the Redeemer. The words are so familiar, so commonplace, that one can hardly fix the attention of hearers upon them; but what a key they are to the history of the old and of the modern world! All external plagues, famines, wars, are represented as means of reawakening their faith, of recalling the nation and its members from the idols to which they were bowing down, from the accursed principles which they were exalting to the throne of God. These idols, these accursed divinities, were all connected with sacrifices; they demanded the continual oblation, the fire upon the altar; they demanded the inward offering, the giving up of the spirit to that which was immoral and base. The heart was to confess an oppressor as God; then it must set up some human oppressor, or change the one it had into an oppressor; then it must utter itself in acts of oppression to all beneath. The sacrifice to evil powers embodies all the falsehoods and crimes that are at work in all directions throughout a country; it gives them their sanction, their inspiration; it provides for the degradation of those who are not yet utterly degraded; it hinders all efforts for the removal of the most flagrant outward grievances; it ensures their perpetual increase. It is a Sisyphus toil.

to better the social maxims or the individual morality
of a people which has accepted devils for gods; the
gravitation of the stone downwards is mightier than all
your efforts to force it up. But if you try the other
course, which so many have tried, of denouncing sacrifice as being itself an unreal and mischievous idea,
having nothing to do with the life of a nation or of a
man—will you help the stone to ascend? Is not that
a monstrous attempt to contradict the experience of
mankind, to resist the witness of your own consciences?
You know that sacrifice has been a part of the institutions of every people under heaven; you know that
every better impulse of your own spirits leads you to
it, that every right act you have done has been a
sacrifice.

Oh! then consider manfully if there is not a better
course; if it is not that which the legislator of Israel
took, when he explained to his countrymen in his
own day, when he bade them tell their children in all
days to come, how they might resist the superstitions
of the surrounding world, and in themselves; how
they might go forth to fight with them; how they
might at last extinguish them. By looking upon
themselves as beings surrendered and sacrificed to the
God of Truth, to the Deliverer of men, to Him
who cares for the oppressed, to Him who puts down
the wrong-doer and the tyrant; by feeling that they
held all the powers of their minds and bodies, all
the creatures he had committed to them, all their

outward possessions, as instruments for the great work in which He is engaged; by keeping up this conviction in their own hearts, not suffering it to slumber through neglect of any ordinances that affirmed His righteous government and redemption, and united them to their countrymen as His subjects; by teaching these lessons to their sons, bringing them up as brave, hardy, cheerful citizens of God's kingdom and of that land which He had given their forefathers; by holding all external sufferings and bodily calamities to be nothing, in comparison of the moral diseases which stifle and eat up a nation's spirit; by regarding the one as a necessary effect of the other, and God's blessed method of curing them: thus Moses instructed the Israelites that they might be a nation indeed, one which would be a pattern to the nations, one which, in due time, would break the chains which bound *them* to visible and invisible oppressors. Their patriotism; their heathenism; the victories which they won in their weakness; the contempt into which they fell when they boasted of their strength; the mighty blessings which they have achieved for the world and have bequeathed to it; the curse that has come on their pride, exclusiveness, and money worship; these are the witnesses of the veracity of the history, of the worth and certainty of its principle, which make our petty arguments on behalf of either look very pale and contemptible. But it is not for this chiefly that I refer to them. It is because I think we have here set forth to us the ground upon which every nation stands now—the ground on which our nation is standing; the ground which we must each of us feel to be beneath his own feet, if we are not to rock and reel in any great convulsions which may be appointed for us. Let us understand it well, Brethren; we too are a people dedicated and sacrificed. To some power or other, good or evil, we must be devoted; there is no choice about that. It may be to Baal or Moloch or Mammon. It may be to the Lord God of Abraham; the Redeemer, the Holy One, the God and Father of our Lord Jesus Christ; to Him from whom comes the Spirit of Truth and Freedom and Unity. Our fathers said that it was this God, and not any of the others, to which we were offered up. They said that when we were baptized He who breaks asunder the bonds of the captive, chose us as His redeemed children; that then and there we were sacrificed to Him and signed with the sign of sacrifice, in token that hereafter we should not be ashamed to confess the faith of Christ crucified, and to fight valiantly under his banner against sin, the world, and the devil. That is our national consecration; that is our individual consecration. In the strength of that, we may go forth, we are pledged to go forth, against every false principle, and base, dishonourable practice, that enslaves ourselves and that enslaves the world. In the strength of that dedication and sacrifice we are bound to eschew every kind of worship and sacrifice that is not offered to a Righteous and Gracious King and Deliverer; we are bound to watch and suspect the growth of it in ourselves and in our land,—to combat it, as it only can be combated, by continually remembering the true ground and meaning of sacrifice,—by continually recollecting to Whom it is that we are given up, Who has sealed us, and with what Spirit, as a witness that He has accepted the offering and that we belong to Him. And never for a moment let us try to separate, or dream that we can separate, our individual life from our national. Our vocation is the same in the most private occupations, and when we are fulfilling what are called our duties as citizens. Every duty is a civic duty. We are fighting in our closets for our nation, if we are fighting truly for ourselves; our soldiers should go out to open battle against the foes of freedom and order with the same recollections, with the same sense of self-devotion as that which we would cultivate at home. Commonly they shame us: there is more simple surrender, more casting away of themselves, not for fame or glory, but simply because it is their calling, their plain duty, than we can pretend to in our most sacred private or public acts of devotion. We should try to learn from them this indifference to effect and to consequences; we should try to teach them what the true basis of it is, how it is laid deep in God's own claim that we should be like Him,—that we should be witnesses for Him,—that we should do His work. When once we understand that, self-sacrifice can never be an ambitious thing—a fine way to get the reputation of saints or the rewards of another world. It will be regarded as the true ground of all action; that on which all the blessed relations of life stand; that upon which all the charities and sympathies of life depend; that which is at the same time the only impulse to and security for the hard and rough work of the world—for the reluctant but necessary blows which are inflicted upon the miscreants who abuse God-given power to the service of the devil, and the injury of their fellows—for the wrongs which are endured by those who testify to the world that the works thereof are evil. Sacrifice is the common root and uniting bond and reasonable explanation of all those acts which seem in the eyes of men, often in the eyes of those who perform them, most hostile to each other, but which God sees to be essentially alike, and which in due time justify themselves as proceeding from the same children of wisdom, though one may be said to have a devil because he wears camels' hair, and a mightier than he be called a gluttonous man and a wine-bibber, because He eats and drinks with publicans and sinners. But Sacrifice cannot have this ennobling and mysterious power—it will be turned into self-glory, and lose its own nature and acquire a devil nature—if it is not contemplated as all flowing from the nature of God; if it is not referred to Him as its author as well as its end. Think of this as you kneel at the altar, which is more wonderful than any Jewish altar because it speaks of a finished Sacrifice. Think of it as you eat that feast which is like the Jewish Passover, because it is individual, because it is common, because it testifies of God as a Redeemer, because it testifies of Him as the avenger of all evil; but which is higher than the Jewish Passover, because it is human and universal, because in it we partake of a Sacrifice which has been offered to gather together in one the children of God that are scattered abroad,—offered that they might be able to offer themselves as children to do their Father's work and will.

SERMON V.

THE LEGAL SACRIFICES.

(Lincoln's Inn, 5th Sunday in Lent, April 2, 1854.)

'And the Lord called unto Moses, and spake unto him out of the tabernacle of the congregation, saying, Speak unto the children of Israel, and say unto them, If any man of you bring an offering unto the Lord, ye shall bring your offering of the cattle, even of the herd, and of the flock. If his offering be a burnt-sacrifice of the herd, let him offer a male without blemish: he shall offer it of his own voluntary will at the door of the tabernacle of the congregation before the Lord. And he shall put his hand upon the head of the burnt-offering; and it shall be accepted for him, to make atonement for him. And he shall kill the bullock before the Lord: and the priests, Aaron's sons, shall bring the blood, and sprinkle the blood round about upon the altar that is by the door of the tabernacle of the congregation. . . . . And the priest shall burn all on the altar, to be a burnt-sacrifice, an offering made by fire, of a sweet savour unto the Lord.'—
LEVITICUS i. 1–6, and part of 9th verse.

You must now consider the Israelites as an organised nation. They have the Passover, which is to remind them from generation to generation that they are one people, one with their forefathers, one with their descendants, one because the Lord has redeemed them out of the house of bondage, one because He is their King for ever and ever. They have commandments, which tell them that they are not the subjects of a capricious despot, but of a righteous Ruler, who would have them know the laws by which they are governed. They have an interpreter of these laws, and a set of elders or heads of tribes who work with him in deciding the causes which arise between man and man. They have statutes, applicable to particular cases,—punishments, awarded to specific crimes. They have, lastly, a tabernacle, which goes with the people where they go,—which announces to them the presence of God with them,—which testifies that He is guiding them,—which is said to be a meeting place between them and Him,—in which a whole tribe is set apart to minister,—in which a family of that tribe is consecrated to offer sacrifices. What I am to speak of, to-day, is the relation between these sacrifices and the rest of the polity as I have described it,—the relation between them and the distinct Israelites who formed the congregation. I have taken the first verses of the book of Leviticus as my guide in this inquiry. As far as the principle of the national sacrifices is concerned, they are, it seems to me, all that we want. But they are the introduction to a book, to other parts of which I may have occasion to refer for the illustration of their meaning, and for the purpose of showing how the sacrifices for the nation as a body were connected with the sacrifices for its individual members.

The first words of the passage show us how needful it is that we should understand the principle of the Jewish commonwealth before we examine this institution of it. According to the heathen notion of sacrifice, as we considered it last Sunday, the offerings must be always experiments to obtain some benefit, which the power to whom they are presented can bestow, or to remove some evil which it is likely to inflict. The rules respecting them may have been devised by those whom the people held in most reverence for their wisdom or their sanctity. They may acquire fresh authority from long transmission and observance. But they are always liable to change. New and more extraordinary occasions may demand higher gifts, more august propitiations. Traditions may become more complicated each new stage, almost each new year. The child has experiences unknown to the father. Influences of the heavens upon the earth are detected which had not been before observed. Crimes multiply, and fears multiply with them. Who can tell that the sacrifice, which was available to remove the punishments which threatened one generation, or one man, may not utterly fail for another?

(1.) But here the very same voice which proclaimed the Commandments on Sinai is said to announce the nature of the sacrifices, and how, and when, and by whom they are to be presented. The unseen King and Lawgiver is here, as everywhere, making known His Will. Those sacrifices, which it was supposed were to bend and determine His Will, themselves proceed from it. To vary them at the suggestion of any priest, or council of priests, under any impulse or inspiration of devotion, or gratitude, or fear, or sense of evil, is to depart from His decrees, to commit one of those transgressions which the sacrifices themselves are provided to meet.

Consider how immense this difference is; how the doctrine of Moses reverses all those conceptions, and subverts all those motives, which are supposed by many to be at the basis of sacrifices, which have actually been at work in a vast majority of those who have brought them and enjoined them. But consider how exactly this doctrine accords with that which we found to be involved in the patriarchal sacrifices, when there was no precept enjoining them; how the security of fixed law carries out and expounds the principle to which we found men doing homage when there was no law. The difference between Abel's offering and Cain's, between Noah's and the offerings of the corrupt and violent men against whom he denounced judgments, between Abraham's and those of the cities of the plain,—is precisely that which is maintained in this more advanced stage of society, by the words which were spoken to the children of Israel *out of the tabernacle of the congregation.*

(2.) That they are said to be spoken *there,* is the next point to which I would draw your attention. The tabernacle, as I have just said, was the witness of God's abiding presence with the people, the pledge that they were to trust Him, and that He sought intercourse with them. From thence proceeded those precepts which have reference to trespasses, transgressions, sins; and to the methods which an Israelite, feeling that *he* had trespassed, transgressed, sinned, was to take for obtaining peace and reconciliation. A whole scheme of services, ordinances, institutes, is arranged and appointed under the most awful sanctions, by the Divine King—for what end? That He may re-establish an intercourse between Him and His subjects which has been interrupted; that He may bring back those whose hearts tell them they have wandered.

(3.) Again, it is not an insignificant point that the tabernacle is represented as the tabernacle of *the congregation*. There, where God dwells, is the proper home of the whole people; there they may feel that they *are* a whole people; there they may *know* that they are one, because He who has called them into covenant with Him is One. The more the sense of this unity was realised, the more easy and intelligible would be the words which follow.

(4.) '*Say to the children of Israel, If any of you bring* '*an offering unto the Lord.*' It is not said, 'You *shall* 'bring this offering;' it is said, '*If* you do, then so and 'so it must be brought.' The desire for such sacrifice is presumed. Might it not safely be presumed? Did not the condition and history of every people show that it existed; that it could only be stifled when the strongest and deepest convictions of humanity were stifled? Wherever there was in men *no* sense of thankfulness, of obligation, of dependence,—wherever men were entirely wrapped up in themselves, satisfied with themselves,—wherever they had no sense of the past being connected with the present, and the future with both,—there was no movement towards sacrifice, no effort to make sacrifice. Whoever cherished these feelings amidst the strangest perversions and contradictions, felt sacrifice to be a necessary and cardinal condition of their lives, though it might be turned to the destruction of the impulses which had prompted it. Everything in the position of the Jew was awakening in him the sense of gratitude, of obligation, of dependence. He had been redeemed; he was bound to the righteous Lord who had set him free; he had no hope of life and freedom but from Him. Moreover, he was one of the *children of Israel*; he had obligations to his fathers, to his children; he could not separate himself from his country. He was apprised of relationships which he could shake off; of laws which must execute themselves whether he obeyed them or not—which he was created to obey. In such a man the sense of transgression, of disobedience, is awakened more than in anyone else. His whole education serves to bring it forth in him. Everything tells him what has been done for him, what goodness and mercy are compassing him round; everything witnesses to him that there is a want of sympathy with them in him: everything tells him of an order that is fixed and that is blessed, and that there has been disorder in him. How certain was it that he would seek for some way of ridding himself of his burden, and that he would be ready to ask every person and thing to tell him what that way was. All the nations around would be saying to him, 'Our way 'of shaking off these troublesome thoughts and recollec-'tions, is to offer sacrifice. We go to the priest or wise 'man; he tells us what God we have grieved, how we 'are to make amends to him. We do what he bids us; 'we take it for granted that he has told us the right 'thing; we can then go comfortably to our business or 'our pleasure, and hope that all is right or will be right 'in due time. Of course there are some offences which 'require a greater compensation than others. Rich men 'are better off than the poor: when they have committed 'any huge crime, they can slaughter a whole herd by 'way of satisfaction, or bring some still more precious 'gift. We must do as well as we can. One animal will 'perhaps be reckoned enough in our case, both because 'more are not to be had, and because poverty may have 'had some share in making us go wrong.'

(5.) In many countries this would be the popular language. It would not be exactly so in Egypt; there the animal *worship* would in some degree interfere with the animal *sacrifice*. The ox might rather receive the offering, than be made the victim. The command to the Jew is not that he should offer any peculiar novel sacrifice. He is to take *of the herd and the flock*, the same kind of offering which Noah or Abraham would have presented; he is not to fear to take it, lest he should be extinguishing any divine life. The lesson is a double one. The common things, the most ordinary part of his possessions, are those which he is to bring; that is one part of his teaching: the animals are subjects of man; he is to rule them and make use of them for his own higher objects; that is another.

(6.) He, however, is to understand that the service he is engaged in, is a serious one. He may easily be tempted to regard it as a formality which he is to go through; but which is to be despatched with as little cost to himself, either of outward goods or of thought, as he can spend upon it. He must be reminded that sacrifice upon these terms is a lie. The demand that the victim from the herd shall be a *male without blemish* is a silent admonition to him of this truth if it leads him to reflect and question himself why such a rule should be laid down for him, one part of the object is accomplished; the ceremony is no longer a mere ceremony; the spirit of a man is occupied with it; the offering of the animal, he begins to perceive, is not the chief part of the sacrifice.

(7.) And to assist this conviction there comes in, the clause which sounds so strange in an accurate and formal edict, that he *shall offer it of his own voluntary will at the door of the tabernacle of the congregation before the Lord.* 'After all, then, it is matter of choice 'whether he will perform or neglect this service?'

Certainly: if there is no sense in him of evil done, or evil to be removed; if he has committed no trespass; if he has incurred no defilement; if he has no need of reconciliation;—he is not under any compulsion to approach the tabernacle. If he is a true Israelite, —if he has taken any measure of that which is implied in this name,—if he knows what it is to be a devoted, dedicated being to God, what it is to be one of a congregation, he is certain to feel that he has departed again and again from his right condition. But, as it is needful to assert that all sacrifice proceeds from the will of God, it is equally needful to affirm that the sacrifice is accomplished only by the consent of the will of man; that without that consent it is absolutely without meaning.

(8.) Although, however, there is this vindication of choice in the act of bringing the gift, there is no choice whatever as to the place at which it is to be presented. The words are strict and imperative: '*He shall offer it at the door of the tabernacle of the congregation.*' 'It is a private calamity he wishes to avert; why not offer private sacrifice? It is a sin of his *own* he wishes to be free from; why come forth to make this public acknowledgment of it?' Such questions, according to the heathen views of sacrifice, were unanswerable; the whole faith of the Jew perished if he listened to them. Out of those notions of private sacrifice, grew everything which was superstitious, idolatrous, destructive of a commonwealth. It was not the bond to a common Lord that had been broken; it was an offence that had been committed against some special power,—some avenging deity, of earth or air. It was not the bond to the fellow-citizen that had been broken; the individual could set himself right, without any reference to father, wife, children, neighbours. An altogether confused notion of the nature of evil, a disbelief in the privileges which belonged to the Israelites as a body, a denial that they were a people called and redeemed by the one living God, a growing doubt, therefore, whether there was such a Being— these were the consequences of taking the ox or the sheep to some other place than that in which the Lord God had put His Name.

(9.) The victim was taken to the door of the place, at which all Israelites had an equal right to appear; but the man who brought it *laid his own hand upon the head of it*. He signified that the act was his; that it expressed thoughts in his mind which no one else could know of. The crime he had done, or the disease that was preying upon him, or the bitterness of spirit which he could not tell to another, might all be declared to the searcher of hearts: if *he* could not utter them the act uttered them. He comes in his ignorance, believing there is One who knows him, and has bidden him come. That which is passing in him cannot be weighed or measured. He cannot reduce it under the head of bodily grief, or mental grief, or stings of conscience; he cannot say how much of pleasure and joy are mixed with the suffering, or whether it is good or bad, animal or spiritual. What did he understand of these refinements? What could they have profited him if he had understood them? He sought to have that explained to him which was utterly confused; to have himself set right. There was war in him; he needed peace. Someone was displeased with him; he desired to be reconciled.

(10.) And the words are as precise and strong as can be. '*It shall be accepted for him to make atone-* '*ment for him.*' The reconciliation which he seeks he shall find. God will meet him there. God, who knows what he is,—what he is suffering,—what he has done, —who has appointed the conditions of his existence,— who sees exactly how he has used them or abused them,—to whom the past and present of his life are both open—who has been making him aware of that in which he has been wrong,—of that in which he is weak and is likely to be wrong,—the God from whom he is conscious of estrangement, with whom he is sure that he ought to be at one,—He takes away that which separates them. He accepts this sign of his submission, He restores him to his rights in the divine society.

(11.) And now first it is that we hear of the *priests*, *Aaron's sons*. They have not suggested what the offering shall be, or what is likely to be the best way of making it acceptable. All this is taken out of their hands; they are not even the persons through whom the communication of the divine will is made to the

Israelites; they are the servants of a law, as much as the meanest of the people,—a law which they are to execute, which they must not, at their peril, depart from, to carry out any sublime notions of theirs, to meet any notions which may arise in the mind of any offender. The gift, the place, the atonement, are all spoken of before there is any allusion to them. But when they are introduced, we perceive at once that their office is a most important one; that the idea of the commonwealth and of the sacrifice would be imperfect, nay, self-contradictory, without them. If there was a congregation—if the individual Israelites were not to have their separate sacrifices and their separate gods—then there must be a representative of this unity; there must be one who acted as if they were a body. If the congregation derived its unity from its relation to the invisible Lord who had called out the family and the nation to be His witnesses to the world, then the man who expressed its unity must express its relation to this Lord. There could not be a fear of his ever glorifying himself on either of these positions, while he remembered the other, and while he remembered that they were inseparable. The abstracted Brahmin, standing aloof from the people, may believe that he is absorbed into his God—that he becomes identical with him. The minister of the congregation, the priest who was bound by his calling to feel himself one with them in all their sins and infirmities, had a perpetual witness in himself that he was no God, and that he could not approach to God whilst he supposed himself in any degree divided from God's people. On the other hand, the priest may sink into one of the congregation, using any higher lore he has received only to gratify their tastes and fancies, or to gratify his own avarice and ambition at their expense; the vilest pander to all their most violent passions; interested in keeping them base and ignorant, lest they should see into his hypocrisy and loathe him as he deserves to be loathed. But so long as he remembers that 'holiness to the Lord' is inscribed on his forehead—that he is consecrated as a witness to the people of the actual relation which exists between them and the God of truth and righteousness —and of his will to put away their falsehood and evil, that they may be like Him—this horrible fall becomes as impossible as the other. So that, while the history tells us in plain terms that the Jewish priests were often not better than heathen priests, and when not better were very much worse, it testifies as clearly that their arrogance, and craft, and sottishness came from a disbelief and forgetfulness of their divine and human calling, —not from exaggerating its worth and sacredness.

(12.) And I believe there were lessons taught the priests in this very passage, as well as in other passages of this book, which would recur to them again and again, and smite their consciences, while they went on in an evil course, till their consciences became actually seared, and they and the nation they represented fell together. One of these lessons lay in their hereditary succession. The limitation of this office to a family signified that the priests were not chosen for their individual gifts or virtues, though these would be bestowed upon them freely if they remembered their calling. They took nothing by mere descent from their ancestors; they declared to each new age that the same God who had spoken to their fathers and ruled them, and held intercourse with them, and blotted out their sins, was speaking to *them,* ruling *them,* holding intercourse with *them,* blotting out *their* sins. And lest any family conceit should spring up, as of course it would, out of a vocation which, rightly apprehended, was so subversive of it, they were reminded continually by interruptions in the succession, by the atrocities of priests and the tremendous judgments which followed, how the instrument might be dashed in pieces, that the truth for which he existed to testify might be established.

(13.) The special office of the priest, as it is set forth in this passage, was also, I think, very significant to him of the end for which he was appointed. *He was to bring the blood, and to sprinkle the blood round about the altar that is by the door of the tabernacle of the congregation.* The blood, the Israelites had been told already, was the *life,* which they *were not to eat, but to pour out like water.* It had been said that *whoso sheddeth man's blood, by man shall his blood be shed, because in the image of God was man made, and because of every man's brother would he require the life of man.* This blood, this life, was evidently the most sacred part of the service; it is referred to in every part of the institution of sacrifice; it is connected with purification. Yet it was not mixed with the rest of the offering; it was poured out about the altar, while the mere animal, the dead thing, was offered as a whole burnt sacrifice. I apprehend that there were lessons here never to be forgotten, concerning death and life; concerning the preciousness and dignity of life; concerning the dedication of that to God; concerning the special duty of the priest to be a witness that the living sacrifice is that which God seeks for, that it is this which interprets the mystery of death, that it is this which purifies, that it is this which unites. The hint was given; the priest was to think over it, to dwell upon it, to consider what principles, yet to be brought out and realised, were latent in it. When he tried to do the work which was given him to do—when he entered with most simplicity into all that was weakest, and all that was saddest in those for whom he ministered—when he sought the interpretation of one and the other from God Himself, these lessons became clear to him. Then he was taught to pour out his own life blood, and not only that of the beasts, before the altar; then he was taught that there must be a higher and nobler blood than that, poured out for the whole congregation and for the human race, to purify it of its selfish corruptions, to unite it with God.

Even in the perplexities of the Levitical law, such a priest may have found subjects for reflection and meditation, which may have been, in the end, more profitable and instructive to him than rules which he could at once have understood. It has seemed to many, that the division of offerings into trespass-offerings, sin-offerings, thank-offerings, peace-offerings, is what logicians call a *cross* division; for must not the trespass-offering be also a sin-offering, a peace-offering, or a thank-offering? The classification, though it may offend the intellect, justifies itself to the heart. The desire to express thankfulness may be mixed inseparably with the desire to confess an outward trespass, or a secret sin. But one of these desires is always predominant over the other, and this predominance determines what a man is likely to seek for in a sacrifice if he is left to his own fancies. The divine Legislator meets him with these distinct names; they are what he needs; a more formal and seemingly accurate classification would defeat its own objects. The priest who took these hints as his guides and landmarks, would arrive at a deeper knowledge of himself and of his fellow-men. He would be preserved from the great temptation into which priests in all ages have fallen, of inventing a multitude of rules for cases of conscience, which produce the evil they profess to guard against, which corrupt and enslave the conscience they pretend to purify and relieve.

The mixture of services for what, in the dialect of divines, are called *ceremonial impurities*, that is to say, such as have no inherent moral evil in them, with actual trespasses, has been another complaint against these

Levitical precepts. Here, too, I think, we are forgetting
facts in our eagerness to make distinctions, and thus
lose the real and radical distinctions which we should
discern if we were less impatient. Bodily diseases do
affect the mind in a thousand ways—affect it with fears
of the future, with remembrances of the past, with a
sense of wrong. They look like punishments; it is very
little help merely to tell anyone who is suffering from
them, that they are disguised mercies. If you are
to make him *feel* that truth, you must show him that
the Lord of all cares for all the evils that afflict him;
for every kind of torment to which he is actually subject, whatever name psychologists or physiologists may
please to bestow upon it. You must not leave him to
find out, by subtle self-questioning, whether there is
moral evil in what he has done or thought, or how
much; if you do, he will involve himself in endless
entanglements, from which no maxims or formulas will
set him free. Treat him as such a being as he is;
show that all his experience has been foreseen, and that
it is not a solitary one; let him come and cast himself
before the Lord, and seek the atonement He has promised; so you give him real help, so you make him a
wiser as well as a more simple and true man. That this
is done; that the difficulties which belong to human
beings, and which would lead them to seek all evil helps,
are turned to the account of good; that the rules come
in where they are wanted, and do not attempt what
they cannot perform; that they suggest what they are

unable to teach, and so leave the minds of those who are disciplined by them to expand under higher and freer influences; this is, I conceive, the test of that legislation which is at once human and divine.

The great annual atonement, which is appointed in the sixteenth chapter of this book, carries us a step beyond those daily sacrifices, of which the opening passages speak, though the two parts of the scheme are strikingly in harmony. The general like the individual offerings is grounded wholly upon the will of God; like them, it assumes the nation to be already a holy and sacrificed nation, in spite of the sins of its particular members, and of its own public sins; like them, it starts from the assumption that God is seeking to reconcile those who have wandered, to Himself; like them, it assumes the will of the creature to be the great subject of the reconciliation; like them, it treats the priest as at once representing the holiness of the nation, and as sharing its sins. But with the dead animal is connected a living one, which goes away into the wilderness bearing the sins of the land. The bullock that was slain, the scapegoat that disappeared, suggested to the Israelite these two thoughts. God can entirely take away the evil of a people and of a man. If He takes it away, the Mediator, the sin-bearer, must in some unspeakable manner unite Death and Life.

SERMON VI.

DAVID'S SACRIFICE.

(Lincoln's Inn, 2nd Sunday after Easter, April 30, 1854.)

For thou desirest not sacrifice; else would I give it: thou delightest not in burnt-offering. The sacrifices of God are a broken spirit: a broken and a contrite heart, O God, thou wilt not despise.'—
PSALM li. 16, 17.

WHEN I spoke to you last on the subject of Sacrifice, I was considering the provisions of the Levitical Law. I endeavoured to show you how strikingly those provisions, formal and precise as they were, illustrated the principle of Sacrifice, as we had seen it unfolding itself in the offerings of Abel, of Noah, of Abraham. The national precept carried on the education of the Jew when he was come into new circumstances, but it did not alter or modify any of the lessons which he had learnt among the tents of the Patriarchs. It protected those lessons from perils by which they were threatened; it connected them with the experience which the Israelites had passed through in Egypt; it prepared the way for fresh experiences through which they would pass in Palestine. The more closely we examine the terms of the command which appointed *what* sacrifices should be offered,—how, and where, and by whom,—construing those terms strictly as laws should be construed, the more we perceive how they were directed against the Heathen notions of sacrifice, which spring up so naturally in the heart of man—which foster its pride, and which bring it into slavery—and which had already worked so mightily and fearfully in the world : the more we saw how these provisions asserted the divine doctrine that Sacrifice must proceed from the Will of God, and is perfected when the will of man is subdued to it.

But clearly as I think these positions are established by the plain words of Scripture—still more by all the context of its history, by the errors of the chosen people, and by the effects which ensued when they fell into the habits of the people round about them—I do not wonder that readers have felt something like a shock when they have passed directly from the Law to the Psalms; when they find Kings and Seers apparently disparaging those offerings, which were so precious a part of the divine economy. Our attention has been lately called to passages of this kind—passages which have a startling sound, and which certain critics affirm must have been written by men who, secretly or openly, had revolted from the national faith. The fiftieth and the fifty-first Psalms were chosen for our use last Wednesday morning.¹

¹ On the Day of general Humiliation.

In the first, we find such sentences as these—'*I will take no bullock out of thy house, nor he-goat out of thy folds. For every beast of the forest is mine, and the cattle upon a thousand hills. I know all the fowls of the mountains: and the wild beasts of the field are mine. If I were hungry, I would not tell thee: for the world is mine and the fulness thereof. Will I eat the flesh of bulls, or drink the blood of goats? Offer unto God thanksgiving; and pay thy vows unto the most High: and call upon me in the day of trouble: I will deliver thee, and thou shalt glorify me.*' In such language, there is something like scorn of the notion that animal offerings—the very offerings which the law had prescribed and which the priest continually presented— could be of any worth in God's sight. The argument is stated in the broadest manner, in a way which must have given offence, one would have thought, even to sincere and devout suppliants. And the conclusion, that the offering of thanksgiving, and the calling upon God in trouble, is that which he really demands, must have been urged by a number of Sadducees in the latter days, if there were none in the earlier, as a justification of all that they taught respecting the easiness of the divine requirements and their purely moral character. The fifty-first Psalm is altogether different. *There* is nothing which can be taken for contempt of any vulgar doctrines or practices. The King who speaks is not raised to a higher point of view than his subjects—he is beneath them all. But in the depth of abasement, he seems to arrive at the same discovery to which the other teacher was led by a different route. '*Thou desirest not sacrifice; else would I give it: thou delightest not in burnt-offering. The sacrifices of God are a broken spirit; a broken and a contrite heart, O God, thou wilt not despise.*' These words, though none were ever spoken in the world that could be so little intended to perplex any worshipping Israelite, nevertheless must have strangely clashed with some of his most cherished and familiar thoughts. *Thou delightest not in burnt-offerings!*—Why then, was it said, that the Lord smelled a sweet savour when Noah brought forth the clean beasts after the flood? Why were all the offerings at the door of the tabernacle accompanied with incense which intimated that they were grateful to Him who dwelt there? Why were they called peace-offerings, and offerings of atonement? And supposing that, in some sense, the heart was a better offering than the bullock or goat, must it not, according to all symbols and analogies, be a *whole* heart in order to be accepted? Were not Israelites forbidden to offer anything maimed or broken to the Lord? Were they not to bring unblemished males of the first year? Was it not running counter to all these axioms, and to that which was implied in them, to speak of the heart, bruised, worn, torn in pieces, as the very gift which God desired? I do not see how any Pharisee could have answered these questions. He would have tried to answer them, by saying that the Law was divine and that the Psalms were divine, and that it was not his business to reconcile them, but to believe both. The practical effect of which resolution, I think, must have been that he would believe neither, and would act according to neither, but would believe his own notion of sacrifice, and would ground upon it doctrines and practices which Moses and David would have hated equally. But a simple, childlike man—one of those whom the evangelists describe as waiting for the kingdom of heaven —beginning with a strong sense of the apparent diversity between the teachers whom he reverenced, would gradually have discovered—by suffering as the psalmists suffered—how truly they were the interpreters of the Law, how little it could be understood except by those whom God Himself trained in the school in which He had trained them. Christian men living since the Gospel of the kingdom, for which these men waited, has been proclaimed, have been brought to the same conclusion by the same process. And we, my brethren, may find out, as they did, what the words of these psalms signify, how they illustrate all that we have ascertained about sacrifice hitherto, how needful they are to explain the nature of our sacrifices, how they bear upon that perfect sacrifice, the inestimable benefits of which have been set forth in the Collect for to-day.

I. The fiftieth Psalm exhibits the chosen race as summoned to answer for itself before its divine King. God is calling *to the heavens from above, and to the earth, that He may judge His people.* This people is marked out in the next verse, as *saints who have made a covenant with*

Me with sacrifice. It is assumed, therefore, that the nation is holy, and that God has claimed it as holy by taking it into covenant with Himself. The covenant cannot be separated from sacrifice. I have shown you how this principle was embodied in the institution of the Passover; how the ordinance which established that sacrifice—how every part of the service itself—testified that Israelites were a dedicated, devoted, sacrificed nation. The first-born were consecrated as representatives of the whole people. They were redeemed from death, but not redeemed from this condition. The animal was a dead offering; they were living offerings. The great trial or judgment, then, which the Lord of the land is making of His subjects, has this issue: Have they acted as if this were their state; as if they were dedicated, sacrificed creatures? *He is God, even their own God.* Have they understood this to be the case? have they believed that He was their God, and that they were His saints,—His sanctified, redeemed creatures? Let them not put the cause upon a different issue from this; let them not suppose that God is *reproving them for their sacrifices or their burnt-offerings, because they were not always before Him.* He does not want these; *the cattle on a thousand hills are His.* He wants their acknowledgment of Him, He wants their trust. But what had they to do *who declared His statutes* and boasted of His covenant, yet remained wicked? Did not they know that His purpose in taking them into covenant with Him was to reform them; to separate them from their evil; to deliver them from the adulterous, deceitful, slanderous tendencies of their nature? Did they suppose that God wanted to be fed with their beasts? Did they not know that *they* needed to be made right men by Him? Oh, miserable delusion! they fancied Him altogether such an one as themselves!—one who could be bribed as they were bribed! They had not yet learned, after all His teaching and discipline, that their duty and their blessing was to submit to Him, that He might make them like Himself.

Here is a wonderful exposition of that falsehood which was leading the Israelite astray in all the periods of his history; the falsehood which turned him into an idolater in one generation, into an insolent denouncer of idolaters in another. He did not look upon God as his God, as his Deliverer, as his Judge, as his Reformer; he did not yield himself to Him as His subject, as His redeemed creature, to be purified, to be renewed. He had never understood what it was to be sacrificed himself. But he could, if need were, produce a hecatomb of oxen to be sacrificed: he supposed God's toleration of his sins was to be purchased, and that this was the purchase-money. The mockery of such a notion by the psalmists is terrible, but not disproportionate to the monstrousness of the evil which it was condemning. It is that mockery which comes out of the burning heart of a man who knows God to be righteous and true; and who sees that men are making a god like themselves, and are strengthening themselves in their lies and their crimes by regarding him as the patron of them. But the mockery is only a translation into words of that which is embodied in the whole law and ritual of Israel. The Psalmist draws out the inmost sense of the book of Leviticus, when he says, that '*if God were hungry, He would not tell them.*' In all the institutes which that book contains, God is commanding a people, with whom He has already made a covenant, what they shall do in order to testify that they are in that covenant, and that they have broken it. They are righteous, for He has chosen them and united them to Himself; they have distrusted Him; they have forgotten that they are a righteous people; they have chosen ways of their own. By their offerings of beasts, they acknowledge that it is so; they take up their place as Israelites; He accepts them. What pride and falsehood to suppose that an act, which was the confession of sin, had some meritorious power! What blasphemy to think that the instrument by which God chose to establish peace between Himself and those who had revolted from Him, was a successful contrivance of theirs to conciliate Him and induce Him to overlook their revolt!

II. No one could have taught his countrymen these lessons who had not learnt that *he* needed to be judged and reformed, that he could not judge and reform himself; that the Searcher of hearts, the King of his land, was doing that work for him; that in doing it He was fulfilling the covenant which He had made with the Israelites; that to submit freely and frankly to that process was the man's part of the covenant, was the sacrifice which God above all others demanded of him. And this is the link between the fiftieth and the fifty-first Psalms, which in outward characteristics are so dissimilar, and yet in which we found a striking correspondence on the subject of sacrifice. The circumstances which suggested this last Psalm do not affect its nature, but I shall assume the old tradition, which few have ever disbelieved, that it is the confession of David's sin against Bathsheba and Uriah. We may believe that the King did not say, *Thou desirest no sacrifice, else would I give it,* without having made the experiment. It was a most natural thing for him to betake himself to the Tabernacle which he had frequented before; to make his gifts there more costly than in former days; to persuade himself that if other men's transgressions were forgiven, his, who had fought so many battles for the Lord, and sung so many songs to Him, would certainly be overlooked. Why did not the result answer to his expectation? Why, after the priest had duly presented the whole burnt-offering—had praised him, perhaps, because his devotion and bounty were greater than ever—did he return to his house, with his countenance fallen, with the same weight on his heart as before, with his *moisture* still *like the drought in summer?* That singing men and singing women should not avail to give him ease, he might have expected. But the sin-offering, the trespass-offering, the peace-offering—could not they do it? What did the Law mean—what did the whole service of the Tabernacle, the ordinance of the Passover—mean, if this were the case? This at least was clear: he was *not* at peace. His conscience told him so; his endeavours to persuade himself that the voice which spoke to him there was not the voice of God utterly failed. God evidently did not delight in David's burnt-offering more than He delighted in Cain's.

But the next step was a much longer and harder one. A man who has begun to negotiate and traffic with his Maker will not quickly give up the hope that he shall find something to sacrifice sooner or later which He will be content to receive. To part with this hope, to sink humbly on the knees; to say, *Against thee I have sinned; I have done this evil in Thy sight*—how is this possible;—what brings a man to this? And what kind of offering is this? David knew at last what it was. It was *the sacrifice of God*. He had not brought himself into that posture: God had brought him into it. He had corrected him and broken him. He had prepared the sacrifice. He had shown him that this was what he wanted. This great saint, and singer, and king of Israel, must positively understand that he has nothing whatever to do, but to say, 'I am what thou knowest 'I am. Thou hast found me out. Thou art right, and 'I am wrong. I give up the struggle.' That was the ultimate result. Now he believed that God was a Righteous Being who hated sin, not one who overlooked it in king or peasant, that He was willing to take it away from king and peasant, to give each of them a right heart. That now became his one desire. *Not* to be a deceiver, *not* to keep his secret; but to be a right and true man; to have his inmost spirit laid bare, that every cheat might be purged out of it.

Here was the explanation of the strange fact that a broken heart was better than a whole one; that the maimed offering might be presented by the Israelite, who was to bring only of the firstlings of his flock. The sacrifice was a *more* complete, a *more* entire one, than he had ever yet presented. He had never, even in his days of early shepherd faith, even when he threw himself away in battle, so absolutely and unreservedly given up himself. The discovery that he had nothing to present, that he was poor and worthless, was the discovery that he belonged wholly to God, that he was His, and that his sin had consisted in withdrawing from his allegiance, in choosing another condition than his true and actual one.

So subtle are the inventions of human pride that even these words of David—these words of simple renunciation—have furnished food for it. 'We are to ' bring,' says the casuist, ' humble and contrite hearts. ' And, therefore, it must be ascertained what contrition ' is, and how much of contrition is needful to constitute ' a true repentance, an acceptable sacrifice.' In what delicate scales have men's tears and sorrows been weighed out by divines, to know whether they answered to this standard; how the hearts and consciences of suffering and penitent men have been, not tormented merely—that is nothing—but made utterly insincere and false, by their efforts to apply the rules and test their own condition! And vain it is to point out, in mere words, that as long as a man fancies that he has contrition, or any other present, to bring to God, in order to make himself acceptable, so long he is not really humbling himself; he is not confessing that he is a sinner: he is not giving up himself. Vain it is, I say, to point this out in words, for *these* words may be abused as much as any other. But God makes this known to a man *in fact*; His discipline brings us to understand it inwardly; that discipline cuts through the webs which we weave for ourselves, and breaks the spirit actually, not according to the maxims in books.

And it is by breaking the man's spirit that He restores it to its true freedom and greatness. The child away from its home, seeking paths of its own, joining itself to any citizen of the country in which it is wandering, feeding upon husks, at last hungering and wishing for the bread of hired servants, comes to recollect that it has a father, that it is one of a family. It asks for its home; it finds that the Father has been seeking for it;—in knowing what He is, it begins to know itself. This is the history of King David; and his history is written that each man may read his own in it. The Book of Psalms is the most wonderful book in the world, because it is the most universal; because

in it saints and seers and prophets and kings prove
their title to their great names, by finding that they
have a greater name still,—that they are men; that they
are partakers in all the poverty, emptiness and sinful-
ness of their fellow-creatures; that there is nothing in
themselves to boast of, or claim as their own; that all
which they have is His, who would have all to know
Him and to be partakers of His holiness. And therefore this fifty-first Psalm is, as it seems to me, the
real explanation of all the Psalms, and of the continual
references which they contain to another and higher
King than David. It was, and is most natural, that the
Jews reading of such a King, and honestly persuaded
that he must be what the name *King* imports, should
have rejected the notion of a broken-hearted man—
a man of sorrows—as not at all answering to the idea
of such a ruler and conqueror. Till they are brought
as low as David himself was brought when he poured
out this confession, they will not, from all the arguments and evidences in the world, find how that riddle
is solved; they will not know why only such an one
could be the King, because only such an one could be
the sacrifice. And we too, brethren, we who are wont,
perhaps, to think of Him more as a sacrifice than as
a king, may have need of the same deep humiliation
before we can know what His Sacrifice is, or who could
truly offer it. We may build up for ourselves a notion
of someone who has come to offer a great and gorgeous
present to the Lord of all, which has changed His

H

mind towards His creatures; we may unawares thrust into our Christian faith those heathen notions of sacrifice against which God's witnesses before the flood,—when the world rose out of it,—on the hill Moriah,—amidst the idolaters of Egypt,—in the Wilderness,—in the royal city, lifted up their voices. But if we are brought, as one of the psalmists says that he was, as all really were, to a horrible pit where no ground is, we shall find that there is one Rock, and only one, on which we can place our feet—the rock on which prophets and apostles alike stood—the Name of Him who said, *Lo, I come, in the volume of the Book it is written of me*—not to alter Thy purpose, but—*to do Thy will, O God.*

SERMON VII.

THE LAMB BEFORE THE FOUNDATION OF THE WORLD.

(Lincoln's Inn, 3rd Sunday after Easter, May 7, 1854.)

'Forasmuch as ye know that ye were not redeemed with corruptible things, as silver and gold, from your vain conversation received by tradition from your fathers; but with the precious blood of Christ, as of a lamb without blemish and without spot: who verily was fore-ordained before the foundation of the world, but was manifest in these last times for you.'—1 ST. PETER i. 18–20.

IT is not my intention to dwell at present upon the first of these verses, though I should be very sorry if you did not remember how closely it is connected with the two last. How the death of Christ is the redemption of men, in the strictest and fullest sense of that word, I hope to consider in a future discourse. It is of Him as fore-ordained before the foundation of the world, that I desire, in all fear and reverence, to speak now. I believe the subject rises naturally and necessarily out of that on which I addressed you last Sunday.

The scriptures of the old Testament have led us, step by step, into a deeper apprehension of sacrifice. The humiliation of David, which showed him that he had nothing of his own to offer; that he must come empty-handed, broken-hearted, to receive of God that which He alone could give, a right and true spirit—this humiliation, while it seemed to undermine the legal doctrine of sacrifice, actually vindicated it, and placed it on its proper ground. The corrupt and heathenish notion of sacrifice, against which the law had been protesting, was uprooted by the principle to which David gave utterance in the fifty-first Psalm. Sacrifice was brought out in its fullest and most radical sense, as the giving up, not of something belonging to the man, but of the man himself. Till he made that oblation, he was in a wrong state. When it was made, he was in a restored state, —in the state in which God had intended him to be, a dependent creature, a trusting creature, capable of receiving his Maker's image.

Although this experience was so personal in the case of David, although it must be personal in the case of every one who goes through it, I maintained that it was, for that very reason, human experience. David is taught that he is not better than other men; he is taught that his very sin has consisted in separating himself from other men, in claiming for himself the privilege of doing them an injury; he is taught that he must be on a level with them all before he can be what he ought to be himself. This is one of the paradoxes of life, one which we must be all made in some way to understand. No man has attained the true elevation of humanity till he feels that he is not above any human creature; no one can be really an individual till he has confessed that he is only one of a kind. But with this two-edged paradox, another still harder to take in was involved. If there could be one who never did lift up himself above his brethren, who never claimed to be anything but the member of a kind, must he not be the perfectly righteous man, and yet must he not be in sympathy and fellowship with all sinful men as no other ever was? Must he not have a feeling and experience of their sins which they have not themselves? Is it not involved in the very idea of such a being that he sacrifices himself?

David could not stop here; he had learnt that the sacrifices of God are a broken spirit; he had learnt that God does not only accept this sacrifice, but prepares it. The law had taught him, his shame and humiliation had taught him, that God is the Author of every true sacrifice; that it originates in His will, and therefore fulfils His will. Could it be otherwise in this, the highest case of all? If there ever were such a righteous man, if he ever did offer himself as a sacrifice, must not that sacrifice, in the strictest and most eminent sense, be the sacrifice of God? Must He not, in some wonderful way, prepare it, originate it, offer it?

We sound a great depth here; but it is a depth into which men were led not by speculation, but by misery and anguish, by the sense of sin which was in themselves, by the sense of a death which they shared with all their race. It was not in the schools, from any illuminated or initiated teachers, it was in their closets when they had to confess that all their illuminations and high conceits had failed, when they felt as if they had no standing-ground at all, when they were on the brink of despair, that these truths appeared to them as solid and eternal resting-places for themselves and for all. I say for *all*, because this was the very discovery that gave them comfort, and the only one which could. They were not only taught—'*If* there is 'such a righteous man, *then* he must and will offer such 'a sacrifice as this, and that sacrifice must be a sacrifice 'of God.' But their hearts said also, God leading them to the conclusion, 'Such an One there *is*, and such 'an One will be manifested. His existence is implied in 'all we are thinking, feeling, doing. Some day he will 'make it clear by a transcendent act, an act pregnant 'with the mightiest consequences *to the world*, that 'He is.'

Here, then, is the point at which the Old Testament teaching meets and falls into that of the New. The Church has always recognised it. The fortieth Psalm is quoted in the Epistle to the Hebrews as anticipating and expounding the New Testament idea of sacrifice; it has been incorporated into our Good Friday service for that reason. Although, therefore, I might trace the unfolding of the doctrine of sacrifice through the prophets, and show how diligently they were employed in protesting against the heathen abuse of the idea, in warning their countrymen against the appearances of that abuse amongst themselves, in pointing out the only counteraction of it; yet, as I have travelled over this ground before in sermons addressed to you, I shall assume that the hints which we have derived from so many parts of the Hebrew Scriptures, fairly set forth the principle as it is revealed in them, and shall go on at once to consider how far the lessons of the apostles are in accordance with it.

No one can doubt that this passage of St. Peter is a capital and classical one upon the subject. It is continually referred to as a leading authority; the words, '*Lamb without blemish and spot*,' point at once to the Passover, and to the memorable sentence of John the Baptist when he saw Jesus walk and spoke of Him to his two disciples. Even if the expression, '*precious blood*,' was not introduced into the passage, the association with the Passover would at once prove that St. Peter was directing our thoughts to a sacrifice. The rest of the passage assures us that it is a sacrifice of *God* to which the apostle refers; he speaks of the Lamb being '*verily fore-ordained before the foundation* '*of the world.*'

I must remind you that 'fore-ordained' is not the literal rendering of St. Peter's phrase. Our translators, no doubt, supposed *fore-known* and *fore-ordained* to be equivalent expressions; they understood the *logic* of the predestinarian controversy; for that very reason they were less attentive to a *philological* distinction which we cannot afford to neglect; since conclusions have been founded on the one word, for which the other offers not the least justification. The text has been supposed to mean that, before Adam fell, a remedy was provided in the counsels of God for the consequences of that fall. It was *fore-ordained* that Christ, the Lamb of God, should yield Himself a sacrifice, that those who believed in Him might be delivered from the penalty of the original transgression.

You will all remember how beautifully this divine arrangement is expounded in the third book of Paradise Lost. I refer to that passage, not merely because you must be more familiar with it than with any more formal theological statement, but because, by so doing, I am exhibiting the popular theory to the greatest possible advantage. Milton represents the Father as full of love to His creatures, but as determined to assert the claims of justice and righteousness. Sin, once committed, must draw death and ruin after it. What doctrine more entirely commends itself to our conscience? What doctrine is written in clearer sunbeams on the pages of Scripture? And how much of that which follows is equally in accordance with the testimony that God has borne in His word and in the heart of man:

> ' And now without redemption all mankind
> Must have been lost, adjudged to death and hell
> By doom severe; had not the Son of God,
> In whom the fulness dwells of love divine,
> His dearest mediation thus renew'd.
>   *   .   *   *   *

> Behold me then, me for him, life for life
> I offer; on me let thine anger fall.
> Account me man; I for his sake will leave
> Thy bosom; and this glory next to thee
> Freely put off, and for him lastly die.
> Well pleased on me let Death wreck all his rage.
> Under his gloomy power I shall not long
> Lie vanquish'd. Thou hast given me to possess
> Life in myself for ever. By thee I live.
> Though now to Death I yield and am his due,
> All that of me can die; yet that debt paid,
> Thou wilt not leave me in the loathsome grave
> His prey, nor suffer my unspotted soul
> For ever with corruption there to dwell:
> But I shall rise victorious, and subdue
> My vanquisher, spoil'd of his vaunted spoil.
> * * * *
> Then with the multitude of my Redeem'd
> Shall enter Heaven long absent, and return,
> Father, to see Thy face, wherein no cloud
> Of anger shall remain, but peace assured
> And reconcilement; wrath shall be no more
> Thenceforth, but in Thy presence joy entire.'

This voluntary oblation made by the only-begotten Son, because 'in Him the fulness dwells of love divine'—and attracting the infinite complacency of Him whose image He was—what can so entirely correspond to that idea of sacrifice which we have traced in the older records? Must not this be the very root of all sacrifices, the consummation of all? Why, then, have the most ardent and affectionate admirers of Milton's character and genius mourned over those parts of his poem which contain these colloquies of the Father with the Son? Why did he himself slide into Arianism, in his scientific divinity, though his poetry expressed such a feeling of the perfect unity of the Son with the Father? I apprehend that our dislike of those artificial arrangements which mingle so discordantly with the music of his song, grows in proportion to the awe and reverence with which we accept its inward meaning. I apprehend Arianism is inevitably involved in these arrangements, because they confound time with eternity, and because while we dwell on them we cannot feel, however much we may desire it, that the Mind which demands justice and denounces evil, is one with the Mind in which lives all mercy and forgiveness.

Is this theory, then, found in the words of St. Peter? I know that some neologians of our day will say instantly, 'Of course it is. He was a mere vulgar Jew. 'If you ask whether it is in *St. John*, or in the Gospel 'which passed by his name, the answer might be dif-'ferent.' Such language is very peremptory. But surely it is not enough to make assertions without examining the documents upon which they profess to be founded. Look into this passage. See whether the theory of an arrangement made before the Fall, with reference to it and its consequences, *is* there, or whether we have put it there. See whether what is there does not correspond most exactly with what we find in the disciple who was St. Peter's companion before and after the Resurrection; whether the correspondence does not add one link to the chain of evidence, which shows that he who has given the most simple and childlike record of our Lord's acts and words was not a dry systematic theologian of the second century, who basely and blasphemously forged the name of the beloved disciple to endorse a lie.

There was one, St. Peter says, who was *verily foreknown before the foundation of the world*. What would such words seem to denote, but that there was one whom the Father of all knew, and who, in the fullest and most intimate sense, knew Him, before the *earth or the lowest part of the dust of the world was formed?* What is this but that which the Book of Proverbs had said already, when it spoke of Wisdom as one brought up with Him; His inmost counsellor? What is it but what was afterward gathered up in the wonderful sentence, *The Word was with God and the Word was God. Without Him was not anything made that was made.* The Book of Proverbs goes on to say, that *His delights were with the sons of Men*. St. John had said, *In Him was Life and the Life was the Light of Men*. It must then be all important that men should know Him, from whom their light comes, in whom their life dwells. But how could they know Him? How could they look into the Eternal secret? What apprehension could they have of that life which He had with the Father, that life which does not belong to time and its accidents, that life which can only be spoken of as eternal? St. Peter assumes that we could know nothing of it, that all our guesses about it must be wild guesses, mere dreams derived from our own earthly associations and discoveries, if this life had not been manifested

But the veil, he says, has been withdrawn which hid His divine nature, His relation to the Eternal Father, from us. And how has it been withdrawn? He has appeared in our world, in our nature; He has sacrificed Himself. In that sacrifice we see what He is—what He always has been. His acts here, plain and palpable, done among men, done for men, have shown forth that perfect filial obedience to the Creator of all things, that entire filial union with the Eternal Father, which is the ground of the universe and the ground of our humanity.

I think if we had no other words to guide us than those in the text, we should be forced to put this construction upon them. And then this *fore-knowledge* of which he speaks, instead of being a provision that is contingent upon human events and human will—instead of being an anticipation, which every devout man shrinks from attributing to him to whom all things are naked and open, to whom past, present, and future are one—becomes the communion of will and purpose in the persons of the Godhead, our belief in which saves us from the necessity and the horror of ascribing self-will to the Author of all; and enables us to see how a perfectly loving will can only be uttered and shown forth by one who enters into it, and yields himself to it.

That this obedience should be the means of rectifying the disorders of the universe, of bringing back the state of things which self-will has broken and disturbed, of re-establishing the kingdom and righteousness of God, of renewing and subduing the hearts of human beings, this is what we should with wonder and trembling expect; this is what corresponds so blessedly, so perfectly, to the deepest prophecies in the spirit of mankind; this is the very Gospel which has brought light into the midst of our darkness, life into the midst of our death. But we must not change and invert God's order to make it square with our condition; if we do, it will not meet the necessities of that condition. We must not start from the assumption of discord and derangement, however natural to creatures that are conscious of discord and derangement such a course may be; we must begin with harmony and peace, and so understand why they have been broken, how they have prevailed and shall prevail.

It is for this reason, I conceive, that the apostles, when they dwell so continually upon the effects of the divine and human sacrifice in taking away sin and utterly removing all the effects of it, yet lead us back to a ground of sacrifice in the divine nature; in that submission of the Son to the Father, that perfect unity of Purpose, Will, Substance, between them, whence the obedience and fellowship of all unfallen beings, the obedience and fellowship of all restored beings, must be derived, and by which they are sustained. Believing such a mystery of a Will commanding and a Will obeying, and of a Spirit uniting both, to lie beneath all the order of nature, all the actions of men; there comes forth from both the same testimony to the Creator and the Father.

The poet has boldly spoken of Duty as the lawgiver to which all nature bows, and from which all her grace and beauty proceeds:

> ' Flowers laugh before thee in their beds,
> And Fragrance in thy footing treads;
> Thou dost preserve the stars from wrong,
> And the most ancient Heavens through thee are fresh and strong.

And, doubtless, the more we studied the secrets of nature, and entered into her most intricate relations, the more we should be impressed with the sense of government and obedience—of a law which all things confess, and to which all yield unresisting homage. We should see that life and productiveness are the effects of even and regular submission; that tempests and whirlwinds, and whatever tumults break the monotony of the world, are themselves proofs that it is not under the sway of a dead law, but of a living one; of a *Lawgiver* who guides and controls its energies, and makes them serve still higher purposes of His will. And so we are led from the wonderful machinery and mysterious powers of the physical universe—the wheels within wheels which a living spirit guides, where there is such intricacy and such simplicity—to that moral world, all the elements of which appear to be continually clashing with each other, where disobedience and self-will have tried to make themselves the law. It is through this confusion that the light breaks in which illuminates the other world, and shows us the secret of its loveliness. Men are taught that the death which has come into the world is a sign and pledge that all their life is from God; they come with the dead animal to make that confession and yield themselves to Him. Men, seeing the punishment of a violent and disobedient world, confess by sacrifice that the earth can exist only by submission to a living and gracious Ruler. Heads of families find that sacrifice is the only bond which can keep fathers and children, husbands and wives, brothers and sisters, at one. God calls nations out of a chaos of turbulent, warring elements. They find that sacrifice must keep them from relapsing into endless war. Individuals discover that all right-doing has its ground in sacrifice, and they find, when they have offended, it is because they have chosen to break loose from the law of sacrifice. So it is proved that obedience and sacrifice are the very conditions of truth and righteousness, that they belong to man who is made in God's likeness, because they are involved in the very character and being of God Himself.

This wonderful truth, so utterly contradictory to all the notions which men had formed to themselves of their Creator, when they had supposed Him to be a mere power, who might exercise capricious vengeance upon them, and whom they were to conciliate by their sacrifices;—and yet which was implied in those very sacrifices, and in every act of real obedience and devotion, by parent, friend, warrior, sage—in every act which had been acknowledged as truly acceptable to the gods—in every dream of gods who themselves deigned to be deliverers of men; this truth, I say, had been unfolding itself gradually to the seers and sufferers among the chosen people. The Bible is a history of the discovery. But surely St. Peter's words are true to the letter. The manifestation of this perfect Son of God,—of this Lamb, in whom dwelt the very law of sacrifice, whose whole mind and heart were fashioned into conformity with it, who never swerved, or broke loose, from it—this manifestation was reserved for the latter days. Though men have stumbled, and do stumble, at the records of the life of Jesus of Nazareth; though they can find innumerable reasons for not accepting these records, and though the inconsistent unbelief of Christians has often justified their suspicion; yet there has been a witness, in the hearts of successive generations of poor, and sorrowing, and sinful people: 'This is the history of a sacrifice—of a man who is 'making a sacrifice,—of a sacrifice of God.' They may have been utterly unable to arrange these thoughts in their minds, to explain them according to a theory; and, therefore, they have been ready to accept any theory which has been made for them. But the moral conviction: 'This is the Lamb of God; this is He in 'whom we see the very mind, and will, and purpose of 'Him who created us; this is the Lamb of God, in 'whom we see the perfect surrender of a man to that 'will and mind of God'—this conviction, unable to put itself into words, has breathed itself out in the prayers and agonies of tens of thousands of men and women, on sick beds which no priest has visited, in lonely dungeons which no philanthropist has heard of. The heart and reason have affirmed in opposition to all the cavillings of unbelief, ' He who perfectly sympathised ' with us in our evil, must be the man who is free ' from all evil; He who has entirely given up Himself ' to death, must be the mighty God.'

SERMON VIII.

CHRIST'S SACRIFICE A REDEMPTION.

(*Lincoln's Inn, 4th Sunday after Easter, May 14, 1854.*)

' Forasmuch as ye know that ye were not redeemed with corruptible things, as silver and gold, from your vain conversation received by tradition from your fathers; but with the precious blood of Christ, as of a lamb without blemish and without spot.'—
1 ST. PETER i. 18, 19.

LAST Sunday I inquired into the force of the words which follow these. I wish to consider, to-day, how the sacrifice of the Lamb, who was foreknown before the foundation of the world, is connected with *Redemption*. I desire that we should limit ourselves to that question; reserving the consideration of other subjects, such as Remission, Propitiation, Intercession, for future occasions. Great inconvenience, I think, has resulted from a loose habit of confounding the ideas which these words express, as if they were not capable of separate illustration. I am satisfied that there is no such carelessness in the Scripture use of them; that each has a distinct sense of its own, and will bear and reward, a distinct investigation. Then we shall know how harmonious they are; how they all converge to one point; how they illustrate and unfold the Divine Mind.

But before I enter upon this examination, I wish to show you how the remarks which I made last Sunday, bear upon a topic, which happens to be occupying the minds of many thoughtful people at this time,—a topic in which moral and physical science have become rather curiously blended. Many years ago, a Scotch Divine, whose remarkable abilities were even less remarkable than the benevolence and nobleness of his heart, published some sermons upon the connection of Revelation with modern Astronomy. Assuming, what he supposed to be the settled opinion of scientific men, that our system contains a multitude of worlds, and that each of these worlds may have as many intelligent inhabitants as our own, he grappled with the question: How such a doctrine was consistent with the enormous importance which the Christian revelation seemed to attach to the creature—Man?: How it was possible, that such an insect, as he would appear to be, in the midst of such an universe, could be the subject of a great scheme of Redemption, in which the Son of God was the agent? It was answered, that modern science does not only lead us to think of the great, but of the little; that the wonders of the microscope are as overwhelming as those of the telescope; that it does not diminish our idea of the Creator, to believe that He is contriving for the very minutest of His creatures; that, in thinking so, we acquire a new sense of His wisdom and greatness, as well as of His love; that the economy of our redemption,—place us as low as you will in the scale of intelligences,—make us numerically as insignificant as you will,—may explain the depths of the divine resources to the admiring students and worshippers of innumerable worlds, or systems of worlds.

It has been argued recently, by an anonymous writer, of great talent and most various information, that the hypothesis on which these Discourses proceed is not one which the latest scientific discoveries encourage; that it is more likely that we are alone in the universe, than that we are surrounded by creatures having capacities at all similar to ours; that, if we hold that opinion, we are free from the difficulty, which it required all the ingenuity and eloquence of the Scottish divine to dispose of; that then we may understand perfectly, why our fall, and our sin, and our deliverance, should assume what, otherwise, would seem so disproportionate a place in the divine order.

On the scientific question, I can, of course, presume to say nothing, except that whatever is true must be satisfactory; that the most beautiful dreams and the most exquisite reasonings are good for nothing, if they are at war with that which is; that moralists and theologians never can have an interest in maintaining any proposition that is physically unsound. But as some have thought that Christianity would gain an advantage, if it could narrow the dimensions of the intelligent universe,—that it would be well for us, because we are believers in Scripture, to snatch at the hope, which the probable absence of an atmosphere in the moon holds out, that every part of creation, except our planet, may be tenantless—I think it is very needful, that we should ask ourselves, whether we have this motive for looking unfairly at the evidence; whether, if the next wave of scientific discovery should sweep us from the ledge on which we had found a temporary standing, we should feel our theological position more insecure. I believe that, so long as we fancy our transgressions and sins form the groundwork of the divine Revelation,— so long as we think that the purpose of the Creator was turned into a new and strange direction, by the evils of men perpetrated or foreseen—so long we shall be uneasy when we think that myriads may be living under the law of the same King and Father, of whose history we know nothing. This restlessness will be experienced most strongly by those who feel how glorious a principle that of Sacrifice is; how impossible it is to imagine a blessed world in which it does not exist. For if that which seems to be the source of all good to God's intelligent creatures is contingent upon the existence of Sin, we could scarcely bear—awful and monstrous as the assertion may sound —to conceive of intelligent creatures without sin. But if sacrifice is implied in the very original of the universe—if it is involved in the very nature and being of God—if it was expressed in the divine obedience of the Son before the worlds were,—if the manifestation of it in the latter days, was to take away Sin, because Sin and Sacrifice are the eternal opposites—then indeed we may believe that the telescope will only give us another sense of the truth, which the microscope has already revealed, that every conceivable multiplication of worlds, and of spiritual creatures, will only manifest some aspect of that love which was gathered up in the Cross of Calvary. I do not think that these remarks are a digression from the proper subject of this discourse; I believe they are a suitable preparation for it.

When the Scriptures speak of Christ's Sacrifice as a Redemption, you will find that they give the word its simplest and most natural force. *Blessed be the Lord God of Israel, for He hath visited and redeemed His people,* is the burthen of all the songs of the New, and of the Old, Testament. God is assumed everywhere to be carrying out the deliverance of His people, who are, therefore, assumed, by some means, to have fallen into captivity. The sacrifice is a means to this end; the means which God uses; the power by which He ransoms the enslaved captive.

Set this thought, I beseech you, distinctly before your minds, and then compare it with what you know of the effects which heathens attributed to their sacrifices—yes, and with the notions which you have yourselves connected with sacrifices. There is, at the root

of both, I am satisfied, an acute sense of some oppression, from which the suppliant wants to be set free; and of a Deliverer, who may be willing, or may be induced, to undertake his cause. But does not this thought mingle with the whole service? 'The op-
'pression I am suffering comes from the Lord of the
'universe; from the highest power of all. He has
'laid it upon me: and, in order to shake it off, I must
'first secure the aid of some powerful ally; next, I
'must do a number of slavish acts—acts which I feel
'to be very burdensome and oppressive, but which it
'is worth while to go through, for the sake of escaping
'heavier penalties which may overtake me if I neglect
'them?' Is not this the habit of feeling which you detect in many who submit to religious duties in Christian lands? Have you not detected it in your own hearts? And is it not the very *reverse* of that idea of sacrifice which we should recognise, if we associated it, as the Scriptures do, with the idea of redemption?

Determine, at all events, which view of the subject, whether it agree or jars with our habits, is most consistent with that doctrine of sacrifice which we have been discovering in the Old Testament. The great truth of all which has come out before us, is that the sacrifices were God's sacrifices,—not merely in that they were offered to him, but in that He originated and prepared them. And, when they assumed the most legal and precise form, they were appointed expressly to commemorate a redemption of the Israelites,—a redemption accomplished *for* them with a high hand, and a stretched-out arm, by the Lord God of Israel,—a redemption from an actual tyrant.

Still the thought will present itself: 'Whatever may 'have been the case with the Jews, the redemption, the 'spiritual redemption, we, Christians, speak of, is surely 'from some evil inflicted or threatened by God—justly 'inflicted and threatened—deserved by us, no doubt,— 'but still proceeding from Him.' As the object I proposed to myself was to discover what the Scripture teaching is, I can only answer this question by referring you to the passages in which the word occurs. Take first, our own passage : '*Forasmuch as ye know that ye were not redeemed with corruptible things, as silver and gold, from your vain conversation received by tradition from your fathers; but with the precious blood of Christ, as of a lamb without blemish and without spot.*' There is no difficulty in giving this language a definite signification. St. Peter was writing to a set of people— chiefly Israelites—who were scattered through different provinces of Asia. Their condition explained to him what he had read in the Law and Prophets, what he had experienced himself. The law speaks of the sins of the fathers as being visited upon the children. The Prophets show, how idolatrous notions respecting God, —the confusion of Him with the works of His hands, with the powers of Nature, with evil and malignant persons,—increased from generation to generation; the falsehood of the father growing falser still in the children, till the sense of truth, and with it the sense of righteousness and moral order, became nearly extinct. Such a growth of corruption in habits and notions,— such a continual alienation from the mind of God,—they led, not heathens, but their own countrymen, to expect, if they forgot that they were a chosen people, if they became mere receivers of traditions from their fathers, not believers in the Lord God of their fathers. The moral state of the Israelites, as described in the Old Testament, at various periods, is precisely that of a people sunk in *a vain conversation*—in a low habitual idolatry and heartlessness, which had begun in one age, and had been transmitted, with fresh accessions, to the next. The scattered Jews in the provinces of the Roman empire, whether they retained a strong sense of their separation, and held intercourse chiefly with each other, or whether they mixed with the heathens round about them, must have presented striking examples of this degeneracy. To them St. Peter came preaching of Christ the Son of David, the Son of God, who had come down from heaven, not to do His own will, but the will of Him who sent Him, who had made the one sacrifice which took away the sins of the world. The message was received by some of these degraded Jews. It became to them the message of a new life. The grovelling thoughts of God, which had been accumulating for years in their own minds, which had been the deposit of centuries, were scattered to the winds. The old words, which they had heard, that He was the Redeemer and King of His people awakened to life in them. These words prepared them for the new, and still more astonishing, news, that this King was a Father, that He claimed them as His children, that they might arise and go to Him, in the faith that He had owned them, accepted them, delivered them.

St. Peter could turn to these people, and say boldly: 'You have been redeemed from your vain traditional 'notions, and from the degeneration that was consequent 'upon them; you *know* that you have. And recollect 'now, recollect always, *who* has redeemed you. You 'cannot think that I was the author of the blessing, 'because I declared it to you. My message must have 'been a lie, if it came from me; I was as much in- 'volved in these traditions, as ignorant of God, as you 'were. He has raised us out of that ignorance. But 'consider again the extent of the redemption. I did 'not tell you of a Father, who cared for you, the 'dwellers in Pontus and Galatia, above all the other 'people of the Earth. I told you of a Lamb of God 'who took away the sins of the *world*. It was the 'belief in Him which lifted you out of your miserable 'subjection to visible things, out of your dark and 'slavish notions concerning God, out of your dread and 'horror of Him; are you not conscious that it was? 'You believed that in Him God has manifested His 'own fatherly will; you acknowledge Him who had 'given up Himself, as your King. Hold fast this

'faith; remember, now and ever, that it is God Him-
'self who has redeemed you out of bondage of which
'none can understand the bitterness and cruelty so
'well as yourselves. And the ransom-money the
'price of your redemption, has not been corruptible
'silver and gold. It has been the blood of His
'only Son. He has made this mighty offering of
'that which is dearest to Him, that He might bind
'you to Himself, that He might vindicate His own
'fatherly love to you, and claim you as His adopted
'sons.'

There might arise a great many questions, in the hearts of St. Peter's disciples afterwards, about the meaning and operation of this sacrifice; he might reply to them in various ways, as he does in this letter. But with these questions he has no direct business in the present passage. The one thought, 'You have 'been delivered out of an actual bondage, not an 'imaginary or a technical one; and this has been the 'process of your deliverance,' occupies him here. He connects an experience of their minds with a *fact*. He treats that fact as the manifestation of an eternal law of Sacrifice; of a Person in whom that law was perfectly realised.

I have been anxious that you should dwell upon this particular instance of the use of the word, because it illustrates the practical method of the New Testament teachers, as well as the principle which is embodied in their Gospel to mankind. But I do not wish to rest upon that single instance. St. Paul's circumstances were very different from those of St. Peter: the habits of their minds were different; the people whom they taught were very different.

Let us take an example, then, of the use of the same word from him. He is writing to Titus, who which settled in Crete; the overseer of a Church, in was the Gentile element was probably predominant. St. Paul is telling him, with the authority of an apostle and a father, what lessons he should impart to his flock. Here is the summary of the doctrine: '*For the grace of God that bringeth salvation hath appeared to all men, teaching us that, denying ungodliness and worldly lusts, we should live soberly, righteously, and godly, in this present world; looking for that blessed hope, and the glorious appearing of the great God and our Saviour Jesus Christ; who gave himself for us, that he might redeem us from all iniquity, and purify unto himself a peculiar people, zealous of good works.* Titus ii. 11-15. Here you have a phrase different from St. Peter's,—a more comprehensive one. Instead of '*the vain conversation received by tradition*' we have '*from all iniquity*'—ἀνομίας. But surely the spirit of the two passages is essentially the same. The bondage of the Cretans, as of all men, was to irregularity, disorder and lawlessness. They were slaves, because they were separated from the true spring and source of order; because they were living as if He were not, as if some other than He were, their Ruler, and the

Ruler of the universe. But His grace had shone forth *upon all men*. It was a saving, delivering grace : one that rescued from ungodliness, and from the lusts of the world; one that produced a righteous, self-restraining, manly, devout, life; one that kindled the hope and expectation of a still brighter shining forth of the glory of God, and of Jesus Christ—*who gave up Himself* for the very purpose of *redeeming* us from evil, and *making us zealous of good works*. Here, as in the other case, the redemption is clearly connected with the sacrifice. God is said to manifest His own grace through that sacrifice. Christ surrenders Himself to do the will of God; and the result of that surrender is, that men may be rescued from a state which is contrary to the will of God—a state of separation from Him, and of consequent immorality, lawlessness, and moral debasement.

I have quoted, I believe, the only two passages in which the simple verb λυτρόω occurs, with the exception of one, in St. Luke's report of the walk of the disciples to Emmaus, where they say, ' *We thought that it had been He which should have redeemed Israel.*' There is, however, a very remarkable passage, in the Epistle to the Hebrews, in which the substantive λύτρωσις occurs. It is this, '*That Christ being come an High Priest of good things to come, by a greater, and more perfect, tabernacle, not made with hands,—that is to say, not of this building; neither by the blood of bulls and calves, but by His own blood, He entered in once into the holy place, having obtained* (or found) *eternal redemption for us. For, if the blood of bulls, and of goats, and the ashes of an heifer sprinkling the unclean, sanctifieth to the purifying of the flesh; how much more shall the blood of Christ, who, through the Eternal Spirit, offered Himself to God, purge your conscience from dead works, to serve the living God?'* I must, hereafter, consider this great passage for another purpose; I refer to it now because it connects so remarkably the obtaining of redemption with the offering of the blood of Christ; and because it explains so fully, what the writer's idea of redemption is. He who vindicated for us a right to enter into the presence of God, and enabled us to enter into it—'*He who purified the conscience from dead works, that it might serve the living God*'—He has found the redemption for us. As if he had said—' Do you not know that 'there has been an oppression on your conscience, a 'tyranny which you could not shake off? Do you not 'know that this oppression arose from a sense of sepa-'ration from God, of being at war with Him? Do 'you not know that, while you have that sense, you 'cannot pray to Him as a Father, you cannot serve 'Him as a living God? And can anyone emancipate 'his own conscience from this bondage? Does not 'GOD emancipate it, when, instead of asking you to 'make the sacrifices which you feel that you cannot 'make, He proclaims His gracious will in that Son, who 'perfectly does His will, by offering up Himself?'

When we have entered into these applications of the

word—*Redemption*, and when we have tested them, by considering what vain habits, handed down from our fathers, what iniquity, what bonds of conscience, we have need to be delivered from, and by asking ourselves what but the belief in a sacrifice made by God will deliver us from them;—when we have proved their power in another way, by considering whether there is any power that is effectual to break the chains of superstition, and of moral corruption, which Christian or Pagan nations have inherited, and are wearing—then we may be able to appreciate the force of some of those passages, in which St. Paul carries out the same idea into heights and depths, which at first make us dizzy, and yet which are continually visited by men of all ranks and intellects,— nay, to which they are driven by the every-day sorrows and trials of earth. He speaks of redemption, that is the forgiveness of sins; he speaks of a redemption of the body, which is burdened with the weight of sickness and death; he speaks of a redemption of the whole creation, which is still in travail, but shall be delivered, and shall enjoy the glorious liberty of the sons of God. These are hints of mighty themes upon which I do not purpose to dwell, because I would rather you found out for yourselves how they all belong to the idea of the one Sacrifice, how inseparable they are from it. But there is one help which I can give you in that search, by directing you to some sentences which our Lord spoke when He was Himself on earth. The word λύτρον, which is translated (rightly, I should suppose) *ransom*, was used by Him in one of His discourses, which is reported in the twentieth chapter of St. Matthew. I should like you to reflect upon the occasion on which He used it. It was when the mother of Zebedee's children has asked that her two sons might sit, one on the right hand, and one on the left in His kingdom. The other ten apostles, we are told, showed great indignation at the two brothers. *'But Jesus called them unto Him, and said, Ye know that the princes of the Gentiles exercise dominion over them, and they that are great exercise authority upon them. But it shall not be so among you: but whosoever will be great among you, let him be your minister; and whosoever will be chief among you, let him be your servant: even as the son of man came not to be ministered unto, but to minister, and to give His life a ransom for many.'* I do not think it is just in that place we should have expected to find this phrase. We speak of the unspeakably costly ransom which Christ offered for the redemption of man, and we speak truly. *He* teaches us wherein the costliness of it consisted. He humbled Himself; He became a servant; He was the servant of all. Here was the sacrifice with which God was well pleased; here was the costly oblation; here was the mighty ransom by which the One was able to deliver the many. The lowliest of all was the One who most showed forth the glory of God's love; the lowliest of all was the One who could alone exercise God's power on behalf of His creatures. That power was a redeeming power; that power came forth when the Son gave up His Spirit to His Father; that power becomes effectual for us, when it redeems us from our pride, when it breaks that chain which has kept us in slavery to the Spirit of Disobedience, which has hindered us from serving the living God. We know the meaning of the Ransom, we understand the greatness of the Sacrifice, when we give up the craving to be chief of all, and ask for the Spirit of Christ to make us the servants of all.

SERMON IX.

CHRIST'S SACRIFICE A DELIVERANCE FROM THE CURSE OF THE LAW.

(*Lincoln's Inn, 5th Sunday after Easter, May 21, 1854.*)

'Christ hath redeemed us from the curse of the law, being made a curse for us: for it is written, Cursed is every one that hangeth on a tree: that the blessing of Abraham might come on the Gentiles through Jesus Christ; that we might receive the promise of the Spirit through faith.'—GALATIANS iii. 13, 14.

As I proposed in my last sermon to examine the uses of the word Redemption in the New Testament when it is connected with sacrifice, you may wonder that I passed over such a memorable text as this. I passed it over, because I thought I should treat the subject more fairly, if I confined myself to the word λύτρον, its compounds and its cognates. The verb '*redeemed*' here is not one of these. This, however, is not one of the cases, of which there are many in the Epistles, that offer a fair ground of complaint against the authors of our version, for adapting the same rendering to two different words. It would be difficult, perhaps, to find a better equivalent than that which they have chosen for either expression. The mere word here does not suggest the thought of ransom quite so directly as those of which I spoke last Sunday, it means simply 'to buy out;' but the idea of a slave for whom a friend obtains freedom, not by arms, but by purchase in the market, is always present in it. Although it sometimes occurs without any distinct allusion to price or purchase-money, as in the phrase *Redeeming the time*, yet generally, that is not only implied, but forced upon our notice. It is so in that celebrated passage, in the fifth chapter of the book of Revelation (where, indeed, the simple verb ἀγοράζω is used), '*Thou art worthy to take the book, and to open the seals thereof: for thou wast slain, and hast redeemed us to God by thy blood, out of every kindred, and tongue, and people, and nation.*' It is so assuredly in the sentence before us, where Christ is said *to redeem us from a curse, by becoming a curse* Himself.

I might, therefore, at once assume, that the purchase spoken of here came under the same principle with the ransom or redemption which we read of in the Epistle of St. Peter, and in the Epistles to Titus and to the Hebrews. I might take it for granted, that, in one case as much as in the other, God was spoken of as delivering His creatures from an oppression under which they had fallen, and as bringing them back into their true and rightful service, which is perfect freedom. I might assume that Sacrifice was the method, the only method, by which the chains that bound man's spirit could be broken, precisely because they were chains on a spirit, not on a mere animal. I might trace here, as I traced before, that union and co-operation of the will of the Father with the will of the Son, which was, as St. Peter taught us, before all worlds; which lay in the very ground of creation, but which was never manifested in its fulness till the Son yielded up Himself to the death of the Cross.

I know, however, that there are associations with the phrase, '*curse of the Law,*' which greatly interfere with this belief. I do not say how far these associations are produced, or promoted, by one system of theological teaching or another. I do not profess to trace them to their origin. I am sure that they haunt you and me. I am sure it requires an effort, and a very careful effort, to disengage ourselves from them, because they are intertwined with very righteous and sacred feelings; and because, at the same time, they gain great strength from tempers and habits, which, though not righteous or sacred, are very natural to us all. Every Englishman understands, and confesses, that Law has its root in the mind of God, that it is one great utterance of His mind. He feels that the decrees of Law must be executed; that no tenderness or graciousness towards individual offenders, or towards a multitude of offenders, ought to suspend or weaken their execution. The curse of the Law he feels is something very tremendous indeed; how can it be other than the curse of God? But if it is this, when Christ is said to redeem us from the curse of Law, can anything else be meant, than that He redeems us from the curse which God Himself had denounced, and was prepared to enforce, against His creatures? that He stepped in, as their Advocate, to shield them from His Father's indignation; that He offered His blood which was an adequate purchase-money or ransom from it?

I wish you to perceive, not how startling this view of the subject is, but how readily it presents itself to us as a most logical and consistent explanation of the apostle's meaning; how it conspires with a belief which is sound in itself, and closely akin to the habits of our national character; how it appeals, also, to our sense of an evil in ourselves which requires the most wonderful process for its extirpation. I have no hope of overcoming such influences as these by merely arguing, that, if this be the true and scriptural statement of the case, we must abandon all the conclusions respecting Sacrifice which we have deduced hitherto from an examination of Scripture, and adopt that theory of it which patriarchs, lawgivers, prophets, apostles seem to have agreed in denouncing. Unless this *particular* phrase, *curse of the Law,* and the *special* aspect of redemption which St. Paul connects with it, can be explained, without resorting to the hypothesis I am speaking of—unless the explanation can be shown to be more in accordance with the teaching of the apostles than the popular one—we shall talk in vain about general principles, or inferences from the course of the Bible history. But it seems to me, that, if we will suffer St. Paul to be his own interpreter—not in some other part of his writings, but in that part wherein this sentence occurs—we shall find our way into such an apprehension of the subject, as will make the doctrine of Christ becoming a curse that He might redeem us from a curse, not the confutation, but the most perfect illustration, of the principle, that the loving Will of the Father is the moving cause of the deliverance of man, and of the Sacrifice by which that deliverance has been accomplished.

The Galatians had, at first, accepted St. Paul as the preacher of a Gospel. News concerning the God who made them was what they wanted; that which the tentmaker of Tarsus brought them was emphatically *good* news. He reminds them in his letter what it was. '*God sent forth His Son, made of a woman, made under the law, to redeem them that were under the law, that they might receive the adoption of sons.*' They had a right to believe that. The God of the whole earth had said that He was their Father. It was not a mere name; He had given them a sign of His adoption; He had promised, with that sign, to give them His Spirit in their hearts, that they might call upon Him as their Father. If they believed this message, they received the sign. St. Paul asked them whether they merely received that? Did there not come with it a joy, and thankfulness, and wonder—a filial feeling such as they never had before? But, very soon, teachers came among them, who said that the Gospel was, after all, but a preparation for the Law. They had been, the most part of them, Gentiles, worshippers of false gods, with none of the privileges of the chosen race of the children of Abraham. 'Did they 'really fancy that they were to spring at once into the 'highest condition which human beings could enjoy? 'Did they deem that they were to be in as good a con-'dition as those who had for centuries been under the 'divine discipline, who had the law and covenants? 'What a monstrous supposition! The man who had 'encouraged them in it was manifestly imposing upon 'them, tempting them to their ruin. Baptism was good, 'but it was the induction to a higher good. If they 'would be circumcised, then, indeed, they might benefit 'by the coming of the Christ into the world; for He 'had come mainly to expound the Law, to bring back the 'religion of the old times, which the modern teachers had 'corrupted, to make that the religion of the whole earth.'

The doctrine was most plausible; when is not a doctrine that leads men into slavery plausible? The Galatians received it; the preacher of the Gospel was discarded as a dangerous sophist; the preachers of the Law were hailed as wise and moral guides, who could show those who followed them an old and safe road to heaven. St. Paul meets his opponents in this letter. He asks for no quarter, and gives none. He regards the question as one of life and death; one upon which the moral slavery, or freedom, of the nations of the earth depended. He believes equally that the understanding of the Old Scriptures depended upon it. These Judaisers he will not admit to be Jews; they know nothing of their own privileges, or of the end for which God had chosen their fathers.

To this point he especially addresses himself. They wished to be Abraham's children; they wished all men to be under the Law, as they had been. The two wishes were incompatible. Was Abraham under a Law? No! he was under a blessing. The covenant with him did not mean, if Moses spoke truly, that he was commanded to do certain things, and to leave certain things undone. It meant that the Lord of all declared Himself to him, and took him to be His friend. And the Covenant was to be a universal one. The tenor of it was: '*In thee, and in thy seed, shall all the families of the earth be blessed.*' This was the groundwork of the Jewish nation. This was the groundwork of all the righteousness of its first father. He believed the God who had spoken to him, who had given him this promise! so he rose to the stature of a righteous man. He became like the Being who had adopted him.

But the law, St. Paul goes on to argue, was no part of this blessing. Its function was of a different, a directly opposite kind; *it was added because of transgressions.* And what it did was to pronounce a *curse* upon those transgressions. It denounced death against them. 'What is it then,' he asks, 'that you, the 'preachers of this new Gospel to the Galatians, want 'for yourselves, and for them? Do you wish to be 'under a curse? Is *that* the great benefit which 'belongs to the chosen people, *that* the great boon it 'is to confer on the world?'

The question was a startling one; but it was not merely startling; it came from the inmost experience of St. Paul himself; it appealed to the experience of the Jew. St. Paul had gloried in the Law as much as any of them could do. He had boasted of the wonderful advantage he had over the Gentile world in possessing it. And, by degrees, it presented itself to him as a tremendous sword which was hanging over him; which was ready to slay him, whom it seemed so greatly to favour. In the strictest sense, it *cursed* him. It made him conscious of evil within him which cut him off from God, which made it impossible for him to trust God, though he found that it was the very characteristic of Abraham and David, and of all the heroes of his race, that they *did* trust God. The Jews, generally, might not have felt all, or a thousandth part of what the apostle had felt, because they were less in earnest; but they knew very well that they were not trusting God,—that they dreaded Him, fled from Him, looked upon Him as having given them a Law which they were to boast of, but which they could not keep, which set them above other nations, and made them more miserable than other nations. It could not be otherwise; according to the eternal principles of the universe and of God's nature it could not. Law, St. Paul discovered, serves this purpose in the education of a man or of a nation. It awakens the sense of evil; it shows them that they are at war with themselves and with God; it cannot make them right and good; it cannot bring about any peace between them and God.

Was, then, this effect all that God designed for Jews and for men? Was it the first thing that He designed for them? Clearly not, unless the covenant with Abraham was a delusion. The blessing preceded the curse; the blessing which declared by its very terms that it was for all. If the Jews wished to be children of Abraham, they must assert a higher and nobler position than that of being the receivers and subjects of a Law. They must say: 'God is blessing us, and the world 'through us; God is calling upon us to trust Him, as 'the source and root of all blessings. And this Law, 'which comes with its tremendous curses, is part of 'our discipline, to teach us what our condition is with-'out God; what we are when we are not trusting 'Him; when we are seeking to make ourselves righ-'teous in any other way, but by believing in His righ-'teousness. The Law is our schoolmaster, to bring us 'to the knowledge of that Mediator in whom the pro-'mise was made. It was a secondary subordinate dispen-'sation, of infinite worth as a means of leading us to that primary truth of our relation to God in this Mediator, 'on which the covenant with Abraham stood; apart 'from which it would have had no force or validity.'

The more you read this Epistle to the Galatians, the more, I am persuaded, you will see that the argument of the apostle, from first to last, is a refutation of the doctrine, that we are first to learn what God is, what His will is, from the Law which curses, and then to ask whether there is no escape from its terrors and its penalties. He insists upon the priority of the Covenant to the Law, of the blessing to the curse. He insists upon it, that the blessing, which appeals to faith and trust, expresses the mind of God, and that the Law, which appeals to fear, is made necessary by the false condition into which men have brought themselves through distrust of His promises. And then he announces Christ, the Mediator, as coming forth to fulfil the blessing which God had laid up for Men in Him, and to redeem them from the curse and separation which they had brought upon themselves. '*He has redeemed us from the curse of the Law, having been made, or become, a curse for us.*' The curse which the Law pronounced upon men was death, death in its most odious, most criminal, shape; and He underwent it, an actual, not a fantastic crucifixion,— the sentence of the rebel and the slave. Do you ask how this act effected the purpose of redeeming any, or how many were included in the benefits of it? The question is, indeed, most difficult, if by redemption you understand *in any sense* the deliverance of man out of the hand of God, the procuring a change in his purpose or will; then there is need of every kind of subtle explanation to show how the means corresponded to the end. But if you suppose that it is the spirit of a man which needs to be emancipated, a spirit fast bound with the chains of its own sins and fears, then I do not see what proof, save one, can be of any avail, that a certain scheme of redemption is effectual. Appeal directly to the captive. See whether the announcement, that the Son of God has died for him, does dissolve that horror of God, that feeling of him as the tyrant, the forger of bonds, the inventor of a curse, by which he has been possessed.

If the spiritual bondage is not real, of course the spiritual redemption is not real. But the whole history of the world, of every portion of the world, for six thousand years, proclaims that it is real; that this is the bondage from which men are seeking by all contrivances to break loose; that all material bondage is but the accident and result of it. If the way of deliverance from it has been found out in some corner of the world, civilised or uncivilised—if it is a way that is available for human beings actually tormented with the sense of evil, actually dying,—then let us know the way, let us try it. But the sacrifices that ascend from ten thousand altars to powers of sky, and earth, and air, to the Spirit of Evil far more than to the Spirit of Good, declare: 'We have not found it; we never shall; till 'you can tell us of some sacrifice which shall be of 'God; one which proceeds from His will, and not ours; 'one which fulfils His will and not ours.'

It is such a one of which St. Paul speaks, when he declares that '*Christ has redeemed us from the curse of the Law, having become a curse for us.*' It was the enunciation of his old message with a new clause, which the objections of his opponents had brought out, and which deepened and strengthened that to which it was added. He had preached to the Galatians of a Father who had sent His Son into the world; he had bidden them take up their place, as sons of God. The Judaisers would cheat them of that position, and send them back to the Law. St. Paul declares, that the act which proclaimed them sons was an act of redemption from the Law. It had been a useful pedagogue; it denoted that they had not yet been recognised as children; that they were still in servitude. Now the hour of emancipation had arrived. The Son of God had owned them as kinsmen. In death, He had proved Himself their brother; in rising from the dead, He had claimed His Father as their Father.

I need not tell you what is involved in the use of this Roman comparison. The emancipated child always had been a child; he did not become so when he was allowed to put on the manly gown; that was only the time when, his preparatory discipline having been completed, he could be safely trusted with the knowledge of his dignity, when he could do the acts of a freeman and a citizen.

St. Paul takes the analogy in the length and breadth of it. There was a period, during which it was needful that men should be learning their condition; should be working through many strange experiences to the discovery that they were spirits; should be feeling after the Father of their spirits. During that time He was not forgetting them. When they were stooping most to visible things, when they were least aware of their high parentage, He was awakening to them desires which nothing they saw or heard could satisfy or could quell. By laws He was controlling their indulgence in things mischievous to them; was making them aware of their own low tendencies; was teaching them to shudder at the sight of themselves. Then, sending forth His Son in their likeness, He raised them to the state for which He had created them; He redeemed them from the vassalage into which their own sins had brought them; He redeemed them from the vassalage which he had Himself ordained for their education. They were no longer under the Law as a curse; they were no longer under the Law as a pedagogue. They could not any longer contemplate death as God's curse, cutting them off from Himself, for Christ had endured it. They could not any longer submit to be servants of a rule, for Christ had come to make their state filial, to give them the spirit of power, and of love, and of a sound mind.

St. Paul was, at least as well aware as we can be, of the false inferences which might be drawn from this Gospel, of the miserable notions of liberty which might be built upon it. He is occupied, in the latter part of this Epistle, in protecting his doctrine against these dangers; not by weakening and diluting it, but by bringing out, in its full strength, that promise of the Spirit, of which he speaks in the last words of my text. The Spirit of Christ could not lead them into any of the acts which were inconsistent with the life of Christ. The Spirit of God could not tempt them to violate any portion of the Law of God. He would teach them to delight in that Law after the inner man, as David did, because it discovered God's will to keep his creatures from the evils which enslaved them and separated them from Him. They could carry out in their conduct the highest meaning and intent of the Law, having that love to each other which is the fulfilment of the Law. '*But*,' he says, '*if you bite and devour one another, take heed lest you be not consumed of one another.*' If you exhibit all the mind and temper of the flesh, against which the Law is directed, assuredly you bring yourselves within the curse from which Christ has redeemed you. But is that the effect of your believing the Gospel, or of disbelieving it; of acting as if Christ had redeemed your race, and brought it nigh to God, or of listening to teachers who lead you to suppose that you are at a distance from Him, and that He is your enemy?

Which doctrine caused the Galatians, in the first century, to bite and devour each other? which causes English Christians, in the nineteenth century, to do the same?

SERMON X.

THE SACRIFICE OF CHRIST A PROPITIATION.

(*Lincoln's Inn, Sunday after Ascension Day, May 28, 1854.*)

' Therefore by the deeds of the law there shall no flesh be justified in his sight: for by the law is the knowledge of sin. But now the righteousness of God without the law is manifested, being witnessed by the law and the prophets; even the righteousness of God which is by faith of Jesus Christ unto all and upon all them that believe: for there is no difference: for all have sinned, and come short of the glory of God; being justified freely by his grace, through the redemption that is in Christ Jesus: whom God hath set forth to be a propitiation through faith in his blood, to declare His righteousness for the remission of sins that are past, through the forbearance of God; to declare, I say, at this time his righteousness: that he might be just, and the justifier of him which believeth in Jesus.'—ROMANS iii. 20–27.

MY special object in this sermon is to consider the meaning of the word *Propitiation,* which occupies so prominent a place in the passage I have read to you. But you will observe that the idea of *Redemption,* which has occupied us for the last two Sundays, is as much dwelt upon here as it was in the Epistle of St. Peter, or in the Epistle to the Galatians. The two words evidently point to different necessities of man, to different aspects of the divine purpose. Yet they are brought together; the apostle treats them as inseparable. It is in Sacrifice they find their meeting point.

I could wish that you would read the letter to the Romans by the light of these sentences; that you would trace the principle which is unfolded in them, as it works itself out through all the reasonings, exhortations, expositions of national and human history, and revelations of personal experience, which are found in that wonderful book. But I shall be content if you will fix your minds on these two or three verses, and will notice a few of their more obvious characteristics.

(1.) The first that would strike you is, that the *Righteousness* of God is the subject, the groundwork, of the apostle's discourse. He assumes that it is the purpose of God to make his own righteousness known. He assumes that what man wants is that his righteousness should be made known. Nor does he for an instant distinguish between the revelation of God's righteousness and the revelation of Himself. He supposes that God is the righteous Being; that He is this, and nothing but this; that to be acquainted with Him is to be acquainted with Right in its very essence and substance, with that Right which is the ground of all we think, and do, and are.

(2.) Next he affirms the *Law* testifies of this righteousness of God, but that it does not bring any man to the knowledge of righteousness; on the contrary, it

L

brings him to the knowledge of sin. You will remember that this was one great point in the argument which the apostle held with the Galatians, and with the teachers who wished to bring them under the Law. The Law, he showed them, could not make any man right; could not bless any man. Its office was to make him feel that he was wrong; its power lay in its curse.

(3.) Thirdly, he says that the righteousness of God manifests itself in another way than by Law, namely, in the Person of Jesus Christ; and that, so manifested, it *is* effectual to make men righteous; it *is* effectual to confer a blessing. And this righteousness, he says, comes *through the faith of Jesus Christ.* I will not stop to dispute whether he means through the faith which Jesus Christ had in His Father—that is, perhaps, the more obvious and natural construction—or through the faith which a man has in Christ; for I think that one meaning involves the other, and that neither will be complete without the other. At any rate, he affirms that this righteousness came through Jesus Christ upon all who believe, all who confess it, and trust it when it is manifested in Him; upon all, without exception, because *all have sinned, all have come short of the glory of God*; all are convicted by God's Law, whether delivered in stones, or only speaking in the conscience, of having that in them which is at war with this righteousness.

(4.) As this righteous Being makes men conscious

of their evil by the Law, and manifests His righteousness to them in His Son, so He is declared, in the next verse, *freely to justify them by His grace, through the redemption that is in Christ Jesus.* I must remind you, that the word *justified* is the cognate verb to the adjective which we translate *righteous*. I do not say that the translators ought to have kept up the analogy of the words; perhaps they could not; perhaps they attempted it more than we suppose, seeing that the *just* man and the *righteous* man were more nearly identical in their days than they are in ours. Still I do not doubt they put a force upon the phrase '*justified,*' which would not have been expressed by the phrase *made righteous*. They were afraid to use that form of expression, lest it should seem to intimate that men became righteous in *themselves,* and are not, as our Article expresses it, ' accounted righteous only for the sake of Jesus Christ.' I believe that fear had a most reasonable ground; though there may have been another fear as reasonable, to which they were not equally alive. They dreaded lest men should fancy they had a righteousness of their own; and that dread no one could entertain so strongly as St. Paul. But they did not tremble as much as the Apostle did, lest men should suppose that the judgment of God was not *according to truth* lest they should ever charge Him with acting upon a legal fiction. St. Paul discovered that frightful mistake in his own countrymen; they thought they were better than the heathen, because God was favouring them, and treating them as righteous, while they were committing the same evils as other men. His whole reasoning, in the second chapter, had been aimed at this delusion; he had been affirming the commonplace, which had become a paradox, that good is good in a heathen, that sin is sin in a Jew. He could not advance one step in making them understand his Gospel, while they held the contrary opinion. When, therefore, he goes on to speak of God justifying the Jew and the heathen equally, he has prepared both to understand that they can have no *real* righteousness but that which they derive from God; and that they possess it in Him by renouncing it in themselves; that they have it when they trust Him; that they have it not when they distrust Him. And, connecting this with the manifestation of God's righteousness in his Son, he affirms that God has freely justified them, or made them righteous, in that Son; that in Him He has acquitted them of their transgressions, and owned them as belonging to Him. If they believe that this is the intent of His acts, if they acknowledge this to be the object of His revelation, they rise up right, true, justified men.

(5.) Next, then, St. Paul says, that this righteousness and justification comes upon them *through the redemption that is in Christ Jesus*. The word, you will perceive, carries precisely the signification which it bore in all the cases we have examined hitherto. They who were enslaved by the *vain conversation handed down from their fathers*, who had thought of God as like themselves, who had regarded Him as an enemy, were ransomed by the precious blood of the Lamb from that intolerable bondage; those who were chained by their own *iniquity* were enabled to lay hold on a righteousness that was not their own, and yet which they could claim as their own; those who felt that *the Law* was *cursing* them, and cutting them off from God, were brought nigh to God, were able to call Him Father. This, which we found St. Peter and St. Paul asserting so emphatically in the other passages, comes out, if that is possible, more clearly, more fully, here. God is Himself the Redeemer, the Deliverer, of a spirit out of the fetters which it has forged for itself. He delivers it in the way which it feels and confesses to be the only possible way. It could not know God, it could not be released from the self-will which is contrary to God, if He did not meet it in sacrifice, if He did not Himself make the sacrifice which it can accept as the fullest revelation both of His righteousness and of His forgiveness.

(6.) We are thus brought to the words, '*Whom God hath set forth to be a propitiation through faith in His blood, to declare His righteousness for the remission of sins that are past, through the forbearance of God.*'

You are aware, probably, that many have objected to our version of the word ἱλαστήριον, and have contended that 'mercy-seat' should be substituted for it. You may think perhaps, since I have dwelt so much upon the desire to make the powers above or beneath *propitious*, as the characteristic of Heathen sacrifices, that I should eagerly join in this complaint, and urge this alteration. But I do not feel the least tempted to take this course. It seems to me that our rendering is, on the whole, a right and satisfactory one; and that we should lose, not gain, if we forgot that the word had presented, and did present, to the minds of those whom St. Paul was addressing, whether they were his own countrymen or Gentiles, all the associations which had belonged to the most degrading devil-worship. I do not conceive that it was the function of an apostle to cast aside old forms of expression, and to strike out new in a mint of his own. I imagine that he was to take those which he found, just as they were, defaced by the wear and tear of centuries, debased by the adulterations of the weak and of the wicked, of the dupe and the impostor, and to bring out, by severe tests, the pure metal, as well as the image and superscription with which it had been originally stamped. He did recollect, doubtless, thankfully and wonderingly recollect, the mercy-seat in the tabernacle and the temple, as expressing the true idea of propitiation. But he did not look upon that mercy-seat as enshrining a peculiar, esoteric doctrine, with which the world at large had nothing to do. He who had established the mercy-seat was the Lord God of that earth from which the foulest steam of human sacrifices was ascending to the Baals and the Molochs. He was testifying, there, that from Him came freely down the blessings which they were hoping to buy of these gods; that He blotted out the transgressions of which the worshippers were seeking, by the cruellest oblations, to escape the penalty. And now the God of Israel, and the gods of the nations, were no longer standing aloof in distant defiance; they were in closer conflict than when Dagon fell prostrate before the ark. Christ had come to fulfil the promises made to the fathers. Christ had come a Light *to lighten the Gentiles.* Hebrew was no longer the tongue in which the mystery of a living and righteous God was to enshrine itself. In the language of Heathen civilisation, in the beautiful forms which generations of polytheists had consecrated to the service of demigods, of beings like themselves, was the Eternal Son, the brightness of the Father's glory, to utter His voice, and claim the homage of those whom he had not been ashamed to call His brethren. What business had those to whom this new and mighty instrument had been intrusted, to cast away any one of the modes of thought and speech that had received an idolatrous taint and impregnation? Why was the Spirit given them but that men might hear, in their own tongue, purged and regenerated, as the lips that spoke it were, by His living presence and power, the wonderful works of God?

Far then from pleading that the words ἱλασμος and ἱλαστήριον had not the sense which we should gather from all the history of the Heathen world that they must have had, or that this sense was not one which would naturally suggest itself to the readers of the Epistle, baptized men though they were, I would earnestly press the reflection on you, that any other view of the case is incredible; and then I would ask you to observe with what a divine art and wisdom the apostle vindicates the word to a Christian use, showing that for that use its Heathen signification must be—not modified—but inverted.

The opening of the twenty-fifth verse at once explains the method of the apostle's teaching: '*Whom God hath set forth to be a propitiation.*' Try, if you can, to translate that language into the Heathen notion of a propitiatory sacrifice. You want something to make God propitious, or favourable, to you. You wish you could find something mighty enough, transcendent enough, which you might be sure would have that effect. Does St. Paul follow out this line of thought? Does he say, 'The mighty transcendent means of bringing 'God to be at peace with you is here'? No! but he introduces HIM as *setting forth* to us the One all-sufficient, all-satisfactory evidence that HE *has* made peace with us. Placing himself on the old Jewish ground, affirming that all good must come down from the Lord of all, that He must be the standard of righteousness, and the author of righteousness, to man, the standard and the author of *forgiveness* to man, he raises that principle to its highest power; he affirms that the barrier between God and His creatures is removed by

Himself, is removed freely without money and without price, and that the act of His Son in shedding His blood is the authentic declaration of that removal. He does not stop here; as a Jew he could not, still more as a believer in Jesus Christ he could not. The mercy-seat in the tabernacle was not merely a sign that the Jews were adopted and acknowledged as a righteous nation by God, and that He was willing to restore those who had forgotten their high calling; it was the witness of a fellowship and intercourse between Him and His people. *There will I meet with thee,'* was the form which denoted its perpetual purpose. Christ's death could not, according to St. Paul, be a propitiation, if it did not prove and declare Him to be the Mercy-seat, the living Mediator, in whom God meets with His creatures, and in whom His creatures meet Him.

(7.) I reserve this great subject of Intercession for another and fuller consideration. But I could not pass it over, lest the words, *faith in His blood,* which are such prominent words here, should be emptied of one most practical and blessed part of their significance. If we do not receive that blood as the sure witness that we are admitted into God's holy and blessed presence, that we have the awful privilege of drawing nigh to Him always, we cannot be said to believe in it; it does not give us that trust in God of which sin has robbed us. I am quite willing, however, to dwell chiefly, though I dare not dwell exclusively, on the *remission of sins that are past,* as the effect of this *declaration of God's righteousness.* Never, for a single instant, ought we to make light of that craving for pardon, that sense of an infinite burden of evil already committed, which has given rise to every confessional and penance that has existed, or does exist, in the world. There are some who would persuade us, that to dwell on that which has been, is a mere device of priestcraft; that, provided we can do the right thing now, we may be well content, whatever we may have to reproach ourselves with, in the years that are gone by. To them the prayer of the Psalmist, '*Remember not the sins of my youth,*' seems to be the utterance of a vain and self-tormenting superstition. Dear brethren! do not let us delude ourselves with these half-truths, which sound so exceedingly plausible, which prove, in experience, so utterly worthless. We *do* feel the sins of our youth, we are assaulted every day and hour by thoughts, words, acts, which we have left years behind us. Do we think we get rid of these facts, by adopting a theory that they mean nothing? But what a melancholy thing it would be for us, if they did mean nothing! What a proof it would be that man is a being who does not look before and after; that he has not the conditions of a rational, voluntary, spiritual creature! Ascribe to him these conditions, and of necessity he becomes incapable of forgetting that which has been once a part of himself, that which has belonged to his own substance; it cleaves to him; centuries and millenniums cannot divorce it from him. And, oh! are we not deeply and awfully aware that recollections which we would give worlds to preserve, recollections of forms and faces, and loving words spoken, and loving acts done, may pass away from us, almost, it would seem, into utter darkness; while words and acts that we should like to bury thousands of fathoms deep, survive, and reappear, like the ghost of Banquo, at men's feasts —at God's feast—to make the present and the future dark alike?

What avails it to talk against priestcraft when these things are so? I admit that priestcraft makes enormous, frightful, use of these states of mind; but if they were nothing, if they could be cast off by an easy effort, or charmed away by a little metaphysical talk, all its devices might be treated with very great indifference. How do they come into operation? how is it, that, in its very worst form the *trade* of the Priest, as distinguished from his glorious and divine *vocation*, may be as mischievous and as gainful a one now as it was in any past generation; that it may be most successful with the most refined classes of society?

If those old recollections, which come back with such appalling force, belonged altogether to ourselves, if they pointed to no One against whom we have sinned, I suppose that suicide would be the continual refuge from them. And yet what a refuge! How completely the prince of Denmark expressed the madness of that experiment, when he said that there might be dreams, and more frightful dreams, in the sleep after death than in any before it. But the supposition is an impossible one. Everyone does connect the images of the past distinctly or indistinctly with God; his theory may be an atheistical one, but the fact of conscience, the sense of evil, brings back the phantom which he thought he had banished for ever. It comes back as a phantom. As such, the false priest speaks to it. He devises means for making the man less afraid of the dark image which he has cast from himself. He tells him that there is a chance of the past being overlooked, that this act and that act increases the chance. And in the meantime, the man actually feels a relief from having told his wrong. The clearing of the breast *has* helped him, he is sure of that. And the punishment that has been imposed upon him is not without its own comfort. It is a witness to him of moral discipline. It suggests thoughts of a process by which not merely the past evil may be cured, but by which *he* may be cured. What a dawn of light is this! How it might brighten into perfect day, if there was only a voice to say to him, *God hath set forth His Son as a propitiation, and a mercy-seat, to declare His righteousness for the remission of the sins that are past.* If God could be declared to the man as the Propitiator —as the Being who puts away sins *because* He is righteous, *because* He would not have the man tied and yoked to evil, *because* He would make him his free and true servant; if instead of this declaration being merely made in words, the *fact* of Christ's death could be proclaimed as the sure declaration of God's righteousness in the forgiveness of sins ; how would the man feel that neither suicide nor atheism was the refuge from the past, but faith in Him who knows it all, who is, and was, and is to come; faith in Him, as manifested in the sacrifice of His Son; faith in Him, as desiring to make us partakers of His own righteous mind! How naturally would this faith find its full expression in confession to Him who so thoroughly understands the length and breadth of the evil, who sees it not, as man sees it, through the blundering, stammering phrases of the penitent, and who so much more desires the deliverance and reformation of the offender than he has even yet learned to desire it ! How cheerfully should we, holding fast this faith in such a Being, accept His punishments—of whatever kind, they be,—as the tokens that he is educating, disciplining, purifying the child whom He has adopted!

But the theory of a propitiation, not set forth by God, but devised to influence His mind,—of a propitiation that does not declare God's righteousness *in* the forgiveness of sins, but which makes it possible for Him to forgive sins, *though* He is righteous,—this scheme changes all the relations of the Creator and creature; this scheme does build up a priestcraft which subverts utterly the morality of the Bible, because it first subverts its theology.

I know, brethren, that it would be easy to obtain a

favourable hearing from a Protestant people, if I were to denounce this priestcraft as it presents itself in Romish countries, or among those who imitate Romish practices. I do not think I underrate that danger, or regard it as a distant one. On the contrary, I feel sure that the confessional and the whole scheme which is connected with it, must prove stronger than that which we oppose to it—and that atheism may prove stronger than either —if we do not earnestly consider with ourselves whether we are not sanctioning the principle which supports all the practices we condemn; whether we are not practically renouncing the faith of our forefathers, while we are ready to denounce our brethren for forsaking it in name. Those mighty words, *'That he might be just, and the justifier of him which believeth in Jesus,'* are entirely stripped of their meaning by the strange interpolation of the word *yet*. They are supposed to say that God is *just*, and yet that, in consequence of Christ's offering, He *can* justify those who believe in Him. Thus the whole argument of St. Paul, the whole Gospel of St. Paul concerning GOD, is deliberately effaced and contradicted. God does not manifest His righteous will and purpose, His righteous character, in the death of His Son; but, through the agency of that death, a certain notion of justice, quite distinct from the righteousness with which St. Paul uniformly identifies it, is satisfied; and so a certain portion of mankind may be excused the penalty of their past ill-doings. It is only the accidental blending of this opinion with a higher faith, which is utterly at variance with it, that has ever served to make it effectual for any moral purposes. It will be found more utterly powerless for such purposes, more perilous to morality, more perilous to all reverence for God, to all belief in Christ's sacrifice and satisfaction, every day and hour. It must bring forth its proper and legitimate fruits in the most degraded, most heathenish kind of Romanism —such a form of it as has not existed in any previous century—or else it will drive men into the most defying reckless infidelity.

But there is hope, not only for ourselves, but for all. If we will go to the law and testimony, instead of merely boasting of them, and declaiming against others for not going to them,—if we will let the Bible speak to us in its own clear, broad, intelligible language, and will let it hew in pieces all the notions and traditions by which we have been corrupting and disguising the truths that would have made us free, we shall again have a Gospel, not for Protestants, but for Romanists, Jews, Turks, Infidels, for all who have been setting up a righteousness of their own, and yet prove in a thousand ways that they can never be satisfied till they submit to the righteousness of God.

And then the words of the beloved disciple will be found to be in perfect harmony with those of the Apostle of the Gentiles. I shall have to speak hereafter, for another purpose, of those words in which he declares, that *we have an Advocate with the Father,*

Jesus Christ the righteous, who is the propitiation for our sins, and not for ours only, but for the sins of the whole world. But I cannot pass them over here; because, if you will read them in connection with the first chapter of the Epistle, you will see how marvellously they sustain that doctrine of propitiation which St. Paul preached to the Romans. The object of St. John is expressly to bring a *message* concerning *Him who was from the beginning*; to proclaim Him as *the Light, in whom is no darkness at all*. And Jesus Christ is set forth as the Propitiation by the Great Father of all, that He might be declared in this character, that the sins of them and of the world might be taken away. It may be that this Gospel sounds even broader, freer, than St. Paul's. But it is not really so. In the fifth chapter of the Epistle to the Romans he declares, that ' *as by the offence of one, judgment came upon all men to condemnation; even so by the righteousness of one, the free gift came upon all men unto justification of life.*' We cannot enlarge the force or application of such a Gospel. God will confound us, if we dare, by any arrangements of ours, to narrow it.

SERMON XI.

THE SACRIFICE OF CHRIST THE PURIFICATION OF THE CONSCIENCE.

(Lincoln's Inn, Whitsunday, June 4, 1854.)

'For when Moses had spoken every precept to all the people according to the law, he took the blood of calves and of goats, with water, and scarlet wool, and hyssop, and sprinkled both the book and all the people, saying, This is the blood of the testament which God hath enjoined unto you. Moreover, he sprinkled with blood both the tabernacle, and all the vessels of the ministry. And almost all things are by the law purged with blood; and without shedding of blood is no remission. It was therefore necessary that the patterns of things in the heavens should be purified with these; but the heavenly things themselves with better sacrifices than these. For Christ is not entered into the holy places made with hands, which are the figures of the true; but into heaven itself, now to appear in the presence of God for us; nor yet that he should offer himself often, as the high priest entereth into the holy place every year with blood of others: for then must he often have suffered since the foundation of the world: but now once, in the end of the world, hath he appeared, to put away sin by the sacrifice of himself.'—HEBREWS ix. 19-26.

IF the Church called upon us to accept a certain set of opinions, each denoted by a certain specific name, it would not be fitting that I should continue my dis-

courses on Sacrifice when we are keeping Whitsuntide.
The death of Christ we should regard as one subject,
the descent of the Spirit another; to mix them together
would be an outrage upon theological order. But since
we are taught to look upon every high festival as an
occasion for celebrating the Eucharist—since this particular festival is one of those for which a special
thanksgiving is appointed in our Communion Service—
we are reminded that we cannot separate the Sacrifice
of Christ from any part of our faith, or any act of our
worship; that it is the interpreter of all, the bond
which unites them together.

And, since Whitsunday is the day which speaks of
the establishment of God's new covenant with men,
'*I will put my laws into their hearts, and in their minds
will I write them,*' there is another reason for speaking
to you from the passage which I have chosen. That
passage refers, as the chapter from which it is taken
refers, as the whole of this Epistle refers, to the difference between the old covenant and the new; between
that which is said to have been established by law, and
that which is said to have been confirmed with an oath;
between the covenant of servants and the covenant of
sons. This is the primary subject of the text and of
the letter. If you would understand the other part
of it, the part which I am most anxious to bring before
you this afternoon, that which speaks of the remission,
or taking away, of sins, and which is the proper sequel
to what was said at the close of the passage I considered

a week ago, you must attend to this portion of the writer's statement first. He does not begin with speaking of the blood which purged the vessels of the tabernacle, or of the blood which washes away sins. He begins from the words of Moses, '*This is the blood of the testament which God hath enjoined unto you;*' he compares that with the blood which is the bond of the higher and diviner covenant, or testament. If we follow this order, in considering the lessons which he teaches us, we shall enter, I think much more fully and satisfactorily into the meaning of this book, which is commonly and rightly regarded as the book, on the whole question of Sacrifice.

I. (1.) First, he describes to us the character of the Mosaic economy in the words, '*When Moses had spoken every precept to all the people according to the Law.*' Here we have the Legislator, the man who is telling the people what they are to do, and what they are not to do. He does not speak of himself. They are not his own decrees which he is proclaiming; they are the eternal laws of God's government. He who breaks them violates his allegiance to God, and incurs death. They are not precepts for one man here, and one man there, they are for *all the people*. Each man, by being a man, comes under the obligation of observing them.

(2.) But, next, we are told that Moses declared the people who were subject to this Law to be under a divine *covenant, constitution* or *testament*. I use all three words, not meaning to determine which expresses best the sense of the original. Perhaps there is something in the phrase which cannot be adequately expressed by any one of these English parallels. We have need to draw something from each of them. It is a *constitution,* or order, which God has established, which He has created them to obey. It is a *covenant,* for it is grounded upon a previous promise, and assurance that they are His people, and that He is their God. It is a *testament,* because both the curse and the blessing of it are in some wonderful manner connected with death.

(3.) This is the third point upon which the writer of the Epistle dwells, and it is a cardinal one. '*Moses took the blood of calves and of goats, with water, and scarlet wool, and hyssop, and sprinkled both the book and all the people.*' Here the death of certain victims, the blood which is shed when they are slain, is made the pledge and assurance that God has taken them to be his servants. This is their consecration; by this they are sealed, redeemed, devoted to Him. I have no need to dwell more on this topic; I have dwelt upon it so recently and so frequently; I have shown you that the Passover service implied this sacrifice and dedication of the whole people to God. He took them by that act to be His; He acknowledged that He had redeemed them for His service. They were as much given up to Him as the animal was given to Him. They were not slain as that was slain; but the sprinkling of the blood, which was, at once, the sign of the death of the creature, and in which was its life, was the witness that they were offered up as sacrifices to God, that they had no life but what He gave them, that that life was to be used for Him, restored to Him.

(4.) This blood was, therefore, a sign of purification. They were holy creatures; God has made them so; for He had bound them to Himself. They were holy, for He was holy; and everything they had to do with was holy. Whatever they used was a vessel of ministry, an instrument given them by God for His Service. It was sprinkled with the blood with which they were sprinkled; it had the same token of dedication, consecration, sacrifice, which they had; it was redeemed from all corrupt uses, as they were.

(5.) Then he goes on a step further. '*Without shedding of blood is no remission.*' Here we pass from the making of the covenant to the transgression of it. The people are a holy, dedicated people. They have been told what acts are in conformity with this condition, and what are at variance with it. They can disobey the Law; they can break the covenant, if they choose. God is holding them by His living bonds to Himself; but those bonds may be snapped. They can come under the law of death if they like it. Each man of them, at some time or other, *does* like it. He tears himself from the right order; he takes the curse instead of the blessing; he becomes its bondsman. The act done, the result is inevitable. Right cannot become wrong, or wrong right. The fetters of evil are no imaginary fetters, but most real. Can the man break them? Does he wish them to be broken for him? God promises him *remission,* the sending away of his transgression. The blood which was the sign of his union to God, is also the sign that that union is renewed. The blood of the calf was sprinkled on him once, as the token of his union to God and his purification. The calf must be presented again, its blood must be poured out before the altar—in token that he submits, —and desires to be treated again as an Israelite,—in token that God puts away his offence and treats him as an Israelite. '*Without shedding of blood there is no remission.*'

Here the case for the old covenant is closed. Each one of these particulars has been distinctly brought before us, and pressed upon our attention; we are made to feel how they bear upon each other. Then the writer passes to the contrast. We are to learn how each of these ordinances, so true in itself, so full of purpose and significance, is unfolded, and the inmost power and principle of it brought forth, in the Gospel of the Son of God.

II. (1.) '*It was therefore necessary,*' he says, '*that the patterns of things in the heavens should be purified with these; but the heavenly things themselves with better sacrifices than these.*' I am sure the question must sometimes have occurred to a reader of this sentence: 'How can *heavenly things* need to be purified 'at all? Are they not pure in themselves? And what

'can these heavenly things be? What have we to do
'with them? How can we be interested in them?'

I hope no one will dismiss these inquiries from his
mind till he has got some satisfaction upon them. It
is not a subject on which we should tolerate loose or
vague notions.

If you will recall the phrase which occurs, not once
or twice in the Gospels, but in almost every parable
and discourse of our Lord's, *'the Kingdom of Heaven;'*
and if you will try to ascertain from any one of those
parables or discourses what force it must bear; you will
not think that the writer of the Epistle to the Hebrews
is using strange or unfamiliar language here. If the
Kingdom of Heaven is *' like a Sower who sowed good
seed in his field,'* or *'like treasure hid in a field,'* or *'like
a merchantman seeking goodly pearls,'* it must denote,
one would suppose, the spiritual world, in contrast to
the natural world. The spirit of man contemplated as
the subject of God's teaching and government, must
be one of the heavenly things which may be likened to
the things of earth; which may dwell among them, but
which cannot be confounded with them. To these the
writer of the Epistle must refer; these he must compare with other things, which he calls the images or
the *patterns* of them. The one he must speak of as
belonging expressly to the new and higher covenant,
the other to the old.

You shall hear how he illustrates his own meaning
in an earlier passage of this chapter, one to which I

alluded in a former sermon, and of which I shall have more to say hereafter: '*But Christ being come an High-priest of good things to come, by a greater and more perfect tabernacle, not made with hands, that is to say, not of this building; neither by the blood of goats and calves, but by His own blood He entered in once into the holy place, having obtained eternal redemption for us. For if the blood of bulls and of goats, and the ashes of an heifer sprinkling the unclean, sanctifieth to the purifying of the flesh; how much more shall the blood of Christ, who through the Eternal Spirit offered Himself without spot to God, purge your conscience from dead works to serve the living God?*' I do not quote this passage now on account of its allusion to the blood of Christ, but that you may see what the things are which the writer affirms that this blood is to purify. The *conscience* is that thing which is set in contrast with the *flesh*. This is that in man which is related to heaven, to the invisible, to God the Judge of all; as the hands and feet are related to the earth on which we tread. Although it is of heavenly origin, although it testifies of a relation to that which is perfectly pure and holy, it is affirmed to need purification, to require that God Himself should purify it and redeem it, and claim it as His servant.

(2.) Now, that which is the instrument of purifying this spiritual or heavenly thing, must be, the writer affirms, *better* than that which purifies the mere earthly thing which is the pattern of it. The distinction is one which we have traced already through various passage of St. Paul's writings. It is a distinction which every man recognises in himself, when he begins to reflect. 'The acts which I do, fall under the cognisance of law; 'they are performed through the agency of my body; 'they belong to the outward world. But *I*, the doer 'of these acts; *I*, from whose thoughts and will they 'proceed; *I*, from whom the good or the evil of them 'must come; *I* cannot be the mere subject of the law 'which pronounces whether they are right or wrong, 'which awards to them praise or punishment. I over-'look these acts; but I must *be* overlooked by Him 'from whom that law proceeds. I want to know how 'He regards me. I doubt Him, suspect Him, fear 'that He regards me as an enemy. I know that He 'must consider me not merely as a wrong-doer, but 'as being wrong myself. I dare not face Him. I want 'to hide myself from Him, to find some secret place 'where He cannot discover me. It is my *conscience* 'which is thus skulking, and cowardly and base. It 'is that which wants to avoid the light, all the while 'that it confesses the presence of the Light. It is that 'which wishes to disbelieve in the truth, to disbelieve 'in God. Is it not defiled? Does it not need some 'wonderful purification? And can *the blood of bulls* '*and of goats, and the ashes of an heifer sprinkling the* '*unclean*, purify it in any wise?'

Some say, that if God pleases that they should, perhaps they might; the writer of the Epistle mocks at their seeming piety. He says, again and again, it is not *possible* that they should do this. Deny the words, if you please, but they are written. The writer is speaking of a God of righteousness and order, of a God who had made a creature in His own image; and he says it is not possible, it cannot be, that such a creature should be purified by a mere decree. The blood of bulls and goats cannot make us clean. We *must* have a better sacrifice than these.

In the pattern with which the writer presented us, we are led, first, to think of the Covenant, by which God had declared the people of Israel to be holy, and which He had sealed and confirmed with blood. This is also the first point to which he has called his reader's attention in the counterpart. A great part of the Epistle is occupied with an argument to prove that the old Covenant implied an actual Mediator; that no legal enactments and arrangements could create a union between God and man; that they presumed one, and pointed to one. The revelation of this Mediator he has assumed in the fifteenth verse, as the foundation of the New Covenant or Testament. We cannot be satisfied, so the writer reasons, with anything less than such a revelation; with anything less than the assurance that there is a real High-priest, not one established by a formal ordinance, not one sprung from an earthly tribe,—a living Son of God. But seeing that the same conscience which makes this great demand, witnesses also of the transgressions which have separated us from God, there could be no revelation of such a Mediator, he goes on to maintain, which did not imply a redemption '*of the transgressions that were under the first Testament.*' The man had been convicted of evil acts by the divine Law; had been convicted of a positive alienation of mind and heart from Him who had given that Law. To be told that the transgressions were forgiven, was good; this was what the sacrifices under the Law had told him; but it was not enough; it was chiefly precious for the hint and hope it gave of something more. The alienation must be removed; the man himself must be atoned with his Maker. This was a far deeper, and more wonderful thing than the mere pardon or oblivion of offences. No arbitrary sign or token could denote this reconciliation; no sacrifice that was merely offered by the sinner, even though it was fixed and established by God. There was need of '*better sacrifices*' than these. I scarcely need stop to remark, that by '*better*' the inspired writer means not higher in degree, but different in kind; he does not oppose one amount of costliness to another; he opposes a living, voluntary sacrifice to a dead, involuntary one; he contrasts the sacrifice of one who stands in an actual relation to God and to man, with the sacrifice of something which implies no such relation, which is a mere thing that a man can use or destroy at his pleasure. Only a living sacrifice, he intimates, could be the bond of a living covenant between man and his Creator, of a covenant which should declare that their union stood on an eternal, unchangeable ground, that it was upheld in a Divine Person, the High-priest of the universe.

(3.) That this is the primary idea of the passage, the next sentences abundantly prove: '*For Christ is not entered into the holy places made with hands, which are the figures of the true; but into heaven itself, now to appear in the presence of God for us.*' The great question of men in all ages was: 'Who shall ascend into the 'Heavens for us;—who shall break the great barrier 'which separates us from the Invisible Ruling Power; 'from that pure and holy Being of whom our con-'sciences speak, before whom they tremble?' In this question the great contradiction was implied, that the man felt he belonged to this heavenly world; that it was his proper home; that he could not live without God; and that he was a hopeless exile; that he must wander abroad, and find comfort where he could, amongst things which were beneath him, and for which he did not inwardly care; that God and he must be at strife, now and ever. This was the mournful wail which was going up from the old Heathen world; which was expressed in every kind of sacrifice that cried for mercy to gods conceived or inconceivable; which was expressed in every form of sensual indulgence and gratification; the heart testifying: 'We must have 'earth, for we cannot find heaven; we must eat husks 'of swine to the fill, for, oh! how dreadful it is to 'remember, even for a few minutes, that we have the 'responsibilities of men—of spirits!'

And this was the answer: 'The Father of all, who
'seemed at so vast a distance from you, in that cold,
'dreary heaven, and yet whom you tremble lest you
'should encounter in every dark night, beside every
'tomb; whom you dread as the author of your misery
'and death; as one who may inflict a deeper misery,
'a more hopeless death upon you hereafter, has sent
'His only-begotten Son to take your nature upon Him,
'to die your death. He has been here in these dark
'nights, amidst these tombs; He has been *in* the
'tomb; He has risen out of it; He has gone, not into
'some figurative holy place, but into the actual holy
'place, which your hearts tell you of, which all temples
'and altars and priesthoods witness of. Christ is with
'God His Father. And now the Father, in whose
'presence He is, declares that sacrifice of His to be the
'bond of peace between Him and you. That is the
'pledge and witness of His covenant with you; with
'your own very selves; with that in you which has
'shrunk ·from Him, which has wished that it could
'banish Him. The blood, not of goats or calves, but
'of His own Son, of the Eternal Mediator between Him
'and you, is the assurance that he regards you as His
'sons and daughters; that He gives you the Spirit of
'His Son in your hearts; that your sins and iniquities
'He remembers no more.'

(4.) This was the Gospel to the heathen world; this was the ground of a Church on earth, of a society of men who could claim a filial relation to God, who could recognise this living sacrifice as the reconciliation of earth and heaven. But the writer of the Epistle knew too well, too experimentally, what the tendencies of the human heart are, how ready it is to disbelieve in the liberty with which God has made it free, and to forge chains for itself, to stop at that point which might serve the proper climax of his great argument. He adds—'*Nor yet that He should offer Himself often, as the high priest entereth into the holy place every year with blood of others; for then must He often have suffered since the foundation of the world: but now once in the end of the world hath He appeared to put away sin by the sacrifice of Himself.*' He knew well that in the Christian Church, amongst baptized men, amongst those who had come under the new covenant, in that Church of Palestine to which he was writing—though it dwelt on the spot where the one offering had been made, where apostles had first proclaimed the ascent of Jesus Christ as the eternal King and Redeemer, and the Giver of redemption, where the Spirit had come down to witness a fellowship for all nations, of a union of the world that is seen with that which is unseen —though all the events which the Gospel proclaimed had only been a few years ago transacted—he knew well that there and then were those who would crave for the signs which spoke of an unaccomplished sacrifice, for the hope which the blood of the ox and calf gave that the transgression of the day *might be* blotted out; for the promise which the entrance of the high priest into the holy place held out, that heaven *might* at some distant day be opened to those who would bring penitence and sacrifice enough to purchase an entrance into it.

All these delusions and diseases of the heart, conscious of *part* of its misery, unaware of its *great* necessity, were rampant then, would be rampant, he was sure, under every form, in every section of that Christendom to which he looked forward. And therefore he sets down this great warning, this mighty assurance and comfort, to all who will receive it, that the Mediator, He of whom all covenants and sacrifices had been testifying, for whom all periods had been waiting, had been manifested once in the crisis or winding-up of the ages to put away sin by the sacrifice of Himself. Supposing a merely formal sense is given to the word *sin*—supposing it is taken to mean the violation of some decrees which have been imposed upon men by the will of a Being who could decree whatever he pleased—this announcement could give no rest to the conscience. But he has guarded himself against this perversion of his meaning; his whole Epistle has been one continued protest against it. Sin has been brought before us in its inward radical signification; sin as the disease of the will; sin as conscious separation from a pure and holy will. Every attempt to substitute any less inward and essential definition of its nature for this, the writer discards, because he is a practical man, who in presenting an actual remedy for an actual disease, which he must trace to its principle, which he cannot hope to cure by treating some of its superficial symptoms. Any attempt to substitute a less universal and essential definition for this, he discards likewise, because he is a divine, because he has a message from God to His creature, because he dares not betray his trust and misrepresent the Lord who has made him the steward of His mysteries. But taking *this* to be the sin which man needs to be freed from, from which God desires to set him free, he declares that the one Sacrifice, made once for all, is the assurance of a union and reconciliation with God, and therefore of the full remission of sins. He proclaims it in this character to the world; he lays it down as that which makes the new covenant *well ordered and sure*, for all nations, for all mankind. But in doing so, he testifies how the sins of each day,—the conscious evils of those who have broken the covenant of their God,—who feel that their continued transgressions are as great as those of the heathen, and less excusable,—who feel that their inward alienation from God is as deep and thorough as that of any heathen can be—may obtain this perfect remission. As the blood of calves and goats, with which the Jewish testament was sealed, which had sprinkled *the people, the book, and all the vessels of the ministry,* was also the sign that the particular offences against that covenant were forgiven; so the blood of the Son of God, which is the pledge of our original adoption to God, the witness that we are His accepted children, is that which purges the conscience from *dead,* selfish *works, to serve the Living God.*

Receiving it as the seal of an everlasting bond that was established before the foundation of the world in the well-beloved Son; receiving it as the witness that God is the same yesterday, to-day, and for ever—the same in His hatred of evil—the same in His desire to deliver men from it;—this blood becomes that remission of sins, that purification of the spirit from the guilt or guile which is the essence of sin, that assurance of divine forgiveness for the acts which have flowed from it, that token of restoration to the house and family of the Father from whom we have wandered, which nothing else in heaven or earth could be.

And wherein lies its power? The writer of the Epistle asks *you* the question. He knows that you can answer it. He knows that there is One standing at the door of your hearts with a light to show you what is in them, with a voice that is bidding them open to receive Him. The light which shows you your evil is the light of His own and His Father's love; the voice by which He wooes for admission is, 'Have I not sacri-
'ficed Myself for you? Does not my blood say that
'Sin and Death are not your masters? Does it not
'say, There is an eternal life in Me, of which you are
'the inheritors? Am I not willing to come in and sup
'with you, to give you that bread which is my body,
'that wine which is my blood, as the assurances of
'forgiveness, of a death to evil, of a new birth to
'righteousness? Have I not ascended on high that

'the Spirit in which I offered Myself to God might come among you, and might sit in tongues of fire upon you, to make you the witnesses of my death, of my life, to the world?'

SERMON XII.

CHRIST MADE SIN FOR US.

(Lincoln's Inn, Trinity Sunday, June 11, 1854.)

'For he hath made him to be sin for us, who knew no sin; that we might be made the righteousness of God in him.'—2 COR. v. 21.

THIS verse is commonly interpreted by the addition of a word. He hath made Him to be a *Sin* OFFERING *for us, who knew no sin; that we might be made the righteousness of God in Him.* You will not suspect me of objecting to the word which this paraphrase introduces. I have endeavoured, for many weeks past, to show you that the revelation of God is the revelation of a Sacrifice. And though I have maintained that sacrifice is entirely independent of sin—that the most pure and perfect state we can conceive, is the state of which sacrifice is the Law,—I have contended, as strongly, that nothing but sacrifice can take away sin. This was the subject of my sermon last week. We learnt from the Epistle to the Hebrews, that Sin lies much deeper than the offences and transgressions which are the outward manifestations of it; that it has its seat in the Conscience. The legal sacrifices, the Epistle taught us, were good, as means of doing away with *transgression*, of restoring the offender to his right position as a member of the divine commonwealth. But sacrifices of this kind, he said, were totally inadequate to take away *Sin*, for they could not reach the conscience. The sacrifice of a Son who came to do His Father's will, who entirely gave Himself up to do it, did reach the conscience; it did take away sin. How rightly then may this sacrifice be called a Sin-Offering! What possible objection can any reader of Scripture raise against such an expression?

But this is the very reason why we should be most careful not to alter the language of the Apostle, or to substitute for it language of our own. We have seen what errors men have fallen into, in their attempts to conceive the nature, and object, and effects of sacrifice. We have seen how much it has been the design of God's revelation of Himself to deliver us from these errors, by setting forth its true relation to Him and to man, to the perfect righteousness and to the creature who has wandered from that righteousness. We have seen with what carefulness Evangelists and Apostles have brought out before us one and another aspect of this offering, contrasting it with the counterfeit notions which men had devised for themselves.

This is, evidently, one of the passages which is to instruct us in the character and effects of the Divine

Sacrifice, which is to show wherein it consists, and for what end it was presented. How dare I, then, put in the phrase which I want to have explained, as if I understood it sufficiently without the Apostle's help ? To make me know what God's Love to man was, how *He reconciled the world to Himself*, St. Paul says, *He made Him to be sin for us, who knew no sin.* That I may not be forced to inquire what these wonderful words import, I coolly and deliberately take all the force out of them. He sets me before a startling antithesis, that I may meditate upon it. I destroy his antithesis as if it were an idle figure of speech, and insist that the same word should mean two different things in two different clauses of the same sentence. Could you bear to see any writer who was *not* an Apostle, whom you did *not* recognise as a canonical writer, treated after this fashion ? Would you not say to his interpreter, ' Either the man whom you undertake to expound is ' not worth your trouble ; he is one who uses words at ' random, he does not understand himself ; or else ' you are behaving most unfairly and irreverently to ' him ; you are not grappling with his thoughts, but ' putting yours in the place of them ?' Is the case altogether changed because we are listening to a man who is uttering, as we believe, the oracles of God ; because he is speaking of the question which most of all concerns us, and on which we are most liable to make mistakes ? Are we at liberty to play with his modes of speech just as we please, to thrust in among them any inane tautological formula,—as if for the very purpose of escaping from the truth which he would make known to us?

No one can seriously think over these words, '*He hath made Him to be sin for us, which knew no sin,*' without feeling that the paradox which is in them is meant to be in them ; that the apostle purposed to force it upon our attention ; that if he could have avoided it he would ; but that he had no way of avoiding it, without mangling and distorting the message which he was appointed to deliver. If you read over the memorable passage with which this sentence winds up, beginning with those words in the second chapter, in which he speaks of his ministry *as a savour of death unto death, and of life unto life*; in which he declares that he does not *corrupt the word of God*, but that *as of sincerity, as of God, in the sight of God, speaks he in Christ*; you will scarcely persuade yourselves that he ended with a mere verbal contradiction which was to surprise us, and which he expected us to find some easy method of explaining away. Between these two points of his discourse, he has been speaking of the *ministration of righteousness* and the *ministration of condemnation*; of *the glory that was under* a veil, and of that which was unveiled, and therefore might be presented *with plainness of speech* ; of *renouncing the hidden things of dishonesty ; of commending himself by the manifestation of the truth to every man's conscience in the sight of God.* He has been declaring that *all must be manifested before the judgment-seat of Christ; that if he is beside himself it is to God, that if he is sober it is for their cause; that the love of Christ is constraining him, because he thus judges, that if One died for all, then were all dead; and that he died for all, that they which live should not henceforth live to themselves, but unto Him who died for them, and rose again.* He had just been gathering up all that he had written, all that he had ever spoken to the Corinthians, in the words, '*All things are of God, who hath reconciled us to Himself by Jesus Christ, and hath given to us the ministry of reconciliation; to wit, that God was in Christ, reconciling the world unto Himself, not imputing their trespasses unto them; and hath committed unto us the word of reconciliation. Now then we are ambassadors for Christ, as though God did beseech you by us: we pray you in Christ's stead, be ye reconciled to God.*' The verse before us is the climax of these vehement protestations, of this appeal to God's judgment, of this declaration of God's will to men as accomplished in Christ, of this earnest exhortation to men not to refuse the gift which has been bestowed on them. Can you seriously believe that at this moment he adopted a phrase to describe the work of his King and Redeemer, which was strange and ambiguous, either from carelessness or through the paltry vanity of a rhetorician?

No, my brethren, this is doing just what the Apostle is protesting that he dares not do, what he wants us not to do: *It is handling the word of God deceitfully.*

We may think that it is our business to extricate the writers of the New Testament from apparent contradictions; but we have no such vocation. They are as well aware as we can be, that their language sounds perplexing; they know that it must sound so. All sin is contradiction; if you speak of it, you must denote it by words that cross and seem to confute each other. Unless men were spirits, you could not complain of them for acting as beasts; unless they proved every moment that they were framed for fellowship and mutual dependence, you could not blame their selfishness; if you were not sure that they were intended to obey God's gracious will and to walk in His ways, you could not accuse them of ruining themselves by determining, each one of them, to have a will and way of his own. You may get rid of the strife by ignoring either set of facts; by assuming that there is no moral order, or by pretending that it is not resisted. The man may come to think his transgressions are themselves laws; the delusion is easy enough, it is one of the signs of his derangement, and he may adapt his phraseology to this conception. It may be consistent with itself, but for that very reason, it will be inconsistent with much of what he feels and knows.

Keeping these thoughts in mind, and beseeching the Holy Spirit to lead us into those depths, in which, without His guidance, we must be utterly bewildered and lost, either through the cowardice which shrinks from the light, or through the boldness which stumbles on in the darkness, let us ask what St. Paul can intend by saying that Christ was *'made sin for us, though He knew no sin.'*

1. There was a time in our Lord's life on earth, we are told, when a man met Him, *coming out of the tombs, exceeding fierce, whom no man could bind; no, not with chains.* That man was *possessed by an unclean spirit.* Of all men upon earth, you would say that he was the one between whom and the pure and holy Jesus there must have existed the most intense repugnance. What Pharisee, who shrank from the filthy and loathsome words of that maniac, could have experienced one-thousandth part of the inward and intense loathing which Christ must have experienced for the mind that those words expressed? For it was into *that* He looked; *that* which He understood; *that* which in His inmost being He must have felt, which must have given Him a shock such as it could have given to no other. I repeat the words; I beseech you to consider them; He must have felt the wickedness of that man in His inmost being. He must have been conscious of it, as no one else was or could be. Now, if we ever have had the consciousness, in a very slight degree, of evil in another man, has it not been, *up to that degree,* as if the evil were in ourselves? Suppose the offender were a friend, or a brother, or child, has not this sense of personal shame, of the evil being ours, been proportionably stronger and more acute? However much we might feel ourselves called upon to act

as judges, this perception still remained. It was not crushed even by the anger, the selfish anger, and impatience of an injury done to us, which, most probably, mingled with and corrupted the purer indignation and sorrow. Most of us confess with humiliation how little we have had of this lively consciousness of other men's impurity, or injustice, or falsehood, or baseness. But we *do* confess it; we know, therefore, that we should be better if we had more of it. In our best moments we admire with a fervent admiration—in our worse, we envy with a wicked envy—those in whom we trace most of it. And we have had just enough of it to be certain that it belongs to the truest and most radical part of the character, not to its transient impulses. Suppose, then, this carried to its highest point, cannot you, at a great distance, apprehend that Christ may have entered into the sin of that poor maniac's spirit, may have had the most inward realization of it, not because it was like what was in Himself, but because it was utterly and intensely unlike? And yet are you not sure that this could not have been, unless He had the most perfect and thorough sympathy with this man, whose nature was transformed into the likeness of a brute, whose spirit had acquired the image of a devil? Does the coexistence of this sympathy and this antipathy perplex you? Oh! ask yourselves which you could bear to be away; which you could bear to be weaker than the other? Ask yourselves whether they must not dwell together in their highest degree, in their fullest power, in any one of whom you could say, 'He is perfect; He is the standard of excellence; 'in Him there is the full image of God.' Diminish by one atom the loathing and horror, or the fellowship and sympathy; and by that atom you lower the character; you are sure that you have brought it nearer to the level of your own low imaginations; that you have made it less like the Being who would raise you towards Himself.

2. I have taken a single instance, because you can better apprehend the whole truth in that instance, and because from it you may understand that I am not speaking of abstractions, but of that which concerns us as human beings, as conscious sinners. But now carry on your thoughts beyond that particular man with the unclean spirit: carry them to any man in the crowds whom our Lord fed, and to whom He preached: carry them to these, because they were specimens of the race; because His knowledge of their evils is that which He must have had of the evils which are in all the world; because His sympathy with them is the sympathy which He must have had with all who bore their nature; —and then you will, I think, begin to doubt whether St. Paul could have diluted the language which you find in the text without cheating us of a divine treasure. If he had said that Christ took upon Him *all the consequences* of our sins, would this have been an equivalent for the words, '*made Sin?*' There might be a deep meaning in that assertion. The sympathy which I have

spoken of, extended, as we know, to all the ills of which men are heirs. The evangelist says, speaking of His healing the sick, *Himself took our infirmities and bare our sicknesses*; as if every cure He wrought implied an actual participation in the calamity. He endured in this sense the consequences of sin in *particular* men; He endured the death which is the consequence of sin in *all* men. But men have asked more than this. Their superstitions show how much more is required to satisfy them; they have asked for some god, or demigod, who could not only sympathise in their sorrows, but in their evil; they could only conceive of sympathy coming through participation of it; the gods must do like them —be like them, or they are cold and distant objects of reverence. The demand is indeed monstrous; all the perverseness and bewilderment of sin lie in it. But to get rid of the falsehood of the desire, you must vindicate its truth. Here is the vindication; He knows no sin, *therefore* He identifies Himself with the sinner. That phrase, *identifies Himself with the sinner,* is somewhat nearer, I think, to the sense of the apostle than the phrase, *takes the consequences or the punishment of sin.* But still, do you not feel how much feebler it is than his, feebler in spirit more even than in form? It conveys no impression of the sense, the taste, the anguish of sin, which St. Paul would have us think of, as realised by the Son of God,—a sense, a taste, an anguish, which are not only compatible with the *not* knowing sin, but would be impossible in anyone who did know it. The awful isolation of the words, '*Ye shall leave Me alone,*' united with the craving for human affection in the words, '*With desire I have desired to eat this Passover with you,*—the agony of the spirit which is gathered in the words, '*If it be possible, let this cup pass from Me,*' with the submission of the words, '*Not as I will, but as Thou wilt,*'—above all, the crushing for a moment even of that one infinite comfort, '*Yet I am not alone, because the Father is with Me,*' when the cry was heard, '*My God, my God, why hast Thou forsaken me?*'—these revelations tell us a little of what it was to be made Sin; if we get the least glimpse into them, we shall not dream that the Apostle could have spoken less boldly, if he was to speak the truth.

We might for a moment wish to translate his language into that which we find elsewhere, respecting the *taking*, or *bearing* of sins. The force and the worth of these expressions I believe to be unspeakable; they correspond to some of the most inward and deep, however perverted, necessities of the human spirit. A man feels that he is carrying a burden; it is his own; no one can share it with him; his friend, his wife, does not know what it is; he asks to be freed from it, but that seems asking to be freed from himself. Is there one higher than himself who knows what it is, really, actually? Could he bear it? could he take it away. The question is asked with strange and awful doubt. How can that be possible? how can I transfer to another that which is so absolutely and inherently mine? Yet there is such a necessity for a friend who would be willing to do this; such a witness that there *must* be one willing and able to lift us out of misery by any participation in it, that the heart bounds even at the distant rumour of an act which declares that its hopes were not delusions. There is no selfishness in that first exulting bound; it is the deliverance from selfishness; the recognition of one in whom selfishness has no place; who can do all and suffer all for love. But selfishness may soon intrude itself into these thoughts, and may convert the whole message of a sympathising friend who *bears our burdens, and so fulfils the law of love,* into a scheme by which we escape from the penalty of our misdoings through His endurance of it. Even that scheme is so closely involved with the sense of an infinite Charity and Compassion, has so evidently risen out of it, that no one should touch it with a rude or careless hand. Till we are convinced that the tree is dying from the pressure of the fungus which has attached itself to it, we cannot have courage to incur the risk of tearing one from the other. And if we make the attempt, it must be with no instruments of ours. A man using carefully the Scripture language, and the Scripture analogies—resolving to follow them steadfastly out— and then applying them, first of all, to the detection and exposure of his own crude notions and fancies, will acquire by degrees the power of discerning between that, in the popular statements respecting Theology, which he must cling to for life and death, and that which he must part with that he may preserve the rest.

The text is a strong instance. Those expressions concerning Christ bearing sins, which we meet with so often, sound much less difficult and more natural than the apostle's phrase, *being made Sin*. But if we look seriously at that, we find it explains the others, and gives them the full force, which, in our use of them, they are apt to lose. We quickly attach to them some coarse and material sense; we suppose it is possible to transfer that which belongs to the conscience and spirit, as we might give up a schedule of debts to one who undertook that he would discharge them. Comparisons which, if they are resorted to with exceeding caution, sometimes assist the fancy, but which do not go directly home to the man himself, the actual sufferer and sinner, may so entangle us, that they take the place of the very truths which we would illustrate by them. But the words, *made sin*, carry us out of these and beyond them; they lead us directly to the spirit of man; they become monstrous if they are tried by any other tests than its tests. So tried, they set forth just that which man asks heaven, and earth, and hell to tell him of—one who knows all his evil, one who enters into it, feels it, because He is *not* soiled and debased with it; one who does this, because in no other way can He raise a voluntary and spiritual creature out of a voluntary and spiritual death to a right and true life.

For the Apostle goes on, '*that we might be made the*

righteousness of God in Him.' Here, as everywhere, St. Paul declares that it is the end of all God's acts and dispensations towards men, to make them righteous; to bring them out of that condition which they have chosen for themselves,—the condition of distrust, alienation, sin,—and to bring them into that state for which He has created them, of dependence, trust, union with Him. He is declared, here as everywhere, to be the only Reconciler of His creatures. Here, as everywhere, they are assumed to have no righteousness but His; none but that which they obtain by owning Him and confiding in Him. The giving up of His Son to take upon Him their flesh and blood, to enter into their sorrows, to feel and suffer their sins; that is *'to be made Sin:'* the perfect sympathy of the Son with His loving will towards His creatures, His entire sympathy with them, and union with them; His endurance, in His inmost heart and spirit, of that evil which he abhorred; this is God's method of reconciliation; by this He speaks to the sinful will of man; by this He redeems it, raises it, restores it. The acts which express His love to man; the acts by which the Son of God proves Himself to be the Son of man; these are the means of destroying the barrier between heaven and earth, between the Father and the children; the means of taking away the sin of the world. In each man the sin—the alienation and separation of heart—ceases, when he believes that he has a Father who has loved him, and given His Son for him; when he confesses that this

Son is stronger to unite him with his Father and his brethren, than sin is to separate them; when he is sure that the Spirit of the Father and the Son will be with him to resist all the efforts of the spirit of enmity and division to renew the strife.

But this faith of the individual man implies much more than the deliverance of his own soul. In the great annual act of atonement among the Jews, the priest laid his hand upon the head of the scape-goat and confessed over him *all the iniquities of the children of Israel, and all their transgressions and all their sins, putting them upon the head of the goat, and sending it away into the wilderness, that he might bear their iniquity into a land not inhabited.* Thus the whole body of the people were taught that God, who had accepted them as a holy people to Himself, purified them, as a body, of that which had set them at war with Him. The individual Israelite could not be satisfied with his own sin-offering or peace-offering, unless he was thus assured that he belonged to a redeemed and purified society. In like manner there is no sure peace and freedom for the conscience of any one man under the New Covenant, while he thinks only or chiefly of peace and freedom for himself. The sin which he supposes he has cast aside will appear again; it will seem to him as if it was not the blood of sprinkling, but his own momentary act of faith, which had purified him from it. But if we believe that Christ has taken away the *sins of the world*, we are led to a deeper and safer foundation upon which our hopes may rest. For then we see beneath all evil, beneath the universe itself, that eternal and original union of the Father with the Son which this day tells us of; that union which was never fully manifested till the Only-begotten by the Eternal Spirit offered Himself to God. The revelation of that primal Unity is the revelation of the ground on which all things stand, both things in heaven and things in earth. It is the revelation of an order which sustains all the intercourse and society of men. It is the revelation of that which sin has ever been seeking to destroy, and which at last has overcome sin. It is the revelation of that perfect harmony to which we look forward when all things are gathered up in Christ; when there shall be no more sin, because there shall be no more selfishness; when the law of sacrifice shall be the acknowledged law of all creation; when He who perfectly fulfilled that law—the Lamb that was slain—shall receive blessing, and honour, and glory, and power; when the confession of His Name shall be felt and known to be the confession of the Father of an Infinite Majesty in whom He delighted, and of the Holy Ghost the Comforter, who proceedeth from Them, and with Them is worshipped and glorified for ever.

SERMON XIII.

CHRIST'S SACRIFICE THE PEACE-OFFERING FOR MANKIND.

(Lincoln's Inn, 2nd Sunday after Trinity, June 25, 1854.)

'Wherefore remember, that ye being in time past Gentiles in the flesh, who are called Uncircumcision by that which is called the Circumcision in the flesh made by hands; that at that time ye were without Christ, being aliens from the commonwealth of Israel, and strangers from the covenants of promise, having no hope, and without God in the world: but now in Christ Jesus ye who sometimes were far off are made nigh by the blood of Christ. For he is our peace, who hath made both one, and hath broken down the middle wall of partition between us; having abolished in his flesh the enmity, even the law of commandments contained in ordinances; for to make in himself of twain one new man, so making peace; and that he might reconcile both unto God in one body by the cross, having slain the enmity thereby: and came and preached peace to you which were afar off, and to them that were nigh. For through him we both have access by one Spirit unto the Father.'—EPHESIANS ii. 11-18.

THE name Atheists—'*without God*'—which St. Paul here bestows on the Ephesians, before they became Christians, is the very one by which they and the other heathens described the Jews, and still more the Christians. The absence of all visible images was conclusive evidence to the idolaters of the second century, and probably also of the first, that the disciples of Jesus had renounced all worship and believed in nothing. That the charge should be reversed, that those who acknowledged a multitude of gods should be spoken of as having no God, and this in a letter addressed to the inhabitants of a city with an illustrious temple, and an image that was said to have fallen down from Jupiter, is very startling.

The word is made more pointed and remarkable by that which accompanies it: they were without God *'in the world.'* The world had seemed to them full of gods. It comprehended, of course, not merely the earth upon which they trod, but the firmament, the sun, and moon, and stars, whatever seemed necessary to complete the order, whatever ministered to the wants of those who dwell on this planet. Each grand object that men beheld denoted a god; was probably the habitation of a god. Every hill had its own ruler; every river and fountain had someone who had caused it to spring forth, and who presided over it. Could men who thought this be without God? Had they not rather an excuse for saying that those who emptied the universe of its celestial character, who denounced the worship under hills and green trees, merited that stigma?

The Apostle, who had declared in the Epistle to the Romans, that through his countrymen *the name of God was blasphemed in all lands*, knew what pretext there was for this opinion; how much Jews had actually done to shake the faith of other people, giving them nothing in the place of it. He knew, by still more terrible evidence, what a deep-rooted Atheism there was in the hearts of some who were sons of Abraham, and were signed with the sign of his covenant. He knew it, for he had felt it; he had been conscious of Atheism,— of something more than mere negative Atheism. There had been in his spirit such a horror of God, such a wish to be rid of Him, as he could never have ascertained, by mere observation or discourse, to exist in any human creature. And what made this discovery more dreadful to him was, that the very aspect of the Divine Being from which he shrunk, was that in which it was the glory of his country to present Him. A mere power he could have faced; it was from the Righteous King and Lawgiver, of whom the commandments spoke, that he could have wished the mountains to hide him, even if they crushed him.

But if it were so, why did he speak of the Gentiles as being *without God?* Why did he treat it as a great calamity of theirs that they were *aliens from the commonwealth of Israel?* Because, brethren, it was through this tremendous experience that the Apostle was brought to understand what manner of Being it was who had revealed Himself to his fathers, and why they had testified so continually, *He is a God nigh, and not afar off.* He found that it was a Father of spirits who had been declared to the chosen race: that He had chosen them as witnesses of His government over their spirits; of His presence there; of His care for them; of His sympathy with them. He found that this was the meaning of the Covenant of Promise which he had given them, the meaning of all their history and discipline. He found that it was the meaning of that Law which had seemed to put him at such a frightful distance from God, to pronounce him an enemy of God. It showed that there was in him and in every man that which God hated, and which hated Him. It showed that this was the very thing from which God had separated them and redeemed them, and which He was teaching them to regard as He regarded it.

Now, then, it could not but appear to him Atheism—living without God—for men to have ten thousand gods in the world, on the outside of them, while the God of their spirits, *in whom they were living and moving and having their being,* this Lord and Ruler of themselves, was not known. St. Paul did not slight, as his speech in Lycaonia so clearly shows, any of the tokens which God was bearing *by rains and fruitful seasons,* of His presence with men in one country or another. But these tokens, as he said, were so many calls and messages to the spirit of man, to turn from dumb idols to Him who was feeding the body with bread and the heart with gladness. He did not slight, as his speech at Athens shows still more evidently, the testimonies of poets, or philosophers, or mythologers, to the truth that men were God's offspring, or that there was *an unknown God,* and that *He was not far from any of them.* But all these testimonies were so many proofs that to make God *in the likeness of art and man's device,* was to project Him to a distance, that they might flee from Him and not be haunted by His presence. It was the impulse of an atheistical spirit; the more that impulse was obeyed, the more atheistical, the more alienated from the righteous God, the God of the hearts and reins, they must become. And while this godlessness continued, they were also hopeless. They were seeking to escape from themselves, as well as their Maker; to avoid looking at the realities of their own condition. They had an inward certainty that they could not do so always; that some day the truth would meet them, and force them to confront it. The future, therefore, was drearier and darker than the present. So, he said, it *had* been with the Ephesians; they knew that it had. What had caused any difference in their state of mind? The same revelation which had brought Saul the Hebrew from a state of inward war to peace; from an unutterable dread of God, to trust in Him as a Father. '*Now in Christ Jesus, ye who were sometimes far off are made nigh by the blood of Christ.*' He, from whom they were turning away,— to shun whose presence they would have taken the wings of the morning, or have made their bed in hell,— presented Himself to them as one who was seeking after them, claiming them as His children, sending His own

Son to earth, to death, to the grave, to hell, that He might fetch them home. The blood, the actual human blood which had been poured out, testified of a human life in Christ—of an union with them. But the love which came out in His death, signified a deeper life— the life of God. It was the love of a Father, exhibited as Love only can be exhibited, in sacrifice; it was the love of a Brother, reflecting that love, consummating the sacrifice in death. It spake not to the eye that gazed on idols of wood and stone, nor to the slavish fear that crouched before powers in earth and sea and air. It spoke to the man himself; to the being who used these eyes; who was beset with these fears. It roused him to the recollection of the Being about the bed and about the board, who could not be beheld in the likeness of anything above or beneath, whom the heart trembled to hear of, and yet in whom it was created to trust and to live. It assured him that there was One in whom that Being could be well pleased; One in whom He could meet His creatures; One who had poured out His life-blood, in obedience to His will, for their sakes. The Cross, the blood, said all this, and infinitely more than this, to the spirit that had been losing itself amidst world gods, and was just beginning to dream of its Father's house. St. Paul knew how poor words were as a translation of all the secret love-messages and pledges which the blood of Christ carried to the wanderer. He resorted to explanations when they were necessary; he always joyfully returned to the language which implied an act, sufferings, a person. The Spirit who governed him would not suffer his explanations to put themselves in place of that which they were to explain, or to hinder the direct communion which the living symbols expressed and kept up.

St. Paul's own education as a Jew, enabled him to see a further truth which the Gentile, however simple and serious his faith might be, was only beginning to apprehend. The *Covenant of Promise—the Commonwealth of Israel*—witnessed that God had adopted and still cared for Israelites, stiff-necked as they were. That had been a source of comfort and pride to him till he had perceived that the law demanded actual righteousness; and certainly not less from the Jew than the Gentile. Then the thought of a formal covenant could no longer sustain him, or in the least diminish his terrors. Now when he had seen in the cross of Christ the full revelation of the God of Abraham, he perceived also the deep and true foundation of that divine election, which he had taken to be artificial and arbitrary. The Cross told him in whom it was that God had elected them, in whom He had blessed them with all spiritual blessings. It showed him the Eternal Mediator, the Living Word, in whom God had created the worlds, in whom He had held converse with the sons of men. It unfolded the mystery of the past; the Law, the Prophets, the Priesthood, the Sacrifices. But it took away the exclusiveness, the merely Jewish character, of them all. They were witnesses of the

Man, in whom God looked not upon the sons of Abraham, but on the sons of men, in whom He *would at last gather together all things, both which are in heaven and which are in earth.*

This revelation or manifestation of Him in whom God had chosen the Apostle of the Gentiles, in whom He had chosen Hebrews and Gentiles equally *to be holy and without blame before Him in love,* is the peculiar subject of the Epistle to the Ephesians. That being the case, if the dry and artificial rules and arrangements of divines had governed the mind of the Apostle, we might expect to find less in this book concerning the Atonement, or reconciliation by the Cross of Christ. That doctrine, one might suppose, would be treated of somewhere else; it would not intrude itself while a different portion of the system was receiving exposition. But the method of St. Paul, as anyone who reads any of his Epistles with seriousness will soon convince himself, utterly repudiates those trammels. He is teaching of God, and Man; what the relations between them are; how it has pleased God to establish them, restore them, make them known; He is not announcing certain conceptions which we may reduce under classes or formulas that we find convenient. I am far from wishing you to forget the names and titles by which, both in popular and learned treatises, what we call the doctrines of the Gospel are denoted. They may be of great value to us, if instead of translating the New Testament phrases into them, we ask the New Testament to tell us what they signify, to show us the bonds of living connexion between them, to remove the confusions which torment us when we think of them. For this purpose I have considered those different aspects of Sacrifice, which associate themselves with Redemption; with the deliverance from the curse of the Law; with propitiation; with remission of sins; with Christ as the Lamb known before the foundation of the world; with Christ as made Sin for us, though He knew no sin. It has been impossible, in reflecting on any one of these thoughts, not to speak of *Reconciliation*. The idea of it is involved in each one of them. But, as I observed before, though the *Peace-offering* under the Law implied the existence of sin, and a desire to be delivered from it,—though the *Sin-offering* implied a want of peace, and a search for it,—still they were kept distinct in the Mosaic economy, and their separation served a wonderful purpose in the education of men—leading them to perceive the different needs of their spirits, and how He who had awakened them, was supplying them. For the same reason, we are underrating the power and results of the all-perfect Sacrifice, if we assume that, because there can be no Redemption or Propitiation without Reconciliation and Atonement, we have, therefore, no need to give the last a separate and solemn consideration.

Though I took an unusually long passage for my text, it might be better for the sense of it if I had gone further back still, and led you to reflect on the connexion in which it stands with the fourth verse. '*God, who is rich in mercy, for His great love wherewith He loved us, even when we were dead in sins, hath quickened us together with Christ (by grace ye are saved).*' That verse removes all doubts about the question, whether the Apostle is here, as in the Second Epistle to the Corinthians, representing God as reconciling the world to Himself, or whether he has departed from all his usual habits of thinking and speaking, and is, for once, supposing the first movement to be from the side of man. There is nothing in the verses I have read which could in the slightest degree warrant the supposition. But when it is said, in the fifteenth verse, that Christ has abolished *the enmity, even the law of commandments contained in ordinances, that He might make in Himself of twain one new man, so making peace, and that He might reconcile both under God in one body by the Cross*, there is an opening for a theory drawn from the heathen notions of sacrifice; we can make the Apostle's words, by a few outrages upon their letter, and by destroying their spirit, echo and confirm it. Taking them with those that precede them,—recollecting that the aim of St. Paul, in all his letters, has been to trace the whole economy of the universe, and of the redemption of men from their wicked works and the enmity which they had caused, to God's original purpose, to His creation of man in the eternal Son— we gain a glimpse of the nature of Christ's peace-offering, and of its effects on mankind, which illuminates all the past history of the world, as well as all the saddest experiences of individuals.

The Gentile was seeking God where He was not to be found, invoking Him when He was not near. Conscience made a coward of him; he was afraid of the Lord of his spirit, whose rebukes sounded so alarming; he made himself other lords out of the things which he looked upon, and asked them to save him from himself. The Jew, unable to find a refuge in the forms of the world, forced to think of God as speaking to him and commanding him, would fain have destroyed the Being who, he thought, was ready at any moment to destroy him. God presents His only-begotten Son to both, as the true image of Himself, as the perfect Righteousness which the Law enjoins; He gives Him up for all, as the assurance that there is a bond between Him and His creatures, which no rebellion of theirs, which no law of His, could set aside. By this mighty offering, He breaks down *the middle wall of partition* between those whom He seemed to favour and those whom He seemed to curse. The blessing of the one is found to be a curse, unless it has led him to the living trust in God, not in his own privileges. The curse of the other is found to be a blessing, if it has led him, in weariness and sorrow, to cry for a Teacher and Deliverer of his spirit. One Man is proclaimed as the King and Saviour of both. The signs of His royalty, the marks of the Victor, are the prints of the nails. By these he establishes His right to the trust and the obedience of His creatures; by these He justifies His eternal relation to God. These are the sure testimonies that God has atoned MAN to Himself; that there is no distinction of favoured or neglected race. *He is our Peace*; the centre of union and fellowship between the tribes of the earth; the Destroyer of whatever there *was* in themselves, of whatever there *seemed* to be in the divine ordinances for the teaching and correction of men, which set them at war. Humanity, which had heretofore stood in these apparently hopeless divisions of Jew and Gentile,—while yet it was evincing itself, by the most undoubted proofs, to be essentially the same in both—the same in its conscious evil, the same in its certainty that this evil was the strife against a good, for which it was created—humanity henceforth stands united in Him. *He has made in Himself of twain one new man, so making peace.* Henceforth, to treat any man as an alien from God, as cut off by any legal sentence from Him, was to deny Christ's death; to say that God had not made the great Peace-offering; that the Cross had not removed all which gave one advantage over another.

'*For*,' he goes on, '*through Him we both have access by one Spirit unto the Father*.' This is the climax of the doctrine, and yet also the foundation of it. The access to God is the highest conceivable blessing which any creature could obtain. To have the right of approaching Him without dread, to be warranted in calling Him, Father,—to be sure that that which binds us to Him is mightier than all that is making us feel at a distance from Him,—this is that fruit of the Atonement which, if we really knew our own wants, we should perceive must be greater than all others. And yet it is beneath all the rest; no other has any reality apart from it; the peace with our fellow-men, the freedom from terror of the future, the hope of good things to come, all lie in that. It is *not* possible to conceive of an atonement with man, which has not its basis in an atonement with God. It *is* possible—for it has been done—to conceive of an atonement, which means the removal of the punishment or consequences of the war into which man's distrust of his Creator has brought him, without the ceasing of the war itself. But such a conception sets at nought the meaning of words; the teaching of Apostles; the needs of man; the Gospel of God. It is a dead formula of the schools, which, because it is of itself soulless and skinless, the hearts of men fill out with their own great cravings and hopes, with their terrible sorrows and fears; and so turn it sometimes into a living faith; as often into a dark superstition; a scheme for persuading God to be at peace with that evil against which He has declared eternal war; a scheme for proving that He is still at enmity with a great majority of that race with which He has made peace in the blood of His Son.

I know too well what a temptation there is in all our hearts, to think that such words as the Apostle uses are not altogether safe words; that we must contract his amazing declaration, that *all* barriers have been taken away, that men are reconciled and atoned to God in Christ; that this Atonement is the fulfilment and manifestation of His original purpose, when He created all things in Christ; that He is Himself the Peace-maker—the Author and Finisher of the sacrifice. Every harsh and selfish word we speak, and act we do, our indifference, coldness, hardness of heart, makes the feeling stronger that there must be some exaggeration in these phrases, or that we have misunderstood them, or that they do not apply to us, or that we ought not to hold them forth as true to other men. But if a thousand internal demonstrations have convinced any of us that the hardness, coldness, cruelty of heart grows stronger and nearly invincible, as we forget or disbelieve the fact of this Peace-offering, and the truth of the eternal union between God and His creatures in Christ, which it implies,—and that the only cure for them lies in casting aside all notions that we can make that peace for ourselves which God has made, and all dream that it has been made for us more than for any outcast in the world,—we may well be afraid of yielding to a conviction which is most natural, just as every sin is natural, but which, no one who has traced its workings in himself can believe to be salutary and divinely imparted.

If we set before ourselves some higher result of our religion than this, '*I will arise, and go to my Father;*'

if we suppose that there is some better morality than that which comes from the Spirit of Righteousness and Truth; some more exalted divinity than that which brings us to renounce ourselves and put our trust in God; we shall be continually thinking that a message, which only tells us that God has made peace with us in His Son, which only speaks of a divine Sacrifice offered once for all, which only declares that through Him who has offered it we have *all access in Spirit to the Father*, is not enough for us: that we must find out some mode of applying that Atonement otherwise than by presenting ourselves and the universe in the strength of it before God, some other way of cleansing our consciences from dead works than by receiving this assurance that He would have us serve the living God. But, if we are in the world to live, and act, and suffer, this, I think, will do for us; and nothing less than this will. We shall not want to find out from some subtle divine why the righteous Law of God made a sacrifice necessary. The Law of God will tell our hearts better than we can, that there is something wrong in them. It will tell them, that that wrong comes through separation from a living God; from our selfishness and unlovingness. And, therefore, we cannot, if we let our consciences and reasons speak, be slow to confess that it is He who must make peace with us; and that there can be no sign of peace so fully expressing His nature, so exactly meeting our evil—so mysteriously extracting it—as this of sacri-

P

fice. If we want more, God will teach us more as we pray to Him, as we present to Him the Sacrifice which taketh away the sins of the world, as we offer up our own bodies in sacrifice. If we want more, God will teach us more when we do not shrink from carrying the words of reconciliation to them that are afar off, and them that are near; when we show by tokens which men can understand, that we do believe that Christ is their peace, and that the peace which is in Him passes their understanding and ours; but that it can keep them and us in the knowledge and love of God, and of His Son. The text I have been speaking from this afternoon, declares to us the true foundation of the modern world. The old world existed to testify of the distinction between God and His creatures; of the separation which sin and death had made between them. Its lessons can never be obsolete; every day should make us understand better their deep and eternal import. The new world exists to testify of the atonement of God and His creatures, of their union and fellowship with each other, on the ground of the Sacrifice that He has made. When we enter into the greatness and glory of our own position, as a Church bearing witness of the Atonement to mankind, we shall have such a sense of the awfulness of God's Nature and Being as we never had before; we shall have such a sense of the evil which sets men at strife with the goodness and blessedness, which is embracing and seeking to subdue them, as we never had before.

We shall not strive to build up the wall of partition between men which He has broken down, but we shall feel and confess, each in himself, as we never did, the opposition between the spirit and the flesh. We shall not put Adam in the place of Christ, or build our morality and divinity on the fall which proclaimed men sinners, when Christ's obedience has proclaimed them righteous; but we shall feel more than ever what that sin is, which leads men to distrust Him who has taken it away. We shall not doubt that Christ is, and ever has been, the perfect Mediator between God and man, and that in Him all have access by one Spirit to the Father; but we shall ask ourselves with tenfold earnestness, how it comes to pass that we live so atheistically, so hopelessly, in the world,—how it comes to pass that we can bear to act as aliens and outcasts, when we have been made fellow-citizens with the Saints, and of the Household of God.

SERMON XIV.

CHRIST'S SACRIFICE A POWER TO FORM US AFTER HIS LIKENESS.

(Lincoln's Inn, 3rd Sunday after Trinity, July 2, 1854.)

'Let this mind be in you, which was also in Christ Jesus: who, being in the form of God, thought it not robbery to be equal with God: but made himself of no reputation, and took upon him the form of a servant, and was made in the likeness of men: and being found in fashion as a man, he humbled himself, and became obedient unto death, even the death of the cross. Wherefore God also hath highly exalted him, and given him a name which is above every name: that at the name of Jesus every knee should bow, of things in heaven, and things in earth, and things under the earth; and that every tongue should confess that Jesus Christ is Lord, to the glory of God the Father.'—PHILIPPIANS ii. 5-11.

I HAVE spoken to you of various effects which the writers of the New Testament attribute to the sacrifice of Christ, and have inquired how they connect the effects with the cause. Here St. Paul speaks of a certain state of mind which he wishes the Philippians to possess. He had been exhorting them '*to do nothing through strife or vain-glory; but in lowliness of mind each to esteem the other better than himself.*' He had bidden them '*look not every man on his own things, but every man also on the things of others.*' Very desirable advice, which they had, perhaps, often heard before, of which they knew the value, by the mischiefs which followed when they disregarded it. But what help lies in such experience? Who can keep the commandments the more, because he hears them twenty, or fifty, or a thousand times, and because he finds the inconvenience of breaking them? Things are done through strife and vain-glory by those who have all good maxims by heart; there is an inclination in each man to esteem himself better than others, which gives way to no aphorisms, and to no evidences that they are better than he is. Is there any stronger power before which it may give way? St. Paul believed there was: if he had not, he would have been silent; for he knew what was in others, as well as in himself; and he had no pleasure in tormenting them, or in making professions which he could not perform.

(1.) '*Let this mind be in you, which was also in Christ Jesus.*' So our translators render the passage; faithfully, I think, to the spirit, if not to the letter, of it. The apostle tells the Philippians, as he told the Corinthians, that they may become actual partakers of the character or mind of Christ; nay, that if they were not partakers of it, they were misunderstanding their own position; they were choosing a position which did not belong to them. The thought that was in Christ— the thought that possessed Him, he declares to be the right thought, the true thought; that which should possess and govern all human beings, that to which all things above and beneath must at last be subjected. And he then goes on to show us what this thought or mind of His is, and how it expressed itself.

(2.) '*Who, being in the form of God, thought it not robbery to be equal with God.*' Those who object to the doctrine of the Church concerning the unity and consubstantiality of the Son with the Father, claim that this passage should be translated differently; that it should be taken to mean, *He did not eagerly grasp at being equal with God.* I do not think that they gain much for their cause by that alteration; there are philological difficulties in the way of it; still, on the whole, it more nearly corresponds with the tone and purpose of this passage, than the ordinary version. '*Being in the form of God,*'—being, as the Epistle to the Hebrews puts it, '*the brightness of His glory, and the express image of His person,*'—it was, nevertheless, not His way of proving His divinity, to grasp at divine power and glory. That was the lofty ambition of the sinful creature: '*We shall be as gods, knowing good and evil.*' He gave precisely the opposite sign and testimony of what He was. He emptied Himself. He gave up the bright and glorious form. '*He took upon Him the form of a servant.*' The earthly creature wished to assert its relation to God by climbing to the stars. The heavenly Being, '*He who was in the form of God,*' asserted His relation by stooping; by depriving

Himself of that which was His; by adopting conditions that were altogether unlike His.

(3.) We are not to make this statement stronger and more startling, by substituting our notions for St. Paul's. The heathens, we know, dreamt of gods who became incarnate in brute creatures. That would have seemed to them a much greater abdication than the one which is spoken of here. If we adopt the theory of Sacrifice, which creeps into all our minds—a theory which represents it as most heroical, when it most contradicts our reason—that conclusion must also be ours. But the apostle could conceive of nothing higher or more blessed than God's order; every departure from it, under whatever pretext, must be evil. Here was none. Christ, being the perfect image of the Father, was the image after which men were created. The relation between Him and our race was implied in its existence. If His voice called all things out of chaos, it gave *man* the power to name things, to know each other, to confess a law. To become one of the race when He was the Head of it—to become a servant when He was the Lord—this was an act of deep and loving condescension: but there was nothing in it irregular and anomalous; the glory of it is, that it is the fulfilment of an original and divine purpose—that it is the means of removing the discord and anomalies that were resisting that purpose. How necessary it is to keep this distinction in remembrance, you will perceive as we proceed.

(4.) St. Paul explains further his expression, '*taking on him the form of a servant,*' by another: '*being made in, or having become in, the likeness of men.*' You will not imagine that St. Paul could intend, by this language, to give any countenance to the notion which gained so much hold in the Church afterwards, that Christ was not *really* a man, but only had the *appearance* of a man. That notion he often repudiates in direct terms; every word he writes denounces it implicitly. But the likeness of *men* stands in vivid contrast to the form of *God.* He was the original man, the type of all creation; as it is expressed in the Epistle to the Colossians, '*the first-born of every creature.*' Now he assumes the condition of individual men; he puts on the fleshly accidents which belonged to them, as He had before stood to them in the closest spiritual relation. In the words of the Epistle to the Hebrews, the second and third chapters of which should always be read in illustration of this passage: '*Forasmuch then as the children are partakers of flesh and blood, He also Himself likewise took part of the same.*' I do not quote the end of that verse, because that assigns another effect of the death of Christ, of which I hope to speak next Sunday. But the taking part of the flesh and blood, of which the children were partakers, those '*whom He was not ashamed to call his brethren,*' those whom He was to *claim* as children of His Father, because they always had *been* so,—this is another way of stating the truth, that He *came in the likeness of men.*

(5.) He goes on: '*And being found in fashion as a man, He humbled Himself.*' To be in that fashion, in that earthly mortal mould, was the commencement of the humiliation, but not the consummation of it. He did not, when in that fashion, take any of the higher, grander, positions which sinful and dying men could still vindicate for themselves. He did not become a statesman, or warrior, or poet. But, entering into all human experiences and thoughts — understanding, therefore, inwardly, what these differences are among us, and how we feel them—He yet claimed the peasant condition instead of them; a position which identified Him with *all* men, with the lowest men, instead of one which raised Him above any. And this whilst He was doing regal acts, and was suspected of wishing to make Himself a King; while He was enduring the jealousy of popular teachers, because the people felt Him to be a Prophet; while the Priests were hating Him, as one who had Holiness to the Lord really inscribed on His forehead.

(6.) He felt all these reproaches, and knew what was to be the issue of them. Death, therefore, was before His eyes; not merely the ordinary death which He had implicitly taken upon Him when he was made flesh, but the death of a criminal—'*the death of the cross.*' He was '*obedient*,' the apostle says, even to death; not as some one may, perhaps, suppose the word to mean, obedient *to* death, as if that was His master, but obedient to His Father, to the point of undergoing death, even though it involved agony and the sense of desertion.

(7.) This obedience, so carried out to this final point, is the reason, St. Paul says, why *God has highly exalted Him, and given Him a name that is above every name.* His prayer was—'*I have glorified thee on the earth: I have finished the work which thou gavest me to do. And now, O Father, glorify thou me with thine own self, with the glory which I had with thee before the world was.*' Of that prayer, his words and acts, as they are recorded by the evangelists, are the exposition; every one of them is the glorification of His Father, the sinking of Himself. The Sermon on the Mount is nothing but a setting forth of the name, and kingdom, and will of His Father, —of His desire to make all holy as He is. Every deed of love to those tormented with plagues and sicknesses, every parable to the multitude, every discourse with His disciples, was *letting His light shine before men, that they, seeing His good works, might glorify His Father in heaven.* That was the work which He came to do, and which He finished when He gave up the ghost. The perfect Son, by His obedience, had revealed the perfect Father; the Absolute Goodness had come forth in all the relations and sympathies of the man. One act of self-assertion, of self-glorification, would have dimmed the image, would have made the vision of truth and love which was presented to the creature imperfect. There was no such act. All was self-denial, self-surrender; the love of the Father worked mightily and unresisted in the heart of the Son, till it was broken and offered with the whole body and soul as a complete sacrifice. And then came the triumph of the man, the restoration of the creature made in the image of God to its native home, the exaltation of the body redeemed from death to the right hand of the Father. *God has highly exalted Him* in that flesh which He had taken, and has given Him a *name* above angels, and principalities, that *at His name, and in His name, every knee should bow*; that all creatures should feel and confess Him—not as the Word, the Son of the Father, only, but —as Jesus the crucified to be the Lord, the King and Ruler of men ;—still to the glory of Him whom He has glorified, from whom He came, in whom He dwells, *to the glory of God the Father.*

(8.) This, then, is the mind or thought that was in Him ; this is the mind or thought which has vindicated itself against the high, self-exalting thoughts, by which men have been divided from each other, by which they have defied God. When St. Paul preached Jesus Christ, and Him crucified, he preached that in obedience, humiliation, sacrifice, dwelt the mighty conquering power—that power against which no other in earth or heaven could measure itself. And his words have not been confuted by the experience of ages ; they have been confirmed by the facts which seem at first sight most at war with them. Do you ask why the soldiers of Islam, in the first centuries after Mahomet, or in any subsequent centuries, prevailed against those who had the sign of the Cross on their banners? The only answer that can be given is, that there was more of this thought or mind of Christ, more of humiliation, and obedience, and sacrifice, in them than there was in their opponents. They prevailed not through their denial of Him, but through their implicit recognition of Him. So far as they had zeal, faith, union,—so far as they sought to magnify God's name, and to give up themselves, they were His soldiers, not the Prophet's; they succeeded because the incarnate Son of God was highly exalted, because there was a name given Him which is above every name. Because all power was given Him in heaven and earth, He would not suffer those who called themselves his servants to blaspheme His Father and to corrupt His brethren. Go through the history of the world, of the Church, of individuals, you will find it the same. So long as you creep along the ground, and ask why this man, or this party, or this faith, overcame, and that was subdued, you may be continually disposed to doubt and arraign the Providence that directs all things, to charge God foolishly. But ascend above the mists of earth to the clear heaven where Christ sits at the right hand of God, and the eternal Law becomes manifest which brings these discords into harmony. The Will that rules the universe, the Will that has triumphed and does triumph, is all expressed and gathered up in *the Lamb that was slain.* Beholding Him, you see whence come the peace and order of the world, whence comes its confusion. The principle of sacrifice has been ascertained once and for ever to be the principle, the divine principle; that in which God can alone fully manifest His own eternal Being, His inmost character, the order which He has appointed all creatures, voluntary and involuntary, to obey. The *name of Jesus* is the name to which all the intelligences of the universe refer themselves, and all the energies and impulses of the unconscious creation. They bow *to* it, as denoting the only source of their strength; they bow *in* it, as containing the only secret of their humiliation. If they did not confess Jesus to be the Lord of all, they would fall into all strife and separation, each seeking to be Lord himself, each supposing that the more he could lift up himself, the more he could depress his neighbour, the greater would be the triumph, each discovering at last that in this effort lies all weakness and ruin. If they did now bow in the name of Jesus to God the Father, they would never feel that He WAS their Father, and that they were His children, that He had given them their distinct tasks to fulfil, that He was imparting to them a common Spirit. This, therefore, is the law of the heavenly world; knowing which, we need not care how little we know about hierarchies of angels, and their attributes and relations; because we are sure that this must be the centre of their unity; that they must do the commandments of Him who gave Himself up to die, hearkening to the voice of His words; that as He did nothing through strife and vain-glory, so neither can they; that as He was lowly, so must they be; that as He lived for others, not for Himself, that must be their life; that they must be ever acting, because He is inspiring them with His ever-acting love; that they must be always at rest, because He is ever resting in His Father's love.

(9.) Such a vision of the victorious, all-governing thought or mind of Christ is brought before us in this passage; but the vision was good for nothing except as it carried home the word to the heart of the Philippians—*'Let this mind be in you, which was also in Christ Jesus.'* And in these words there lies the greatest wonder of all. That angels and principalities should have the mind of Jesus Christ—that *they* should be like Him, and do like Him,—this is conceivable; but that a set of jarring people—Jews, Greeks, Romans—with exclusive national feelings each with a separate interest and prejudice of his own, should have this one mind; that it should be reasonable, that it should be possible to bid them have it, this is what we find it so hard to believe. And it is hard, and it was as hard for them to believe it as it is for us. We understand, as we read St. Paul's Epistles, what work an apostle had to keep peace in the Churches,—yes! and how very poorly he could perform the work. The great discovery he made was, that he could not perform it at all; that there were elements of strife in himself, and in those to whom he wrote, which no skill or arguments of his could bring into order. The difficulty was not less with baptized men than with others; it was greater. Their spirits had been stirred to their very foundations;

it was not only the ordinary strife and self-interest of the world which were exciting them to war: a host of new thoughts had been awakened within them, each of which might give birth to heresies and hatreds. Oh! what remorse and misery would have been in the thought of having founded societies with such principles of sorrow and mischief in them, if he had not felt that beneath them all lay that uniting mind of Christ, that divine Sacrifice, the name which can make the proudest spirits bow. But these He had been sent to proclaim in the midst of a fighting world; in them, he was certain lay the secret of eternal power and reconcilement. He could say to them all—'You have these different 'purposes, and notions, and interests, and wills; all 'attempts to stifle them because they are inconvenient, ' to crush them under some general rule, to adjust them ' by some benignant compromise, has always proved 'abortive, and always will. Instead of extinguishing ' them, I have been the means of awakening you to a ' consciousness of them. But I have done this, because ' I know who is at the centre of all these different lines ' of thought, and purpose, and will of yours; in whom ' they all meet; I know whence those springs of life ' within you, which seem so full of turbulence, proceed. ' I can tell you who is ruling you, and with whom you ' are fighting. I can tell you how the power which is ' in the Ruler of heaven and earth may become a power ' in you. The meaning of your baptism, of your calling ' to be members of a Church, is, that He makes you

'sharers of His own mind; that He promises you His
'Spirit every day and hour to overcome that in you,
'and you, and you, which is disposed to set up a sepa-
'rate mind, a mind of your own, in opposition to it.
'The best good tidings I can declare to you, and to the
'universe, is that you need not do that. You can be at
'peace; He has made peace for you. You can give up
'yourselves; He has given up Himself for you. You
'can claim your place in the heavenly order, and
'harmony; He has brought you into it, breaking down
'the barrier of self-will which made our world an exile
'from it.' After eighteen centuries, do the words sound
more hopeless than ever? Does it seem more incredible
than ever that there should be peace in the world, quite
incredible that there should be peace in the Church?
Do you begin to despair of it in your households, in
your hearts? I would not make anyone think less
sadly of the strife which he sees around him, and feels
within him. The more sad it makes him, the more
seriously he will ask himself—'Whence comes it?
'what is it that we have lost? what is it that we want?'
And the answer will come in due time; it comes from
want of a *Centre* of Unity. That Centre men will seek
for, high and low; in one sect and school, then in
another; in one dogma and another, in one man and
another, in one city and another. They will seek, and
will not find, till they come to the cross of Christ, till
they ask for the spirit of self-sacrifice; till they believe
that He is highly exalted in order that He may bestow

it upon His Church and family, and that He will bestow it upon that Church and family when they confess that God has sent His Son to be the Deliverer of it.

The aspect of Sacrifice which I have been considering to-day, is closely connected with that of which I spoke last Sunday. Of Christ, the Peace-offering, the Atonement of God with man, and of man with man, St. Paul spoke of to the Ephesians. Here he connects that peace-offering more directly with the sin-offering. The sin of the world is its self-will, its self-gratification. The Apostle bids us behold the Lamb of God who takes away that sin by obedience to His Father, by emptying Himself of Glory, by humbling Himself to the likeness of the lowest of His creatures. By that sin-offering, He proves Himself to be the Lord of all. When we yield ourselves to Him as the Lord of our spirits, He gives us His lowly mind, and so gives us peace. But the passage to-day brings out more distinctly than the other did the truth which our Lord taught His disciples, when He *took a little child, and set him in the midst of them, and said, Verily, I say unto you, Whosoever shall be converted, and shall become as this little child, the same is greatest in the kingdom of heaven.* ' What can we do ?' we sometimes ask, ' when there are so few examples of heroic virtue ' about us ; so few great saints who can enable us to ' see in our common life the mind of Him who wrestled ' with our enemies ?' When God sends us such specimens of Himself, let us be thankful for them ; let us try and learn from them all we can. But, in the meantime, we can do without them. There are children all about us.—Christ bids us learn of them. There are poor despised people all about us.—Christ was of no reputation. There is death among us,—not heroical, but ignominious death; and it was because he underwent such death, that God has given Him a name that is above every name.

SERMON XV.

CHRIST'S DEATH A VICTORY OVER THE DEVIL.

(*Lincoln's Inn, 4th Sunday after Trinity, July 9, 1854.*)

'Forasmuch then as the children are partakers of flesh and blood, he also himself likewise took part of the same; that through death he might destroy him that had the power of death, that is, the devil; and deliver them who through fear of death were all their lifetime subject to bondage.'—HEBREWS ii. 14, 15.

I ALLUDED, last Sunday, to the opening clause of these verses. The words, '*Forasmuch as the children were partakers of flesh and blood, He also Himself likewise took part of the same,*' proved, I said, clearly, that there was a relation between Christ and men which did not depend upon flesh and blood, which did not commence when He assumed our nature, which was the reason of His assuming it. The more you consider the previous part of this chapter, the more, I think, you will feel that it is the intention of the writer to make us conscious of this truth. In the sixth verse he quotes the eighth Psalm: '*What is man, that Thou art mindful of him? or the son of man, that Thou visitest him? Thou madest him a little lower than the angels . . . Thou hast put all things in subjection under his feet. For in that He put all in subjection under him, He left nothing that is not put under him. But now we see not yet all things put under him. But we see Jesus, who was made a little lower than the angels for the suffering of death, crowned with glory and honour; that He by the grace of God should taste death for every man. For it became Him, for whom are all things, and by whom are all things, in bringing many sons unto glory, to make the Captain of their salvation perfect through sufferings. For both He that sanctifieth and they who are sanctified are all of one: for which cause He is not ashamed to call them brethren, saying, I will declare Thy Name unto my brethren, in the midst of the congregation will I sing praise unto Thee. And again, I will put my trust in Him. And again, Behold I and the children which God hath given me.'*

That Christ is here put forth as fulfilling the words which were spoken of man on the creation day; as exercising that dominion over things which was committed to man, finally; as triumphing over the death which denoted the humiliation of man, is evident to the most careless reader. But we are not permitted to stop here. Passages are quoted from the Old Testament, in which the divine Word of God speaks of human creatures as His own brethren, in which He says that He will declare His Father's Name to those brethren, in which He speaks of trusting in God as if He were one of them. That this is the meaning of the writer, there has never, I believe, been any doubt among his commentators. Nor have they failed to perceive that the principle, of which these are instances, may be applied to the interpretation of the Old Testament generally. We have not, I think, followed out the hint which he has given us, as much as we might have done, and as we were bound to do, considering the authority of the teacher. But we have all acknowledged, to some extent, that the language of psalmists and of prophets would be unintelligible, if we did not suppose that Christ, the divine Word, was speaking in them and through them, was discovering His own sympathy with those to whom they were sent, through the sympathy which He awakened in their hearts. If a holy man sorrowed over the sins of his countrymen, or of the world, or of himself, he felt that another, who was higher than he was, had first experienced that sorrow, and had imparted it to him. His joys, his hopes, must have had the same source. No single man could have known them in their depth and power. There must be some one in whom they were all gathered up, some universal Brother, to whom each particular brother owed his place in the family and the affections which corresponded to it.

There must, therefore, be a deep below even this. It is indicated in the words, '*It became Him, for whom are all things, and by whom are all things, in bringing many sons unto glory, to perfect,* or *initiate, the Captain of their salvation through sufferings.*' The ground of that brotherhood, which the passage is setting forth, lies in the will of Him who has created all things. He does not regard men as included in these things. They are sons; they are to be saved or delivered out of the mass of things in which they have lost themselves. He purposes to bring them to glory, to His own glory, to a knowledge of Himself. The Only-begotten is the deliverer. That He may be so fully, He is initiated through sufferings. He enters into the inmost mystery of human sorrow. He becomes acquainted with grief; it is His bosom companion. Men have had familiarity with it in its different forms and measures, He has familiarity with it in its root and essence. To give Him this perfect fitness for His work of a Leader and Saviour—a work which could never be performed for His creatures if they were apart from Him—which implies the most entire fellowship and incorporation with Him, became, he says, the Father of all. It belonged to the character of His inmost being that so it should be. In no way but this does that character and inmost being fully declare itself; this interprets all other manifestations of it. What ultimate explanation, then, must not be weaker and less satisfactory than this— ' *It became Him ?* '

This idea of the humiliation and incarnation of Christ is essentially the same with that in the passage of the Epistle to the Philippians, upon which I spoke last week. The difference is, that Obedience and Humility

were the aspects of the sacrifice which were brought
out prominently before us there—that Sympathy is the
great subject here. That sympathy, as the necessary
qualification of a Priest, as implied in all he does and
all he is, we hear much more of as the Epistle proceeds.
Through it the writer is enabled to teach us a truth,
which when first stated it is most hard to apprehend,
that when the Sacrifice is perfect, and the Priest is
perfect, they must be one. That great argument
I shall not touch upon to-day. There is another presented to us in the words, *'that through death He
might destroy him which had the power of death, that is,
the Devil,'* which will be enough, and more than
enough, for one discourse. It might be expanded
through a series of discourses; the whole doctrine of
sacrifice might be deduced from it; but I only take it
as describing one of the effects of our Lord's death,
connected closely and inseparably with reconciliation
and propitiation, but still distinguishable from
them.

The word *Diabolus* is never used in
the New Testament without a direct reference to its
derivation and meaning. There are other words,—the
Tempter, the Adversary, the Destroyer, which all
point to the spirit of evil; but they denote him by
different characteristics, each of which we have used to
remember, and which we should not mix carelessly
together. The Accuser, or slanderer of God and of
the brethren, is the title which belongs to this

passage. We shall not enter into the sense of it, if we substitute any other title for that.

I. Whatever our theories are about the existence or non-existence of an evil will, about the personality or impersonality of that will, about the influence of that will upon us,—we all know, as a matter of fact, that whispers do come to us—certainly brought from no visible lips,—which take the form of accusations, cruel and malignant accusations, against persons who may, or may not, have done us wrong; who may be our enemies, or who may be very dear to us. All the horrible suspicions and questions which have been wrought into men's brains and hearts, and which have destroyed the peace of their lives,—even if there has been some conspiring human demon, some Iago or Iachimo, to strike the spark, to light the tinder, has yet—we feel it, and we confess it by a hundred phrases— a deeper source. We say it is within us, and we say rightly; but yet we know that down in those depths which the vulture's eye has not seen, there is a slanderous voice speaking to us—suggesting thoughts which we did not originate, which we shrink from, which being rejected, return again; which may cause most anguish and torment to those who most resolutely defy them. I say boldly, these are facts. I do not try to explain them. The Scripture explains them to me, by telling us of an Accuser of the brethren, of one who seeks to divide us from each other; and I accept this statement, not trying to get rid of it by any analyses or refinements, because I can find no other which accounts so well for an awful individual experience, or so well connects it with that which goes on in every man.

2. But the same secret whispers which seek to set a man at war with his neighbours, strive also to set him at war with himself. The discontents, the terrible visions of the past and of the future, which every man has been conscious of—which seem to many as if they made up the sum of their existence—whence do they come? At first we think from without. We lay them to any annoying circumstances, to any disagreeable fellow-creature. The same discoveries, which we cannot be deceived in, bring them nearer home. They must have more to do with us than with anything about us. They seem to move from us, and yet towards us. There springs up in us, we cannot tell from whence, a desire to be freed from this vile state of mind, this self-torment. But the moment the effort at reformation begins, there begins a suggestion of discouragement and despair. The evil that has been done is brought against us; the evil that is with us still, is brought against us. Both are arguments, why we cannot obtain freedom, why we should not crave for it. Is this accusation from ourselves? Is it from conscience? Surely, conscience must be much mixed up with it. But conscience cannot be an enemy of reformation,—cannot bid us continue in evil. It must be one who is perverting all the witnesses of conscience, who is

using them to keep us from ever being what conscience says we ought to become. It must be an accuser, a slanderer;—not one clothed in flesh and bones,—but a spirit.

3. There is one more discovery still to be made. This spirit is the slanderer and accuser, not only of our brethren, not only of ourselves, but of God. Is it not so? Are not we hearing him accused every moment of the day? Is not every feeling of pain turned into an argument that the Ruler of the world has an ill-will to us? Is not every comfort a proof that He is leading us into temptation? Is not the sin of some men a proof that He has created them to perish? Is not the righteousness of some men a proof that He is partial? Is not that sense of evil in ourselves a proof that He has woven nets about us, from which we cannot escape, that He may have the pleasure of destroying us? Is not that consciousness of inability to escape from an evil a proof that He has sentenced us to inevitable bondage? We know that we have had thoughts of this kind, that they come back to us continually, sometimes nakedly, sometimes in fine court dresses. We know from their words and their acts that it is the same with all who belong to our race. Is there not an accuser of God with them continually?

The words of my text point to the greatest and most decisive argument of all, by which this accusation is supported. The Devil, it boldly says, was he who had the power of *Death*. Whatever reason some higher and better teacher might suggest to men for trusting God, for believing that he intended good to them, and not evil—whatever rains from heaven and fruitful seasons might tell them, Death was the answer to them all. That was the great ordinance for the whole race, for the whole creation. That stopped all the projects of the individual man; that made all purposes of improvement abortive; that made schemes for the future, which nevertheless, we must always be devising, ridiculous. That cut off all the bonds of family, of tribe, or nation. That made a man's concern for his children's children idle dreams. That said, Talk of your freedom as you please; there is this death always waiting to crush it at the last. Talk of Nature with its teeming, ever-renewing life; its mornings after midnight, its springs after winter, as much as you will. But this declares,—With men and the inhabitants of the world *you* have nothing more to do. You may go somewhere else, possibly; you may dwell in some unknown solitude. But the thoughts which have been formed in you here, the life you have led here, the persons you have known,—they are over. This is one part of the argument; one demonstration that God meant nothing by the universe He had formed, or that He meant destruction by it; or that His purpose, if it was a gracious one, had been defeated. But there was another road to the same, or a more fearful, result. The accuser could say, 'In spite of all these 'witnesses against you, you have a feeling that you

'shall go on, that you must go on, after this death; yes,
'and that everything which you have been doing, seeing,
'feeling, here, must have an influence on your state there;
'that you can part with nothing. It is true, frightfully
'true. Everything must go on; *you* must go on. And
'every bad thought you have thought, and every bad
'deed you have done, is bound to you now; will be
'bound to you for ever. God has pronounced His sen-
'tence of death upon you for those thoughts and deeds,
'and He will execute His sentence to the utmost. Do
'what you can to hide yourselves from Him. Avert His
'wrath, if it is possible. Forget Him, if you can. Try
'to appease Him, if you cannot forget Him. What can
'be so dreadful as to be brought into His presence?'

Thus speaks the Accuser to you and to me; thus spoke he to the generations of old. The Epistle says that there came forth an answer to his whispers; that the answer is a complete one; that the moment we accept it, his chain is broken for us: because God has in truth broken it for our race. '*By death Christ overcame him that had the power of death, that is, the Accuser.*' By His own death He tore in pieces that web of calumnies against God, as if He were compassing the ruin of His creatures, as if He were wishing them to abide in their evil, as if He were not upholding the order and harmony of His own creation, but was indifferent to it, and was permitting discord to prevail in it. No words could have shown that the Spirit of Lies was the author of the distrust which men felt in their

Creator; that he was separating the children from their Father. A mighty transcendent act must supply the demonstration. God perfects His only-begotten Son through death. That which was said to be the clear declaration that men are regarded by God as enemies, becomes the sign which Christ gives of His Sonship; as the Resurrection is the great sign which He, of whom are all things and by whom are all things, gives that He owns Him as His Son. Christ bears death not in obedience to an inevitable fate, but to a loving will; not because the tyrant has conquered the earth and those who dwell upon it, but as an eternal testimony that he has not conquered it—that it belongs to the Creator, not to the Destroyer. Death seems to make the great and final chasm,—of which all other separations were but dim prophecies,—the chasm between the Father and Him in whom He delighted. Death is made the pledge of Their eternal union; the pledge of Their infinite satisfaction in each other. That union is shown to be the ground of every other. The satisfaction of God in His Son is His satisfaction with the world whose nature that Son bears. His death is the vindication of their death; they have a right to accept it as a sign of adoption, as an assurance of reconciliation; as a proof that God, initiating them through sufferings, is crowning their work, is preparing them for a higher work. They have no right any longer to speculate about individual deaths, and what they denote. Here is the Universal Death—the death of the Head and Brother of mankind; that is the only test and explanation of its nature; that is the only one to which we dare refer when we would understand the meaning of the universe and God's purposes to it. When we fall back upon our thoughts and experiences, and reason and speculate upon them, we fall back into the hands of the Accuser. Then frightful recollections of what we have been, and of the evil we have seen in others, and of the sin of the world, raise such a mist and darkness, as wholly shut God out of our sight. It seems as if each death were sending some new creature out of the region of His government, out of the circle of hope, into an unknown abyss over which some malignant power may preside. This thought recurs again and again, oh! under what multitudes of strange forms and seemly disguises,—cloaking itself with religious, even with Christian, arguments; always with the same effect; always bringing the spirit into bondage to the fear of death, always leading it to distrust of Him who is seeking for His sheep in all the thickets and on all the crags to which they have wandered; who is watching for the children who are feeding upon husks, and perishing with hunger. But when they turn from their miserable attempts to solve the mystery for themselves, to Him who entered into the mystery for them, that He might bring light out of darkness; when they turn to the cross and to Him who died upon it; when they determine to learn there what death is, and what man is, and what God is, there and only there;

then they find their bondage turned into freedom. The incubus that sat upon their hearts and took away their breathing is gone; that which made trust impossible is the warrant for it; the cause of despair is the foundation of hope; that which seemed to enclose us within time, and to make all beyond it terrible, is that which tells us that the Eternal has triumphed, and that Christ has manifested that Eternal Life which was with the Father, and over which death has no power.

And thus we understand those words of St. Paul: *'The sting of death is sin, the strength of sin is the Law.'* Death is utterly horrible as long as it is linked to that distrust of God which is Sin, and the root of all sins; so long as it keeps that up in our minds; so long as it teaches us that our safety is in flying from His presence. And the Law which pronounces us to be sinners, which makes us inwardly conscious that we are, and yet which we are sure proceeds from God, aggravates that distrust; and, if it comes alone, makes us wish that we could be atheists. *'But thanks be to God,'* he goes on, *'who giveth us the victory through our Lord Jesus Christ.'* Thanks be to that God whom we have counted our enemy, who we supposed had pleasure in our death, for conquering the very enemy we accused Him of sending among us. Thanks be to God, for giving us the victory through our Lord Jesus Christ, through Him who has been made sin for us, knowing no sin; through Him who has made the one free, perfect, voluntary sacrifice which takes away the sin of the world. Thanks be to Him for giving us the victory, not over death only, but over him who had the power of death, who changed all the witnesses which God was bearing in our hearts and consciences that we had forgotten Him, and that we could not live without Him, into reasons for turning away from Him. Thanks be to God, that we can now answer the Accuser with these words: 'We know what death is, for Christ has died. ' We know that His death is the proof of God's eternal ' love, the pledge that He has reconciled the world to ' Himself; the encouragement to draw nigh to Him; ' the assurance that a new and living way is opened into ' His Presence, and that in that Presence is fulness of ' joy.' For now the accuser of the brethren is cast down, he that accused them before God day and night. Now we are sure that there is not an accuser, but a Mediator between us and our father; that the Son of God and the Son of man is with us and with Him. By the blood of the Lamb and the word of His testimony, we can answer the charges which the Accuser brings in our hearts against ourselves, for Christ has made us one with Himself; against our brethren, for His death is for us all, the bond of peace between Him and us; against God, for it is God Himself who justifieth us, who then can condemn? It is Christ who points to His own sacrifice for the sins of the whole world; what power in earth and hell can prevent us from drawing nigh in the might of that Sacrifice to the Father of all? And if death does not separate us from Him, or from those who are with us on earth; if the death of the cross is the one way of reconciling us to Himself and to each other—how can it separate us from those who have passed through the veil? Sin is the divider; there is no other. When we eat that flesh and drink that blood whereby the victory has been won, we may be sure that there is fellowship with all, wherever they are, who have overcome. We may not know it, because we have not resisted to blood striving against sin, and therefore do not feel the power and mystery of that Sacrifice which takes away sin. But perhaps if God gives us grace not to love our lives to the death; if he makes us willing to sacrifice ourselves for His glory and the good of men, the communion may become very real even here. Helps greater than the old world dreamed of, when they spoke of mysterious champions descending to the fight, may be granted to those who are struggling hard with the Accuser. At all events they will prevail at last; for God has made the death of His Son the Gospel of peace to men with Him, and the Gospel of everlasting woe and damnation to every power which would divide men from Him.

SERMON XVI.

CHRIST THE ADVOCATE.

(Lincoln's Inn, 5th Sunday after Trinity, July 16, 1854.)

> My little children, these things write I unto you, that ye sin not. And if any man sin, we have an advocate with the Father, Jesus Christ the righteous: and he is the propitiation for our sins: and not for ours only, but also for the sins of the whole world.'
> 1 JOHN ii. 1, 2.

I DO not know whether we ought to complain of our translators for rendering the same word 'Advocate' in this passage, which they rendered 'Comforter' in the fourteenth, fifteenth, and sixteenth chapters of St. John's Gospel. It was not a sufficient reason for introducing a new word, that the subject which is brought before us here is different from the one of which our Lord is speaking to His disciples there. St. John might have thought that it was very desirable and important to denote the Spirit of Truth, who should testify of Christ, who should bring all things to the remembrance of the disciples, who should convince the world of sin, and righteousness, and judgment, by the very same title which he gives here to Jesus Christ the Righteous. Interpreters have no business, in any case, to act as if they were wiser than their author, and to guard against confusion by departing from the course which he has adopted. But, on the other hand, the translators may have felt that the word which they had selected, not without strong warrant of reason, in the Gospel, would not convey the full sense of the Epistle. They must have reflected, that if etymology was the only thing to be considered, no word could be so accurate as Advocate—one who is called to our aid—to represent the force of Παράκλητος. But they may have reflected also that it had acquired, from use, a signification which corresponded far less happily to the description which is given of the work of the Divine Spirit; whereas, every part of that description signifies comfort or strength, which the weak, who are unable to speak for themselves, derive from the presence of a friend and helper. In the passage before us, they may have dreaded less the technical associations with the word Advocate; they may have felt that, in its primary meaning, it was what they required, and that the phrase 'Comforter' would have been quite out of place. I own I should have thought them more cautious and more reverent, if they had chosen their equivalent carefully, and then had rigidly adhered to it, at least when they were translating from St. John; but so much is to be learnt from their variations, not only respecting the processes of their own minds and the history of theology, but respecting the truths which the Bible sets forth, that we may have possibly full compensation for their error, if error it is to be called.

I have touched upon this point, because it has an important bearing upon the meaning of the text, and also because it connects the subject upon which I wish to speak to-day with that of which I spoke last Sunday. The Accusing Spirit who is said in the Epistle to the Hebrews to have had the power of death till Christ tasted death for every man, misrepresents the mind and will of God towards us, the acts and dispositions of our fellow-creatures, our own moral condition. He leads us to suspect an enemy in our Father, an enemy in every brother, an enemy in our own heart. The more we know of these inward accusations, of their subtle complications, of the way in which they pervert the most undoubted facts, and the most authentic witnesses of our consciences into falsehoods, and arguments to evil—the more horror we feel of a power near to us, acquainted with our secrets, bent upon our ruin. We may state the conviction to ourselves in the most various forms; but we have it one and all, and we cannot shake it off. No; nor is there any emancipation from it, but in the acknowledgment of that other Spirit, the Spirit of Truth, who is also with us, who is also acquainted with all that is passing in us, who knows recesses in our spirits which the other does not know, who reveals to us God as a Father; those whom we had taken to be His enemies and ours, as belonging to a family which He has begotten and redeemed; ourselves as members of that family. To have such a Spirit ever near, ever ready to come when we call upon Him, able to lay bare the sophistries by which the Spirit of distrust and lies is urging us to despair, able to show in every fact which is the excuse for his sophistries, arguments for confidence and hope—this, indeed, is the fulfilment of the promise—'*I will send you an Advocate (or Comforter), who shall abide with you for ever.*'

But our Lord says—'*He shall not speak of Himself; He shall testify of me.*' What do these words signify? The accusing Spirit forces us into the understanding of them. He says to us—' You may have good
'desires, right impulses, divine resolutions; these may
'be inspired by some gracious power. But though
'God vouchsafes all these benignant influences to you,
'you are not really nearer to Him than you were before.
'A chasm, which none has traversed, divides you from
'Him. Who shall ascend up on high into that myste-
'rious world of light where He dwells? Perhaps, the
'gifts which He bestows on your minds and hearts may
'have something more wonderful and celestial in them
'than the gifts of corn and wine which He bestows on
'your bodies; but they do not constitute any closer
'bond between you and Him than those do. One man
'has more of them than another, but how miserably
'poor is the condition of the best! What a sense he
'has of insufficiency, of hollowness, of evil! Nay, is not
'this sense strongest in the best? Do not they accuse

'themselves most of being sinners? Is not this the
'only reason why any men in the world have any com-
'fort or repose, that they do not think of God, and of
'their distance from Him, and of the offences they have
'committed against Him? The moment these thoughts
'are awakened, what shame, what misery, what self-
'loathing, what struggles to attain a good that is never
'reached, to avoid an evil that is never escaped, follow
'in every case? Is it less so among Christians than
'others; less so among those who say they have this
'Spirit, this Comforter, with them? Are not the testi-
'monies which He bears to their manifold transgres-
'sions, to the radical evil from which these trans-
'gressions flow, the cause of their unhappiness?'

'*He shall testify of Me.*' This Spirit shall answer these accusations, not by reminding you that you have done one good work or another, or that you had one kindly affection and right desire, or a thousand; that you have different dispositions and affections from your fellow-men, and have had a trust and hope of which they gave no signs; not by such miserable, ragged comfort as this, which fails in every great crisis, which a fit of pain or the recollection of a single evil act or unkind thought, or the discovery of a wrong in yourself which you never knew to be in any one else, or the discovery of something right and good in a man you took to be an outcast from God, which you never knew to be in yourself, or any single revelation of your own character such as God in His mercy will not suffer you to want—may sweep away in a moment. The Spirit of Truth does not sustain His office as an Advocate and Consoler by feeding you with wind; but He says—'The Accuser 'speaks to you as men conscious of separation from 'God. You have that consciousness; you feel that it 'is an evil thing, a sin, to have it. Why do you feel it? 'Because there is a bond of union between you and 'God, because that bond is one which existed before all 'evil was in the world, and because no evil can destroy 'it. Therefore your conscience tells you that you are 'wrong for being separate from God, seeing that your 'right and proper state is one of union with Him; 'seeing that you are created for that state in Christ 'Jesus; seeing that you were redeemed for that state 'in Christ Jesus.'

This is what St. John had been telling his little children in Ephesus in the commencement of his Epistle. He first told them of the Word of Life which had been manifested, of that Eternal Life which was with the Father; that he had heard this message from Him, that God was Light, and in Him was no darkness at all; that he delivered this message to them that their joy might be full, and that they might have fellowship with the Father, and with His Son Jesus Christ; that if they walked in darkness, they would not have fellowship; but that if they walked in the light, as He was in the light, they would have fellowship with each other, and the blood of Jesus Christ would cleanse them from all sin; that if they said they had no sin, the truth was not in them; that if they confessed their sin, God was faithful and just to forgive them their sin, and to cleanse them from all unrighteousness.

In these words, the Apostle, taught by the divine Spirit—the Comforter—does not give them any joy, or peace, or hope, by telling them of some good thing which they had received in themselves, but of a Life and Righteousness which was in God, and which Christ the Son and Word of God, had shown forth; by telling them how they might be raised out of themselves, and be made partakers of it. To believe in Christ as the Righteousness of God, and as the Mediator between God and man, was, therefore, the true deliverance from sin. The blood of Christ, which declared this righteousness, and the union of man with God, cleansed away the sin of all who really sought God, and wished to be in His Light. It assured them that there was no chasm between them and God; it assured them that nothing but a refusal to believe in the message, 'God is Light; Christ has been manifested;' could create the chasm.

And therefore he begins the next passage of his Epistle with the words—'*My little children, these things write I unto you, that ye sin not.*' In this way;—by accepting this great news of God and of His Love, and by turning to God in Christ, you arise out of sin, for you rise not of yourselves; you become righteous, for you become one with Him who is righteous. '*And if any man sin*,' —if he loses sight of this truth, and sinks back into himself, and so becomes evil,—'*we have an Advocate with the Father, Jesus Christ the righteous.*' The final blow is not given to the Accuser till these great words are uttered. At each act of transgression he renews the argument. You are again evil—consciously, inwardly evil. You cannot deny it. After all that has been done for you, the bond is broken again. And then come the old efforts to restore the union, and bring about the reconciliation. The sin-offering and peace-offering must again be presented; the first-born of the body must once more be given for the sin of the soul. The Father of all must be persuaded to forgive the sin which the child has committed; which means to excuse the penalty which the child has incurred.

St. John cuts short all such schemes, and the argument by which they are justified, with the words, '*If any man sin, we have an Advocate with the Father, Jesus Christ the righteous.*' It is not true that the evil act now, any more than before, has severed the bond between the creature and the Creator, between the child and the Father. The Lamb slain before the foundation of the world, the Lamb slain on the cross at Calvary, is still the Lamb in the midst of the throne; He, in whom God created the worlds; He, in whom God has loved the world; He whom God has given up for the world; He is still, as ever, the Mediator, in whom we are at one with Him, in whom we may draw nigh to Him. No possible act by which man denies and sets at nought the eternal law of the universe, can make it cease to be a law. God's constitution cannot perish, because men's consciences tell them that they are violating it, and that by no other law can they live.

He who understands this to be the case, will not endure to remain under the yoke of sin. As long as it is a question, whether he cannot find out some way of adjusting the quarrel, of pacifying the judge, he will tamper with the evil, get as much enjoyment of it as he can, hug it with a mixture of love and loathing. When he knows that there is a way out of it, and that God is leading him along in that way, and that Jesus Christ the righteous is the way, he will desert the false and dark road in which he has been walking, he will begin to think of God as a Refuge and a Father.

Christ speaks of Himself as the Way to the Father. The beloved disciple, who records that expression, speaks of Him as the Advocate, or Paraclete, with the Father. If we apply what was said of the word Paraclete in its other application to this case, we shall not easily suppose that Christ is called an Advocate because He beseeches the Lord of all to do any act which it is not His own perfect Will to do. But He, who knew what was in man, saw how natural such a thought would be to the sensualised and darkened heart. Therefore, he used those remarkable words in his last conversation with His disciples—the one in which He spoke of sending them the Comforter: '*I say not that I will pray the Father for you; for the Father Himself loveth you, because ye have loved me, and have believed that I came forth from God.*' This was said an hour or two before all those disciples forsook him and fled. He surely intended them to understand by it that His Father's love was not the consequence of any act of His, of any petitions of His; but that His acts and petitions were pure, and holy, and divine,—because they were the expressions of the Father's love, because they were the exact and perfect response to it. The same inference follows still more directly from the passage which introduces the text. The whole of it, as we have seen, turns upon the assertion, that Christ showed forth the Life that was first in God; that He brought the assurance, which was so much at variance with the notions of men, that He was Light, and in Him was no darkness.

I am almost ashamed to argue this point with *you*. For when did any righteous advocate seek to pervert the course of law, and to bring any partial influence to bear on the mind of the judge? When did he acknowledge to himself any other object than that of aiding the judge's own desire to ascertain the truth? And if this is so among us, who are so imperfect; if we feel that any other rule than this is immoral, and that all practice ought continually to be rectified by reference to this standard; how can we ever attribute an advocacy to Jesus Christ the righteous, which is of any other character, which would defeat the ends of righteousness? It is most needful that we should clear our minds upon this subject, and should allow no notions which are deduced from the impure habits of earth, to soil our idea of the kingdom and order which is altogether pure and holy. We can cast stones at other people with great readiness; we can complain of the carnal and dark thoughts which prevail in some countries, respecting the intercession and advocacy of saints, and of the way in which those thoughts have darkened the sense of actual right and wrong in the minds of those who cherish them, and have turned them away from the service of God to the service of vanity. We *may* make the complaint, and in fear and trembling bless God for having freed us from some of the temptations to an error, which is akin to all the worst tendencies of our hearts, as it touches very closely upon some of their higher and better aspirations. But if we suppose we are free from the evil part of this tendency, because it can *only* take this form of pleading for the prayers of saint; or that it will not take that form, or some more corrupt and idolatrous form in our country, and our own selves, unless we are watching against the root and principle of it; we shall find, too late, how we have been deceived. So long as there is the least lingering thought that Christ is an Advocate for us, to protect us from the wrath or ill-will of the Father; that He has some affection or tenderness for us which the Father has not; so long there lies in us the germ of all the corruptions that we attribute to Popery; yes, and of all that do exist, and ever have existed, in Paganism. I say *the least lingering thought*; for we are often very indignant when we find our belief put into words. We may say, honestly, we have not meant that; it is too shocking. And yet we may be cherishing a principle, often acting upon it, suffering it to lie side by side with some better one, which we never try to separate from it,—and this principle, if we dared express it, would take the shape we shrink from. I, therefore, earnestly conjure you all, for the sake of yourselves, and of your children, who will surely carry into its developments any falsehood which you have allowed to remain in the seed, that you bring your feeling about this advocacy of Christ to the light and test of the Scriptures. I have tried to show you, for I consider it important to do so in this congregation, that, even if we give the word its forensic signification, it will not support any such conclusion as the one I have condemned, until we have made that signification dishonest and immoral. But, I must again remind you, that this forensic sense does not properly appertain to the original word. The Paraclete is the Advocate only so far as he is the person who may be always called in as a friend, adviser, helper, counsellor. In this sense, the Spirit is said to be a Paraclete. In this sense, if we follow the analogy of Scripture, Christ the righteous is said to be the Paraclete with the Father. In the language of the Book of Proverbs, '*He was with Him, as one brought up with Him before the worlds were.*' In the language of the Epistle to the Hebrews, '*He is the brightness*

of His Father's glory, the express image of His Person.'
To believe that He who has been manifested to us, who has taken our nature, who has died our death, is indeed with Him, and that not as an accuser but a brother; is the sharer of His counsels; the utterer of His inmost heart; that in Him, and not through any other medium, He sees us, so that we may verily claim to be righteous, because He is righteous; at one with each other, because He is one with all of us; at one with the Father, because He is one with Him; this is, indeed, strength and comfort, and a mighty power, for casting down the accuser; a powerful warrant for repelling and throwing off our sins; for flying from every enemy into God's holy presence. It would be an ineffectual defence against one who charges us with that essential radical evil, which is contrary to God's Nature, and makes us incapable of blessedness, to say: 'But we have an Advocate, who urges His 'prayer and His Sacrifice, to save us from the conse-'quences or punishment of this evil.' Such a conception darkens all our apprehensions of the mind of Him with whom we seek to be reconciled, and of Christ who came to reveal His mind. It bewilders, instead of purging, the conscience. But to be able to say; 'We know that there is at the right hand of God one in 'our very nature, one who has sounded the depths of 'death and the grave, and hell; one, in whom He 'delights; one, in whom He has reconciled the world 'to Himself; one, in whom He is eternally reconciled

'to it;' this is emancipation, not from the darkness of the future only, but from the misery of the present, and of the past. In it lies not that peace which the world gives and takes away, but the peace of God which passes all understanding.

And here, then, lies the connection between this subject of Intercession, and that of Sacrifice. That you may feel how they are related, I have joined the first verse of this chapter with the second, though that is one upon which I have spoken already, when I was trying to ascertain the meaning of the word Propitiation, and the use of it in the Epistle to the Romans. We saw there how altogether foreign that idea of the ἱλασμὸς or ἱλαστήριον, which identifies it with some attempt to make God propitious, was from the mind of either apostle. The ἱλασμὸς, or Propitiation—for I did not object to the word when we had found the divine signification of it—*was set forth by God*; it was declared to be, just as the Mercy-seat in the Old Tabernacle was, just as all the sacrifices in that tabernacle were—His own declaration of His own will and purpose to men; His own way of reducing their will and purposes into submission to His, into harmony with His. Christ, in this mighty and wonderful sense was declared to be the Propitiation, because He was the manifestation of God's righteousness in the forgiveness of sin; because His sacrifice and offering up of Himself was at once the most perfect exhibition of the will of the Father, and of the voluntary surrender of the Son to this will, of His delight to do it. Such a Mercy-seat, such a Propitiation, such a restoring of the lost, such a reconciliation of God with his rebellious children, the Cross of Calvary was. The Cross gathered up into a single transcendent act the very meaning of all that had been, and all that was to be. God was there seen in the might and power of His Love, in direct conflict with Sin, and Death, and Hell, triumphing over them by sacrifice. But if this was so, that Cross must testify of Him who is with the Father now exhibiting that obedience of which this was the consummate token. It must testify of Him who lives for ever and ever, upholding all things and all men, by that obedience; who will be always the Mercy-seat, the Propitiation, the Living Bond between God and His universe. The reconciliation has been made in Him, by His Sacrifice. It can continue only in Him; there can be no intercourse and fellowship between heaven and earth, except in Him. Whenever any other way than this shall be devised by men; any way to God by their own high imaginations, or by their intercessions and sacrifices; or by the intercession and sacrifice of any intermediate power and helper; then it must be proclaimed more and more loudly: 'None of these schemes can avail 'you; they will not deliver you from sin; they will 'fasten the chains of sin more closely about you; they 'will bring your consciences into the very bondage 'from which God is seeking to set them free. One

'Sacrifice—the Sacrifice of God Himself—has been
'made once for all. He who has offered it, is the
'Mediator between you and God. You can only know
'what God's mind and will is toward you and to all
'men, when you behold it in His acts—His sufferings;
'these tell you that there is an Unchangeable Friend,
'an Eternal High-priest, in whom the Creator and
'creature are for ever atoned.'

I have touched here upon the topic which I said last Sunday it was a special object of the Epistle to the Hebrews to expound, the essential connexion between the Sacrifice and the Priest; neither being perfected till they were united in the same Person. I shall not follow out to-day that great subject, which has so many aspects, of the deepest concernment for all times, and for none more than ours. But in preparation for what I may, if God permit, say of it hereafter, I would earnestly remind you, that I have been preaching to-day the doctrine which was proclaimed with such power at the Reformation; the doctrine which made the whole world at that time to shake and upheave. I have been preaching it, not as it was preached then in the terms of St. Paul, but in the terms of St. John. There is the most essential and absolute agreement between them. *God the Father has justified us from all things from which we could not be justified by any law. Christ has redeemed us from the curse of the Law, being made a curse for us. Christ has come, made of a woman under the Law, that we might receive the adoption of sons*

s

The Spirit beareth witness with our spirit that we are sons of God. This is St. Paul's Gospel. *We declare unto you the Eternal Life, which comes from the Father, in whom is light and no darkness. We declare unto you Christ the Paraclete with the Father, the Propitiation for the sins of the whole world. And it is the Spirit that beareth witness, because the Spirit is truth.* This is St. John's Gospel. Oftentimes we fancy that we accept the one, while we turn away from the other; but there will come a sifting which will show us whether we believe either. It is possible for men to speak much of justification, and to suppose that it is some act of theirs which justifies, not God Himself; it is possible for them to speak of Christ's redemption, and to suppose that He redeems them out of the hands of God, not brings them to Him; it is possible for them to speak of the Spirit bearing witness that they are sons of God, and to suppose that its witness depends upon some feelings, or tempers, or experiences, which separate them from their fellow-creatures. In that case, the faith which we boast of as having descended to us from the Reformation, is a mere heirloom, not a possession at all; and all the warmth with which we proclaim our determination to keep it, only shows that we feel how insecure our title to it is. And then we must go to St. John's words. We must affront men—for it is the greatest affront to the proud religionist—with the declaration of God's absolute and universal truth and love; with the assertion that Christ is the Propitiation for the sins of the whole world; that He is the Intercessor and Priest for man; and with the awful words—awful to every one who hears them, most awful to us who preach them: *'If a man say, I love God, and hateth his brother, he is a liar; for he that loveth not his brother whom he hath seen, how can he love God whom he hath not seen?'* These words, not by their softness and tenderness, but by their tremendous severity, drive us to some other ground of hope than our own belief or our own feelings. They force us back upon God's love in Christ as the only refuge from our unbelief, as the only power by which we can be reformed. They force us to say, 'Father, we have 'sinned against our brother, and against thee; 'oh, deliver us from our sins—from our distrust, our 'heartlessness, our hopelessness—in Him, and for His 'sake, whom thou lovest, and who, because thy love 'was burning Him and consuming Him, gave Himself 'up for us all, that we might enter into thy presence, 'and be partakers of thy nature.'

SERMON XVII.

CHRIST THE HIGH-PRIEST.

(Lincoln's Inn, 6th Sunday after Trinity, July 23, 1854.)

'For every high-priest taken from among men is ordained for men in things pertaining to God, that he may offer both gifts and sacrifices for sins: who can have compassion on the ignorant, and on them that are out of the way; for that he himself also is compassed with infirmity. And by reason hereof he ought, as for the people, so also for himself, to offer for sins. And no man taketh this honour unto himself, but he that is called of God, as was Aaron. So also Christ glorified not himself to be made an high-priest; but he that said unto him, Thou art my Son, to-day have I begotten thee. As he saith also in another place, Thou art a priest for ever after the order of Melchisedec. Who in the days of his flesh, when he had offered up prayers and supplications with strong crying and tears unto him that was able to save him from death, and was heard in that he feared; though he were a Son, yet learnt he obedience by the things which he suffered; and being made perfect, he became the author of eternal salvation unto all them that obey him; called of God an high-priest, after the order of Melchisedec.'—HEBREWS v. 1-10.

EVERY reader has perceived that two priesthoods are spoken of in this passage, and in the Epistle to which it belongs; one is designated by the name of Aaron;

one, by the name of Melchisedec. But it should be observed, that in the case of the two priesthoods as in the case of the two Covenants, of which I spoke last Whitsunday, we are told, first of what is common to them both; then of the points which distinguish them.

I. Having spoken, at the end of the last chapter, of Jesus as the High-priest who had passed into the heaven; who was touched with the feeling of men's infirmities; who had been in all points tempted like as men were, yet without sin; through whom they might draw nigh to God with full assurance of faith; the writer proceeds to declare the characteristics which must meet in the priest, those which belong to the very nature and essence of his office. *Every high-priest taken from among men, is ordained for men, in things pertaining to God, that he may offer both gifts and sacrifices for sin.* There is great carefulness and elaboration in this definition. Each clause, and each member of each clause, has been weighed and stands out distinctly. Where there is any vagueness the vagueness is suggestive; we see why there could not be greater accuracy without a further and higher explanation; we are led on towards that explanation.

The Jew would feel instantly,—the words of his Law being his instructors,—that he must learn what was implied in the existence of the priests generally, from that which was true of Aaron the high-priest. He must not ascend to him from those who belonged to his race and progeny; he must understand them from what was first declared of him. The high-priest, therefore, forms the subject of the definition; of him it is said that he is *taken from among men*; He must be one of the race; he must not be above it, if by above is meant estranged from it—having interests of his own or a character of his own, which keep him at a distance from any of its members. And this because he is ordained *for men*. He is to act for his people, he is to represent them. Every sentence in the books of Exodus or Leviticus, which treats of the functions of Aaron, assumes this to be the case. He bears the names of the twelve tribes upon his breastplate; each man who comes to the door of the tabernacle claims that he should speak and act for him. He was to speak and act for the nation, and for the individuals who composed it in various capacities. Even the leper who was separated from the congregation, who proclaimed himself unclean, had a right to demand the inspection and help of the priest. But however various, however earthly, some of those duties might seem to be, they all imported that he was ordained for men *in things pertaining to God*. His existence presumed the existence of an Invisible Being with whom men had to do: presumed that this Being was not separate from men, but was governing all, even the vulgarest events of their lives. The priest stood forth before his countrymen as a continual witness of this truth. If God was not; if He was a great way off; if He was only an ultimate postulate, a Hercules' Pillar of the universe; not a living, acting, working Being;

not one seeking to keep up an intercourse with His creatures; then the priest meant nothing. His name and position were a lie; he had no business in the world, and the world had no business with him. Still there is a phrase necessary to denote him, which is perplexing, and which is intended to perplex us. He is *ordained, or set up*. Who ordains, or sets him up? How does he come among a people, or gain any authority over them? Do they establish him? Does a mere law or decree of one age or another establish him? Whence, then, proceeds the decree? How does it distinguish its object? Whence arises the obligation to obey it? These questions must not be answered for awhile. It is the very design of the Epistle to make the Jewish Christian pause and consider whether he knew the answer to them, and how it might be arrived at. In the meantime the writer proceeds to a point in his description about which there could be no hesitation. The high-priest is appointed '*to offer gifts and sacrifices for sins.*' This, all would admit, was his principal, his characteristic, function; whatever else he did must find its explanation in this. The men from whom he was taken, the men for whom he stood, required that he should present their gifts and their sin-offerings to Him from whom they believed their good things came; to Him against whom they believed they had sinned. If he was God's priest, if the office was not a dream, it was not only *man* who demanded the gifts and the sacrifices. God demanded them; God appointed them. Again, whatever was his function—whatever special act he had to do—there was a condition or character presupposed in that work; presupposed in all that had been said of his being taken from men—of his speaking for men,—of his presenting offerings for the sins of men. He must have the capacity of sympathising with them. He must know what they are wanting, suffering, seeking for. This sympathy cannot be limited to the wise, to those who know the right and the wrong, to those who have an apprehension of the Divine Will. It cannot be limited to the well-behaved, the respectable, the orderly. It must be emphatically with those that are *ignorant and out of the way*. And it cannot be obtained at second hand; not through the condescension and tenderness which a being exempt from peril may feel for those who are exposed to it. The only security for the kind of compassion which his service demands from him, is that he himself is compassed with infirmity; that he knows the evil, inwardly, intimately, which other men suffer for, and need to be loosed from.

'*By reason hereof,*' the writer goes on, '*he ought, as for the people, so for himself, to offer for sins.*' The sacrifice is not something which has to do with them and not with him. It has not *more* to do with them than with him. On the contrary, the sacrifice for the nation can only be presented by a man who is one of the nation—a participator in its evil doings, and in its punishments. And he is not fit to present the sacrifice for any individual if he thinks that he is exempt from the secret root of the evil, whence the evil that individual confesses has been derived; if he supposes himself free from the possibility of falling into his evil act; if he does not think that the principle is more malignant, more directly opposed to God, than the act is.

But the word that was left in a certain dimness and mist must be cleared up. The idea of the priest is not *satisfied* by this description of the sympathising man; any more than by the description of the mere official who presents the gifts and sacrifices : '*No man,*' it is said, '*taketh this honour unto himself, but he that is called of God, as was Aaron.*' A great many, unquestionably, had taken this honour to themselves, in every country of the world; they had claimed, on the strength of a sagacity and knowledge above their brethren, a right to teach them about invisible things, about the gifts and sacrifices which would make them most acceptable to the rulers of the world above or below. But they had all *assumed* a vocation; they had all brought tokens, such as they were, of a divine appointment. Only so far as they could make these tokens credible to the people for whom they professed to speak and act, had they been honoured at all. Everywhere, therefore, people confessed that the true priest should come *to* them, though he must also come *from* them—that God must send him; though he must not be a superior angel or demigod, who knew nothing of them and could not care for them. The writer, without saying that the priests of other nations had *not* a divine vocation,—without saying that they may not have mixed the falsehood of their hearts with truths which came to them from heaven,—assumes that the high-priest of *his* nation, that Aaron, was called of God. He was writing to Jews; he had not, therefore, to make good the position. Nor might he, perhaps, have taken that pains, if he had been addressing Gentiles. To each race—to all men—the calling must make itself good by the effect which it produces, by the testimony which is borne of it in the hearts of individuals and in the life of societies; if God does not support it by better evidences than those which are put forth by apologists, *they* will prove very impotent indeed. The Jew, who had been faithful to his light, knew what he owed to the conviction that God had established an intercourse with His creatures; that he had not left them to grope in idolatry and devil-worship—propitiating malignant powers, in groves and high places, with human victims. The Gentile who had been involved in that misery, did not want arguments to persuade him that, if he was raised out of *it*, God must point the way, and lead him along in it. But the Jew *did* want to know that the law, which had appointed Aaron and his sons to their work, had some deeper foundation than itself, or than an arbitrary purpose in the Lawgiver to select one people and exclude others. The Gentiles *did* want to know that the law which appointed Aaron was not one that said

to them,—' You have no part or lot with God; there
'is no priest or sacrifice appointed for you. You
'must go on making priests and inventing sacrifices
'for yourselves, and so become each day more igno-
'rant and out of the way, more alienated from the
'mind and will of Him who created you, more in-
'capable of finding Him out.' I say, both Jew and
Gentile wanted to be told whether there was an actual,
original, eternal relation between God and them; or
whether it was an artificial, legal, formal relation, which
institutions had created, and which would perish if
they perished. But, if possible, the Jew required this
information more than the Gentile; for if no such
eternal relation existed, the holy men of his land had
been walking in a shadow, had been uttering visions
when they had seen nothing; had been deceiving
their countrymen and themselves. Those who put the
Law and the Covenants, and the Sacrifices and the
Priesthood, for the God who had appointed the Law
and the Covenants, and the Sacrifices and the Priesthood, or supposed that they created the bond between
Him and His creatures, of which they bore witness,
were hastening towards the deepest unbelief—far more
rapidly than those who had come to fancy that all the
divine signs and ordinances were mere names and
fictions.

II. Accordingly, this is the subject to which the writer
of the Epistle continually recurs, and which is prominent before all others in our text. But now that we

are come to the point, at which we pass from that which is common in the priesthoods to that which separates them, you will observe how skilfully the transition is effected, and how much pains are taken that we shall not forget the resemblance between the eternal priesthood and the temporary. '*Even so,*' he says, after asserting Aaron to have been a priest who did not take the honour to himself, but was called to it by God—'*Even so Christ glorified not Himself to be made a highpriest, but He that said unto Him, Thou art my Son; this day have I begotten Thee.*' Here was the original and divine appointment,—that which lay beneath the divine decrees and ordinances which had been established upon earth, and which, by their nature, were confined to particular nations and tribes. This eternal and absolute Will of God is the root from which all the order of the universe proceeds. But this Will can only express itself in a divine *Relation*—'*Thou art my Son?*' The Sonship of Christ is the basis of all intercourse between God and man. The possibility of a priesthood—the fact of a priesthood—rests upon that relation, and not upon any law spoken on Sinai, or at the door of the Tabernacle. The writer of the Epistle had been already exhibiting this Sonship as the foundation of the Jewish economy. He now fixes on that part of the economy which, though it had been confined by tribe barriers, had yet always seemed on the point of bursting through those barriers, and asserting its divine character. He takes a well-known passage from one of the Psalms; he claims it as a witness that faithful Jews demanded another kind of priesthood from that which they prized and loved as God's gift,—that they demanded it because God Himself had educated them to feel the need of it. He investigates the nature of the priesthood which the Psalmist must have intended to indicate by the name Melchisedec. He shows, from the time to which Melchisedec is assigned in the book of Genesis, and from the brief record of Abraham's homage to him, that he could not have belonged to the chosen race, or have holden his office in virtue of any tribe designation. Nothing is said of his parentage or birth, or of the origin of his authority—yet he is called a priest. And the Psalmist recognises a priesthood like his, as the one from which every other is derived— as that for which every other must be a preparation. Bringing the two passages of the old Scriptures together, the writer of the Epistle affirms that they explain each other. The order of Melchisedec is established by the words, '*Thou art My Son.*' The manifestation of the Son is the fulfilment of the Psalmist's longing; the revelation of *the priest for men in things pertaining to God*, of Him who is in the truest, fullest sense *called of God to be a high-priest*.

But how could one so called, possessing so transcendent a dignity, sympathise with those that were ignorant and out of the way—not as a stranger, but as one sharing their guilt, compassed with their infirmity? This is the question with which the last passage in the text grapples. '*Who in the days of His flesh, when He had offered up prayers and supplications, with strong crying and tears, unto Him that was able to save Him from death, and was heard in that He feared; though He were a Son, yet learned He obedience by the things which He suffered.*' You will recognise in this description just what every higher painter has striven to set forth in the Man of Sorrows: not only a passive, submissive sufferer; but one who agonised, who resisted unto blood, who trod the winepress alone. The strong crying and tears, the sense of death, are just what the Evangelists present in a few simple, awful words, when they relate the night in Gethsemane; just what the Church has attributed, not to a single moment of our Lord's life in the flesh, but, in a most wonderful sense, to the whole of it. The conflict, as it is set before us, here as well as there, is intensely personal. An unutterable horror is assailing the Son of God; He is crying for deliverance from it. What is this horror; how may we dare to conceive of it? The words on the Cross utter what it was; but for them we must be silent. The sense of separation from the Father; the sense of a mass of evil, around, above, beneath, pressing upon Him, belonging to Him, which was contrary to God, which was tearing the world from God—this, surely, if we may trust the words of inspiration, was that death —that eternal death—from which He cried to be delivered. But in entering into that anguish, in bearing that death, in casting Himself upon His Father to deliver

Him from it, He was entering into human anguish, He was bearing man's death, He was acquiring that compassion for the most ignorant, for those who had wandered furthest from the divine fold, which none can have who is not compassed with infirmity. What sacrifice could be like this? what could a High-priest of the universe offer that was so absolutely His own; so much His very self? And yet, what sacrifice could a high-priest of the universe offer, that was so entirely for the sins of the world? Thus, therefore, is that mighty difference between the two offerings, which I dwelt on in a former discourse, inseparably connected with the difference between the two priests. The one enters into the holy place every year, with the blood of others; the other comes in the end of the world, to put away sin by the sacrifice of Himself. We are told there, that the blood of bulls and calves could not put away sin; because sin is separation from God, and their blood could establish no connexion with God. Here we have the whole reason why His blood *could* take away sin; because He who offers it is one with God; because under all the pressure of that which divides from God, He cleaves to Him, trusting in Him through all, certain that neither life nor death, nor principalities nor powers, shall be able to separate Him—or therefore the nature which He has taken—from His Father's love.

Therefore, these strange, amazing words are added. *'Though He was a Son, yet learned He obedience by those things which He suffered.'* Everything which threatened that obedience, brought it out more fully, more perfectly; each new experience was to Him a new lesson in trust and dependence. Nothing was anticipated; each moment brought its own battle, its own strength, its own victory. The effort of faith that was needed for the boy would not have sufficed for the youth; but it was perfect for its own occasion. The temptation after the baptism could be answered with the words, '*Get thee behind me, Satan. Thou shalt worship the Lord thy God, and Him only shalt thou serve;*' the temptation in the garden could only be met with, '*Father, if it be possible, let this cup pass from me;*' the temptation on the Cross must be overcome with, '*Father, into thy hands I commend my Spirit.*' In each state there is a new exercise of obedience; but the complete Son is only manifested in the final one.

And having been heard in that strong crying, and having been *perfected* through that death, '*He is become the Author of eternal salvation to all that obey Him.*' In His own person He has vindicated for them the right of Sonship; the privilege of fellowship; the salvation from that death which consists in separation from God; the eternal life which consists in union with Him. The Priest has asserted His name, has made the Sacrifice, has established His office. That office is to last for ever; founded upon His filial relation; embodied in His self-oblation; holding mankind now and always to Him who created us in His image, who has delivered us from the foes which assailed His only-begotten Son, who in Him has adopted us to be sons. Oh, never for a moment let us think of the Sacrifice apart from the Priest; or the Priest as separate from those for whom he prayed, that they might be one with Him! Never let us think of the Priest as another than the Son who was before the worlds were; or of the Son as doing any work but that to which the love of the Father called Him, and His own obedience fulfilled!

It is this idea of sacrifice, not as first rising from man to God, but as coming down from God upon man—as exhibited in His acts, as expressing and accomplishing His will—which I have been tracing through the histories of sacrifice which the Bible records, beginning from that of Abel; and which I have contrasted with the proud sacrifice, whereby man seeks to escape from the punishment of the sin he has committed, and to convert God to his own evil mind. All who trusted God and gave up themselves, felt that there must be an obedience, and a sacrifice which was the ground of theirs; an obedience and a sacrifice which was essentially divine, and, therefore, essentially human. We have now reached the climax of these histories. I shall endeavour, indeed, to show you in two more sermons how all our present life, how all our thoughts of that which is to be for ourselves and the world, are determined by this great principle. But for the satisfaction of the awful doubts and anxieties, of which all schemes of sacrifice have been the expression, my text of this afternoon is

T

sufficient. It solves the great sphynx riddle. That riddle presents itself under various aspects to various minds. There are some who feel themselves lost amidst the multitudinous forms of Nature, and of that other world which Art has called into existence; and who ask whether there is no Centre on which the soul can repose, without hiding itself in its own darkness and solitude? Believe that the Creative Word is the source of that endless variety of objects, of those thoughts which are ever creating or begetting new thoughts, and new images; believe that that Word has been made flesh and dwelt among us, and you have the Centre you seek. You need not refuse to reverence Nature or Art, and yet you may find your life and dwelling-place in God. There are some who feel that a crowd of events and incidents and activities is pressing out the life of individuals; that all personal sorrows and hopes are stifled amidst general interests,—and who would fain assert that each soul is sacred and infinite. Believe in one, who *was in all points tempted like as we are*; who bore the sins of each man on Himself; who was heard in that he feared; who has entered into the presence of God, to utter the cry of every captive, to present the blood that is shed for every man; who is yet the King of all, the Head of the Church, the Priest of the Universe; and you can find that the individual man is only the more distinct, and the more wonderful, because he is but one of a Society. There are some who are overwhelmed by the miseries of the earth, on which mountains of evil seem to have been growing, from the day that Adam fell. Believe in that strong crying of the Son of Man, and the Son of God. Believe that it was heard against sin, death and hell; then we shall be sure that every tyranny, and every anarchy, is falling before Him; that every enemy of the earth and of God must be put under his footstool; that peace and freedom must prevail wherever strife and slavery have been, because God has willed it, and Christ has done his will on earth as it is done in heaven.

SERMON XVIII.

THE ADORATION OF THE LAMB.

(*Lincoln's Inn, 7th Sunday after Trinity, July* 30, 1854.)

'Unto him that loved us, and washed us from our sins in his own blood, and hath made us kings and priests unto God and his Father; to him be glory and dominion for ever and ever. Amen.'
REVELATION i. 5, 6.

MANY persons seem to fancy that the Apocalypse consists mainly of prophecies, or intimations concerning that which shall come to pass in the latter days. That it contains such prophecies,—that its lessons respecting the future should be deeply pondered, because they are lessons upon which we may act—not mere guesses about times and seasons, with which we may amuse ourselves—I thoroughly believe. But I do not think we shall find out their precious import, unless we dwell earnestly upon such a passage as the one I have read to you; the language of which, you will perceive, points to that which is, and to that which has been done.

Some may suppose it a mere interjectional sentence,

the expression of a strong passionate feeling, not a part of the substance of the work, not one which can give us any hint respecting its character. The more you read the Apocalypse, the more you will feel that thanksgivings and doxologies of this kind are inseparable from its texture; that you would lose its meaning and purpose if you lost them. Flourishes of rhetoric do not belong to a Bible: they belong, least of all, to that book of the Bible which gathers its previous revelations into one; which explains the very nature of revelation; which shows us in whom, and for what ends, God has revealed Himself, and does reveal Himself in one age or another.

But such a book is the very one, in which words that can no longer be profaned to purposes of ambition and display, acquire their full force as expressions of the mind of God, as the echo of that mind in man. He that bore witness of the Word of God, and of Jesus Christ, and of the things which he saw, had learnt that from that Word all the life of things and of men was derived; that the crucified man was that Word made flesh; that all his visible acts of power and meekness were the outcomings of that which eye had not seen nor ear heard. He had learnt that the Word had been on earth, and suffered and died, that the enslaved spirit and body of his creatures might be set free, that the tongue of the stammerer and of the dumb might be loosed, and might speak plainly. He was claiming the redemption which had been won for him, he was exercising the freedom of a spiritual creature, when he sent back his ascription of praise to Christ, who had loved him and emancipated him.

According to one reading of the text, the word 'loosed,' or ' emancipated,' ought to be substituted for our word 'washed.' I do not say which is the best reading; there are internal, as well as external arguments in favour of each. The word 'blood,' and the analogy to Baptism, made our translators partial to one phrase; the perpetual allusions to Redemption in connexion with sins, may incline some to adopt the other. A more important hint is conveyed by a change of the tense in the preceding word ἀγαπῶντι for ἀγαπήσαντι. 'To Him who loveth,' for 'to Him who loved us.' The present tense seems certainly more in harmony with the spirit of the beloved disciple generally, and with the context of this passage particularly. A third variation in this passage introduces some difficulty into the construing of it; for 'kings,' in the last clause, we are told that we ought to read 'kingdom.' In that case we can only suppose that St. John here, as in many other places, was falling back into Old Testament forms of expression; that the phrase '*kingdom of priests,*' with which he was familiar, was dwelling in his mind; and that he did not take any pains to translate it grammatically into the language in which he was writing. The meaning cannot be essentially different from that which our version embodies. I shall, therefore, adhere to it. Let us now consider the passage clause by clause.

I. '*To Him that hath loved, or that loveth.*' Since there cannot be a moment's doubt that Jesus Christ is the object of this ascription, the thought may easily intrude itself, 'After all, it is to Him, and not to the Father, 'that the most inspired teachers turn in their moments 'of rapture; His love presents itself to them as their 'real strength and consolation; upon it they rest; what 'lies beyond it is dark, if not terrible.' That you may be understood how far this suggestion is reasonable, turn to the opening of the fifth verse; consider the titles by which our Lord is there denoted. Pause especially on the first of them. He is called '*the faithful witness.*' A faithful witness to what? St. John must interpret himself: '*This is the message,*' he says, in his first Epistle, '*which we have heard of Him, and declare unto you, that God is light, and in Him is no darkness at all.*' Or, take the report which he gives of our Lord's own last prayer with his Apostles, on the night before the crucifixion, that which we were reading in our course of lessons yesterday: '*O righteous Father, the world hath not known Thee; but I have known Thee, and these have known that Thou hast sent me. And I have declared unto them Thy name, and will declare it; that the love wherewith Thou hast loved me may be in them, and I in them.*' Jesus Christ according to St. John, according to Himself, is the faithful witness of His Father. The world had not known Him; it had suspected that in Him there was some darkness, some enmity towards His creatures; but He had known Him, and had come

forth to testify that in Him was no darkness at all.
Whatever love there was in Christ was first in Him, with
whom He dwelt, and from whom He came. Whoso
saw Him saw the Father. And so far is the Evangelist
from dwelling upon this love as something separate from
the love of God, as more worthy of the creature's trust
and reliance, that he can only depend upon it and rejoice
in it because he regards it as the perfect image and
reflex of that which is the Nature and Essence of God.

Most true, however, it is, that St. John does demand
a love which has not remained hidden, but which has
come forth into light and manifestation; most true it is
that he only pretends to know the unfathomable depth
below, through that form and those acts which belong
to the region of human thought, and sympathy, and
obedience. Christ has been the faithful witness of the
Father by bearing death, and being the first-begotten
from the dead. Unless He had sounded the abyss of
human misery, He would not have disclosed the abyss
of divine love; unless He had gone through that misery
and risen out of it, He could not have vindicated the
divine love from the greatest calumny of the Evil Spirit
against it. And unless He were indeed the Prince of
all the kings of the earth, He could not have brought
the love of heaven to bear upon the government and
transactions of the earth, nor have offered to the sons
of earth a continual refuge from their oppressors in the
Judge, before whom they are ever standing and receiving their sentence. Be assured, then, that Christ only

can love any because He dwells with Him who is love, and comes forth from Him; and that we never shall understand that love, if we do not behold it in the acts and sufferings of the Mediator.

II. To Him that loveth *us*. What is the limitation of this *us*? How are we to know who have been, who are included in it? St. John was the beloved disciple, the disciple who leaned on Christ's breast at the Last Supper. He does not fear to give himself the name; writing in his old age, with his heart humbled and broken, he still dares to claim it. And why may we suppose that the Divine Spirit permitted this boldness, and urged him to it? I think, because that Spirit was teaching and compelling him, more than all the other disciples, to show forth Christ's love, as having no partial ground, as resting on the eternal ground, and, therefore, as comprehending all within its circle. Supposing St. Paul or St. Peter had used this all-embracing language, it might have been said: 'Yes, but there was a special 'graciousness, a peculiar affection, altogether different 'from that which went forth upon you—how different 'from that which goes forth upon mankind!' St. John can say, 'Even so; I was the object of that affection, 'I was permitted to experience it. I never knew the 'fulness and tenderness of it better than I knew it at 'the Last Supper. And this is my privilege; to announce 'this love to you, that you may share it, that you may 'have fellowship, as I have, with the Father and with 'his Son, Jesus Christ.' I do not know how the axe could have been laid to any notions of a limited love, bestowed upon certain qualities, or attracted by a certain faith, more completely; or yet how it could be shown more completely that the love of Christ is not vague philanthropy, but personal, and living, meeting and awakening all the qualities and tendencies of the creatures on whom it is bestowed. Supposing we had the Epistles and Revelations of St. John, without being told anything of the relation in which he stood to the Son of man while he was upon earth, we might have been lost in the thought of a benevolence too vast and vague for any individual sympathy. If we had the record of St. John's place among the disciples, without hearing him declare the message which he had received from Christ, and which it was his work to proclaim to men, we should have found a precedent and a warrant for all that glorification of different saints, as objects of Christ's partial regard and mysterious favour, which have been so common, and so hurtful, in some parts of the Church; a kind of warrant for the notion, more prevalent in our day and more mischievous, that there are circles and schools which He favours, to the exclusion and condemnation of mankind at large. Now that the individual and the universal are so wonderfully combined in the lessons and the life of the same man; now that we know this to have been the great and distinguishing reward which was conferred on him above others, that he should tell all men what God felt to them, and had wrought for them; we are able to enter through the disciple into the mind of the Master, who suffered for all and for each; through the Master into the mind of the Father, who rules in the armies of heaven, and without whom not a sparrow falleth to the ground.

III. '*To Him that washed us.*' 'Hath washed' might be better, but there is no question that *this* word is in the past. Be the word λύσαντι or λούσαντι, the tense is the same. The Apostle is often very inattentive to tenses; he adopts a Hebrew freedom in the use of them; as if he would infuse into us the great Hebrew truth, that God is, and was, and is to come; that the Eternal has no portions nor divisions. But here he is exact; the washing or the deliverance has been effected; He that loveth us, hath given us this one solid and satisfactory proof of his love, the only one which could enable us to appreciate it, or partake of it.

The second '*us*' must, according to all reasonable interpretation, have the same force and dimensions as the first. Those whom He has washed, or set free, are those whom He loves. Yet there is a pretext for confining the word in the one use, which did not exist with respect to the other. Sins, as I have contended throughout these sermons, are actual, not metaphorical, chains. They bind the spirit as truly, as consciously, as material fetters ever have bound the body. Every one has, in a more or less degree, the sense and certainty of this bondage. The less we have of it, the more passively we are slaves; every attempt in man to raise himself is a tacit acknowledgment of it. But if so, how can we speak of *these* chains as having been actually broken for any one; how can we dare to speak of them as broken for all? Punishment we might think of as remitted for a whole set of beings, for a whole race; but sin, the cause of punishment, that of which each person must accuse himself, which is so intensely individual and inward; how can we for a moment speak of that as washed away, or taken from us, while we feel it in ourselves, while we see it multiplying and bringing forth new fruits in the world?

The question must be asked over again in this year 1854,—it must be asked as if it had never been asked before; though the Bible, the Christian Church, the Gospel which God has sent us to preach, have had no other purpose than to answer it. Unless we have courage to say to men, here and everywhere—to men of whose condition we know nothing, except that it is an evil one—'The chain of sin has been loosed for you— 'you have been cleansed from sins, emancipated from 'sins, by the blood of Christ'—we have no message to deliver from heaven to earth—we should not run—for we have no tidings which our brethren are concerned to hear. Unless we have courage to say in the most respectable, most religious congregation or circle of Englishmen,—' So long as any of you abide in evil 'practices, and habits, and principles, so long are you 'slaves, in spite of Christ's redemption,'—we are false witnesses of God, we are deceiving people with promises that will not be performed, with names and phrases that will prove their ruin. How may two such opposite statements be reconciled? How may we at once say, 'The emancipation has been effected; 'nothing can be more complete: there is a liberty with 'which Christ has made us free, one and all;' and yet acknowledge the more strongly, in the full length and breadth of it, the fact of the world's misery and wickedness; the fact that every man is a participator in it, and must seek every day a fresh purification,—must confess every day how great a weight is sitting upon him,—how feeble all those energies are with which he tries to cast it off?

You will see at once, if you turn to the confessions of different Churches, that they have been exercised with this difficulty, and that every one of them has attempted to assert the fact of a full and complete redemption, without explaining away experiences which it especially behoved them to recognise and to encounter. Our own Church is particularly distinct and strong in affirming the doctrine of the text. It speaks of Christ being 'A 'sacrifice, not only for the original guilt, but also for the 'actual sins of men.' The expression is remarkable: it takes for granted the redemption from original guilt— from *guilt* you will observe, not *punishment*—as that which was the common admitted belief of the whole Church, and goes on to affirm—what had been denied in a most practical manner—what the reformers were especially raised up to assert,—that the sacrifice was *also* the perfect means of deliverance from the sins which men were committing day by day. All I wish is, that preachers and hearers should enter into the sense of these words; that they should not merely repeat them, or confess their adherence to them, while, in fact, they are contradicting them, and setting up a directly opposite doctrine in place of them.

If we try to understand what man is, what the relation between God and man is, from the fall of Adam; if we take that as determining the condition of our race; we set at nought the letter and still more the spirit of our article. We deny that original guilt is taken away by the Sacrifice of Christ; we deny that that Sacrifice has established a perfect reconciliation between God and His creatures. And then whatever efforts we make to give a sense to the other words of the sentence,—however we may persuade ourselves that we do get rid of our actual sins by believing in Christ's sacrifice,—we shall find ourselves in continual embarrassments; explaining away the strong statement of yesterday by the weak one of to-day; trying to persuade men that they are redeemed, and pardoned, and new creatures; and then calling upon them to find reasons and proofs in themselves, which they honestly confess they cannot find, why these blessings, which others have not, belong to them. Whereas, if we will start, as the Church does, from the Incarnation and

Sacrifice of Christ, as being a full declaration concerning man and God; a full revelation of the nature of both, and of the causes which have separated them; a full proof that in Christ they are for ever atoned; then the sins of each particular man are interpreted by that one all-comprehensive statement of our Lord—'*He will convince the world of sin,* . . . *because they believe not on Me.*' There is no original guilt separating our race and kind from Him who created us in His own Son. The Fall is a fact in history, just as the Bible presents it to us; but it is not a fact from which we can dare to deduce the Law under which we are living and acting: for the Bible, in setting forth Christ as the Son of God and the Son of Man, as the Redeemer and Restorer of man to his union with His Father, and to all the spiritual freedom and prerogatives which that union implies, proclaims to us another Law, the only human Law; that law in our members which resists it, and brings us into captivity, being altogether inhuman, one that separates us from our brethren as much as it separates us from God.

Believing in Christ, we believe this; not believing in Him, we treat that law in our members as if it were some fatal necessity which forced us to sin; we yield to it; we become utterly enslaved by it; the appetite in us lives; the man in us dies. And what slays the tyrant and raises the dead? Nothing but this same news. 'Christ has come to deliver you; He has taken 'your nature and died for you.' The spirit, in its deep death-sleep, hears that voice, which had mingled in its dreams with the songs of earth and the laughs of evil spirits; it starts up with a wild fright; it finds that its true Lord and Brother was inviting it back to its native home. And how else does it recognise Him, but by that blood-token, by the hands and side, as having this right over it, this fellowship with it? What can it say but 'Thou hast set us free, Thou hast washed 'us from our sins in Thy blood. This united Thee to 'our death; this is the assurance that we are sharers in 'Thy life.'

IV. It is a King that our spirits cry for, to guide them, discipline them, unite them to each other; to give them a victory over themselves, a victory over the world. It is a Priest that our spirits cry for, to lift them above themselves to their God and Father; to make them partakers of His nature, fellow-workers in carrying out His purposes. Christ's Sacrifice is the one authentic testimony that He is both the King and Priest of men. But since He is come to make them like Him—since He has taken their flesh and blood that they might have His Sonship—they have a portion also in all that appertains to that Sonship. '*He has made us,*' says St. John, '*kings and priests unto God and His Father.*' The kingly right of government over the earth, which was assured to him at creation, is redeemed for him in Christ. Earth is the instrument of his purposes, not the mistress who may command him. But she is so, while he reclaims that other more precious prerogative of ruling himself, which Christ has also asserted for him, which in Christ's might, while he depends upon Him, he can exercise. And so we understand why kingly authority has been so venerable and dear in men's eyes; why it has also been at times so intolerable. While the King acts as God's minister, ruling himself, treating earthly things as gifts and talents for the use of men, he serves to awaken the sense of kingliness in his subjects. They become free in their spirits, and they have the self-restraint, the obedience of men. But when he is a slave, they become slaves; with the restless conviction that they were made for something better, meant to be like him who governs them; with the ignorant and fantastic dream that they should be better, if they could put themselves in his place, and have his opportunities of self-indulgence and self-destruction. He is the true King, who sacrifices himself that he may raise up a generation of kings; who are like him in proportion as they have his spirit of sacrifice.

And so it is with the other office. The Son of God is the Priest for ever, the sympathising Priest touched with the feeling of man's infirmities; because He is filled with the holiness and love of God; bearing the sins, because He is one with the All-Righteous. And he comes to make us priests; to give us all the power of offering up spiritual sacrifices to God; of offering up ourselves; of feeling with our brethren; of bearing their burdens; of entering into the holy place with them and for them; of presenting to them the image of Christ's Father and

U

their Father. Just so far as any priest on earth does this, just so far will he obtain the recognition that is good for him; not a better recognition than His Lord, but one that is the same in kind. He will help to raise up priests to God among those who do not bear that name officially. He will be ever leading men on to that spiritual freedom, without which they cannot serve the God whose name is the Redeemer. And it is because we who are named priests of God have so grievously forgotten this calling; have not believed that we possess it; have brought men into bondage instead of freedom; have neither felt with them nor with him who loves them, and has washed them in His blood! it is for this reason that we hear complaints of our craft which are just and reasonable, though the men who utter them may have a very dim and confused sense of the liberty which they want; and may only desire to be rid of us, that they may not be reminded of their spiritual rights, and may sink into brutes without compunction or remorse.

Therefore, brethren, this is the sum of what the Apostle tells us in this great ascription, and of what I have been trying to say to you in these Sermons on Sacrifice,—that we are all raised to a new and regenerate condition in Christ,—and that this is our true human condition,—and that it is one which we may all of us claim,—and that we shall only claim it when we believe that there is a Son of God and a Son of Man, who has delivered us by dying for us, and when we vindicate as the highest gift He can endow us with, as the greatest fruit of His Cross and Passion, the spirit of self-oblation, the spirit in which He offered Himself to God. Then we shall know that the Gospel is not a cunningly-devised fable; then we shall be certain that the blood has been poured out, that the redemption and reconciliation has been made; then we shall enter upon our kingly and priestly life. And since that life must be for our brethren as well as for ourselves, for men of every caste and character, we ought to know how we have a right to regard them; what we have a right to tell them, respecting themselves and respecting Him who created them. While we are uncertain about that point; while we do not know whether we are to fly from them as devils, or to recognise them as children of one Father; whether we are to esteem them as creatures whom he has doomed to destruction, or creatures whom He seeks to rescue from the destruction into which they fall through ignorance of Him, and of His purposes to them; I cannot understand how we can think one hopeful thought or speak one helpful word. But in believing the fact which our Catechism and our Articles, and the Bible far more mightily than either, proclaim, that man is a redeemed and restored creature, we do not,—as I have tried partly to show you to-day, as I hope more fully to show you next Sunday,—blink any of the facts which prove that the world is lying in wickedness; or check any of the hopes that it is to become a habitation of righteousness; we do not make ourselves fairer than we are; or lead any one to wish and pray less that he may rise to a holier and purer condition of being. The Sacrament of the Lord's Supper gathers up into itself all that I have been saying to you on Sacrifice; yea, and all that the Apostle is saying in the wonderful passage I have been commenting on. And while at that Feast we give thanks for a Sacrifice, an oblation and satisfaction, that has been made once for the sins of the whole world; while we join with angels and archangels round the throne, in praising for that finished Sacrifice which sets forth, as nothing else can, the thrice holy name of God; we come also to confess sins in ourselves, of which the remembrance is grievous, and the burden intolerable. We come to seek a Redemption for our own souls and bodies, and for the whole creation, from that travail and death which the Son of Man underwent for all. We come as citizens of a commonwealth over which Christ is the King of Kings and the High-priest, in which we ourselves are kings and priests; but we come certain that, unless God feeds us with the flesh and blood of His Son, we have no power to fulfil any of our tasks in that kingdom, to enjoy any of its immunities and rights. Our confidence is that He has provided the spiritual food, that He does awaken the spiritual appetite; that the blood of the Lamb which has been shed, has taken away the sins of the world, and that it has ower to take away the bitterness, and cowardice and torpor which are our daily individual sins. We can in that festival, we can in every act of our daily lives, give thanks unto Him who has washed us from our sins, and made us kings and priests to God; we can say, Glory and dominion be unto Him for ever; for we believe glory and dominion are His for ever. And we are sure that to this prayer and ascription of ours, God has given and will give His own Amen.

SERMON XIX.

THE WORD OF GOD CONQUERING BY SACRIFICE.

(*Lincoln's Inn, 8th Sunday after Trinity, August 6, 1854.*)

'And I saw heaven opened, and behold a white horse; and he that sat upon him was called Faithful and True, and in righteousness he doth judge and make war. His eyes were as a flame of fire, and on his head were many crowns; and he had a name written, that no man knew but he himself. And he was clothed with a vesture dipped in blood: and his name is called THE WORD OF GOD. And the armies which were in heaven followed him upon white horses, clothed in fine linen, white and clean. And out of his mouth goeth a sharp sword, that with it he should smite the nations: and he shall rule them with a rod of iron; and he treadeth the winepress of the fierceness and wrath of Almighty God. And he hath on his vesture and on his thigh a name written, KING OF KINGS, AND LORD OF LORDS.'—REVELATION xix. 11–17.

THERE have been many discussions about the time and place in which the battle described in this chapter has been, or shall be fought. I do not know which of the opinions on the subject is entitled to most regard. Each of them, I think, must have its value, for I find it difficult to conceive of any place and of any time, in which the combatants spoken of by the Apostle have not been fighting with each other; I am quite sure the fight will be more terrible before the end comes. Whatever place may not be the scene of it, I am convinced England cannot claim to be that place. To whatever distant times it may be prolonged, I would tell you with all earnestness, that we who are met here this afternoon are in the midst of it now. The thought may be an alarming one—if we lay it to heart, it will be;—but it is also a very cheering one. I know not any which may give us so much purpose and so much hope.

Are there any gifts which we feel to be so needful for us, as these? Are there any which we are so conscious of wanting? What a number of utterly purposeless men and women do we meet with, as we journey through the world! What noble powers do we see going to waste, because there is nothing to fix and concentrate them on one object! What fine affections are squandered upon nothing, or upon a multitude of nothings! What precious stores of information are accumulated only to be dissipated in talk! How, in severe moods, one condemns these misusers of time and opportunities! how, in kindlier moods, one mourns over them! Yet, in the midst of our censures or our sorrow, what proofs we have that we are labouring under the same infirmity! How continually we are reminded that we, too, have been chasing shadows; that we have been drawn aside after one tempting project or another; or that we have been merely revolving in a circle!

How many times our conscience whispers to us, that we have been merely carried along a current of customary notions and observances; that our acts have been determined by accidents and circumstances, not by our will!

And how much has the indifference and listlessness which we witness to do with want of hope? How strenuous, we are sure, some of the laziest people about us might become, if they had but any goal in the distance which might some day be reached. If for a moment they do catch sight of such a goal, if they only fancy that they do, what a movement there is in the midst of their torpor; how the dry bones shake, are ready almost to come together, to start up, to live. But it seems as if these impulses were to become rarer and rarer. We feel sometimes as if we were born into a busy, and excited, and yet into an exhausted age; when men, even boys, have become prematurely wise about the vanity of human wishes; when the words of preachers about the emptiness of pleasure and ambition, and the poor results of study and enterprise, are all too readily taken for granted. I do not mean that we pursue pleasure or profit less, but we pursue them without exhilaration. The appetite must be kept alive by continual excitements. The ordinary tradesman, and the man of fashion, seem as if they both required gambling to give them an interest in their different pursuits, and to preserve them from utter vacuity.

We have succeeded in persuading people that they have nothing to live for, that death has set its mark upon everything. They say, reasonably enough, that they do not want to come to church to be convinced of that, they are convinced of it already. Unhappily, we have convinced them of nothing else. We have spoken to them of a future state, which shall be altogether different from the present state. But, they say, that all the visions we have given them of it, when we wish to describe it in fair and glowing colours, are vague and indistinct; that there is nothing in them which a man, who is either occupied with the world, or sated with it, can take hold of. And if there were, they say they are reminded in all our discourses, that they have no part or lot in these anticipations. The happy future belongs to a few souls, who are fenced round, and distinguished, by inward signs and outward badges, from the race of which it is their misfortune to be members. The future state has nothing to present to that race generally but images of gloom and horror. So men on all sides of us affirm, and whether their complaint is reasonable or exaggerated, true or false, the result is evident. There is a decay of hope, and of all the moral strength which hope awakens. Men are not content with what they see about them, far less content with themselves, yet they do not look for anything higher or better. They do not think it is worth while to struggle to retain that which they have, any more than to grasp that which they have not. They expect changes, they assume them to be inevitable. But they expect no good from them, more than from the continuance of that which they find so wearisome. There is a sleepy, dreary, fatalism into which we are settling down. The sleep is disturbed from without by the noisy clatter of disputing sects, and by the groans of suffering multitudes. It is disturbed from within, by dreams of what we ought to do, of what we might be. We need something more than an earthly or a human voice to break that slumber, and prevent it from passing into death.

I believe that voice is speaking to us in the text. I need not repeat what I have said to you so often, that *the opening of heaven,* in this book, and elsewhere in Scripture, does not imply the discovery of a distant or future paradise, but of that kingdom of God which is in the midst of us; the divine order which is hidden from the eye, but apart from which nothing that the eye beholds has any meaning or substance. What was opened to the Seer at this time was then, as I believe, the mystery of our human condition, of the world within us and without us, of the power which is working for every man and against every man, of the relation in which every man stands to one of those powers and to the other, of the purpose which may govern every man's life, of the sure and certain hope which is set before mankind, a hope of which every man is an inheritor, if he does not declaim his manhood. Blessed be God! it is no sweet Arcadian picture of felicity which is offered to us here. Behind, indeed, there are visions of a most glorious peace, of a wonderful order,

of a new Jerusalem descending from God out of heaven.
But the way to them is through battle and blood. If it
were not so, these visions would have nothing to do
with us. We should say, They may be for some beings
of another mould, but we cannot be intended to realise
them. It is true that the Person whom St. John
saw, when the heaven was opened to him, was the same
whom Isaiah calls the Prince of Peace. But mark how
Isaiah introduces *his* description of that Prince, on
whose shoulder the government was to be: '*For every
battle of the warrior is with confused noise and garments
rolled in blood. But this shall be with burning and fuel
of fire.*' The battle which was to assert the Name, and
vindicate the rights, of the Child that was born, of the
Son that was given, would not be less terrible than
other battles. The very essence of all that was fiercest
in them, would be in it. If all peace was the efflux of
that peace which dwelt in Him, all war would be the
expression and outcoming of that in which He was the
Leader and Champion.

It is then very necessary, brethren, that we should
not lose ourselves in the sublimity of the Apostle's
language; that we should not cheat ourselves with the
miserable notion that he is dealing with fine oriental
hyperboles. We must be assured that he is speaking
of the most intense reality, that he is spurning fictions,
that he would make us acquainted with facts, that his
language is the most divine most inspired he could
find, but that it is only language still; that the truth

it speaks of, the truth which we may know in ourselves and in the history of the world, the truth which we shall certainly know one day to be at the root of both, is far deeper than any forms of human speech. And St. John's is not, as some people may carelessly imagine, difficult or unintelligible language. It is particularly clear and transparent. We may cloud it with our conceits, we may interpose a number of shadows, thrown from ourselves, between it and our consciences; but if we will let it bear directly upon them, they will recognise its force, they will not wait to have it translated into which is feebler and more formal. To some, the language of symbols may seem unsatisfactory; some may even denounce it as idolatrous and profane. They may speak as they like; but if they will have the Bible, they must have symbols; they must be content to let God speak to them through the forms of sense, because they are His forms, and because no others could convey His meaning to the hearts which He desires to take it in, so well as they do.

I do not, therefore, stop to give you some abstract equivalent for the image of a *white horse* and *One that sat upon him.* You know, far better than I can tell you, what an impression of human dignity and lordship that likeness has made upon men in all generations, and does make upon us now. This impression is not the effect of any peculiar or artificial training. You do not receive it from a picture or a piece of sculpture, or because you have been familiar from boyhood with the

Homeric epithet for the hero. That epithet would have no force, if it were not an expression of actual human feeling; if it did not bear witness to that authority over the animal—over all the lower creation—which belongs to our race in virtue of God's original fiat. Here, then, we have the representation of this human authority and vicegerency, the Person in whom it was first vested, by whom it is really exercised, from whom it descends upon mankind, or upon any man.

The first titles by which the Horseman is described are *Faithful* and *True*. The old chivalry recognised and adopted these names. They denoted the knight who knew what his calling was. Gentleness in blood and in behaviour, might be his greatest and most necessary ornaments, but faithfulness and truth were to be the substance of his character. In men, like Louis IX., who at all acted up to their profession, we perceive at once that these words express the ideal which they set before themselves. What we are told here is, that they did not *make* that ideal. It was not a beautiful phantom projected from their own minds, the apotheosis of that which they had thought and dreamed. The Faithful and True Knight actually existed; they were but receiving a few imperfect graces corresponding to His graces,—a few partial treasures out of His fulness.

Oftentimes it was the hardest thing for them to discriminate between the right and the wrong—the false and the true—in the men who served them, and in those with whom they acted. They were sometimes deceived by hypocrites, they were sometimes unjust to honest people. Still they knew they had the faculty of judgment; they were permitted to exercise it in the open tribunal, in the ordinary business of life. They exercised it most safely and rightly towards others, when they dealt strictly and honestly with themselves. But in these secret transactions, also, they were liable to be imposed upon. Bribes which corrupted the judgment might be received with less sense of criminality, when they were pronouncing on their own acts and thoughts. There must be a judge over them, over their subjects, over all men. This Faithful and True Knight, the Apostle says, is the Righteous Judge; the discerner of the thoughts and intents of the heart; the perfectly clear and equitable and effectual divider between that which is, and that which is not,—between the real thing, and the counterfeit which waits upon it.

To believe that there is such a Judge at the heart of society, close to the heart of each man, is an infinite security that the crude and random apprehensions, and the selfish schemes, of individuals, or of ages, shall not have power to make good evil, or evil good, however they may labour to do so. But yet the knight and king on earth demanded more than a judge over him and over his fellows. He felt that their wrongs needed to be redressed, that the weak must be raised, and the giants who trampled on them put down. How noble, often, were his efforts to this end! How salutary the example which they presented to mankind! Yet what confusion was there in the very best of these efforts, when directed by the best men! What an excuse after ages have had for saying, that the devotion and sacrifice which were exhibited in them were thrown away! nay, that they sometimes wrought positive mischief! How certain it is, that when the knight began to idolise his own work, and to perpetuate the mere forms of it, he became himself an oppressor, whom it was right and useful to dislodge by ridicule from the position which he could no longer honourably fill! What need, then, was it, that the true knight should ask in his own day, that the student of history should ask in our day, Whether there is no permanent defender of the weak, no permanent avenger of the evil doer, who knows exactly which are the humble who need protection, which are the proud that need to be abased; who is not misled by appearances in one case or another; who is bound by the forms and circumstances of no period or locality; who can compel the forms and circumstances of all periods and localities to serve His righteous purposes?

In righteousness, says the Apostle, shall this faithful and true Knight, both judge and *make war*. We look upon this great war, which has been waged among men, and upon that. We ask ourselves, Was it just? was it necessary? We are often puzzled for the answer; but we feel that the question is a reasonable one, that there are enormous differences between different wars; that with the objects of some, we can, in a great degree, sympathise; that some we must almost entirely condemn; and yet, that with respect to the actors in one as well as the other, there may be something to admire, something to denounce; and that the habit of pronouncing a promiscuous approbation, under the plea that war is in itself glorious,—or, under the plea that all war is destructive, and, therefore, must be hateful, effaces moral distinctions, and is injurious to the conscience. Then again, how we are perplexed when we find that wars we had reason to think unrighteous have produced blessings; and that wars from which we could not withhold our sympathy, have tended to demoralise a land. All these observations, and the conclusions we found upon them, are utterly bewildering; and the refuge which we seek, in attributing all to a fixed necessity, is more disheartening still. But if there is One who in righteousness maketh war; who is aiming distinctly, and with no double or doubtful end, at the extirpation of falsehood, at the vindication of truth; then we may understand how all things that seem to thwart His purpose, are at last helping to forward it; then we may see, also, why every fraudulent and selfish plan of ours, however it may be designed to defend His power, is stamped with His curse, and is part of that which He is pledged to destroy.

All the time that I am saying these things, I feel how likely you are, because I know how likely I am, to think: 'Yes; this conception of the Apostle's is a

'very fine one. Such a Knight, and Judge, and Warrior,
'men have always talked about, or sighed for. It is a
'proof of their greatness that they can construct such
'a glorious specimen of Humanity, and can invest it
'with Divinity.' A proof of our greatness; Only
take in the sense of the next words,—only reflect on
them till you have made them your own,—and then
say, whether St. John is not making you feel your
littleness, your nothingness, the darkness and evil that
is in you, by bringing before you One who looks into
you, who sees you through and through, who has a
right to command you, of whom you can know nothing,
till He has first known you, and made you know yourselves. *'His eyes were as a flame of fire; and on His
head were many crowns, and He had a name written that
no man knew but He Himself.'* That—that is what you
want; that is what you are trying to conceive of; because he has first conceived you and your whole race.
Oh! if there is no such an One,—no one whom we
cannot measure and fathom, but who measures and
fathoms all that is within us;—no one who is King
over each of us, and over the whole intelligent and
voluntary universe, as well as over all nature—who has
these many crowns;—no one who can say, 'The Father,
'and the Father only, knoweth the Son, as the Son, and
'the Son only, knoweth the Father;' what a mere chaos
is this which we call a creation, what a dream of a
shadow is man!

    The Apostle, St. John, declares that there is such

an One, and that '*He is clothed with a vesture dipped in blood.*' We have heard of His fidelity, of His truth, of His clearness of vision, of His royalty, of His personality. One sign is needful still to identify Him. These garments speak of a Sacrifice. He has been slain—He has given up himself—it is His own blood with which He is stained. This is the token that His faithfulness and truth have encountered the spirit of selfishness, the great enemy of both, and have prevailed; this shows that no one dark film dims the insight of the Judge; that no one partial inclination sways, to right or left, the sceptre of the King; that the Name which He bears is not that of some separate individual, but of *the* Man, the Brother and Head of Men. And that Name cannot, therefore, be expressed in the terms which belong to our nature, though it is so intimately, and inseparably involved with that nature, and with its interests. His Name is called THE WORD OF GOD!

You might have expected, when you had been told of the vesture dipped in blood, to have heard another Name than this; one which speaks of Humiliation, of Sorrow, of Death. But if once we catch the least glimpse into the mind of St. John, we perceive that there can be no gulph between these ideas; that the very object of his whole teaching and life is to bring them together, so that we shall feel that the divine Word can only be known as the Lamb which was slain; that the death and sacrifice of the Lamb are nothing except as they reveal that Filial Word, who was in the bosom of the Father, and who has declared Him.

Dear brethren, if in the few broken hints I have been giving you respecting the nature and effects of sacrifice, I have, in any measure, been able to bring this thought home to you,—to make you perceive that the Cross of Christ makes known to us Him, in whom we are created, Him by whom we consist, Him who is the source of righteousness, of strength, of life to every man, because He is Himself the Eternal Son of God, and because by His acts He declares to us what God is working in us, to will, and to be, and to do—then I am sure, that what remains of this passage will come back to you in hours of overwhelming sadness; when you are thinking of those whom you have conversed with on earth, and whom you see no more; when the crimes and miseries of the actual world, and the centuries during which they have been growing, press upon you with an intolerable weight; when your own feebleness and incapacity for struggling with the pettiest temptation, for overcoming the most ignominious habit, seems to make it almost monstrous that you should be troubled about the transactions of the world, or the doings of other men.

Is it nothing to remember that the Word of God is not now treading the winepress alone, but *that the armies which are in heaven are following Him upon white horses, clothed in fine linen, white and clean?* Is it nothing to think, that every true and faithful man who has ever wrestled with his own evil, and with the evil of his brethren, with the world the flesh and the devil, has been Christ's soldier, cheered by His voice, inspired by His Spirit? Is it nothing to think, that you have seen but the beginning of their warfare,—when they were just learning the use of their arms, and wielding them very awkwardly (and how little did you know, how little they knew themselves, of the severest conflicts they were passing through!)—but that now they have entered upon a new stage of their service, and have profited by their sorrowful experience and many failures, and rule the things to which they often yielded subjection, and confess and obey the Leader, from whose yoke they so often broke loose? Is it nothing to believe, that now they appreciate each other better, and are not misled by appearances, and are not separated by hard thoughts, but feel that a common bond unites them, that the same banner is over them, and that they have been purified by the same blood from the vain wishes and petty vanities which kept them asunder? Is it nothing to think, that now they understand us and sympathise with us, as they could not do before; because, if they are more awake to our evils, they are more earnest to deliver us from them; and because they see us no longer as separate from Him who has loved them and us, and given Himself for us? I say, brethren, we have a right to cherish these thoughts about those who have gone before us. For we are not to judge them by our poor jaundiced sight, which oftener rests upon blemishes than beauties, even when we desire to discover them; but we are to contemplate them in the light of the great Sacrifice; robed and covered with Christ's vesture; we are to believe that He who is in the midst of the throne is feeding them, as He fed them during their pilgrimage through the earth on which He died. If, indeed, they were purchasing a place for themselves there, by their sacrifices here, we might tremble for the best of them; but it is He, the Word of God, who has purchased for them the privilege and the power of sacrificing themselves. He has redeemed them from the miserable death of independence and selfishness, that they may lead the true and pure life of obedience and self-surrender. Do not, then, conceive of them as dwelling in some distant, unknown region, where they possess some felicity from which you are excluded. Think of them as still caring for the earth, and for the country, and village, and homestead in which they learnt their lessons of humility and trust; think of them as struggling that these may become fit habitations for Righteousness and Peace to dwell in.

But if we may comfort one another with these words concerning those who have fallen asleep, what comfort can we find when we look upon this earth, and the portions of it which we have most to do with, and see in them the habitations, not of Righteousness and Peace, but of Tyranny, and Superstition, and Atheism?

What happy dreams of that which has been, or of that which may be to come, can make us endure the sight of that which actually is? No such dreams assuredly can help us much. But these words that tell no dream, that contain no soothing music, that are full of sternness and terror, may be of mighty strength to us, if we will consider them rightly. '*And out of His mouth goeth a sharp sword, that with it He should smite the nations: and He shall rule them with a rod of iron; and He treadeth the wine-press of the fierceness and wrath of Almighty God.*' Cannot we mitigate the severity of this passage a little? May we not make a slight allowance for the Jewish education even of the Apostle of Love? God forbid! As long as there is oppression, and anarchy, and evil in this world of ours, they are cowards, and enemies of their species and traitors to charity, who would wish one word here to be milder than it is, who do not rejoice that every word has its real counterpart. How utterly mournful and unbearable is the history of mankind, if we do not believe that wars, and plagues, and pestilences, that revolutions in kingdoms, that the convulsions of Churches, have been authentic testimonies that the Son of God Himself is calling those whom He had set as stewards over His household to answer for their trust; that He is proclaiming the captive and the slave to be His—the purchase of His own blood; that He is uttering, and bringing forth into act, the fierceness and wrath of Almighty God against those who are destroying the heritage which He has redeemed. Oh, believe that it is not some other, but the Saviour of the world, the meek and lowly Jesus, who is executing this wrath and vengeance of His Father. Ask that it may burn on, till all that is resisting His love, and hindering the manifestation of it to mankind, be utterly consumed. Accept every message of it, when it comes near to ourselves, as a witness that there is some abominable thing, the fruit of our selfishness, which must be destroyed, and which God has doomed. Remember, that when Christ prevails, it is over human wills ; that as long as these are refractory, the battle must still go on; that when He enters His new Jerusalem to claim the triumph of the conqueror, the multitude that go before and that follow, will shout with their hearts and lips, ' *Hosanna! Blessed is He that cometh in the name of the Lord.*' And, therefore, whatever holds the will in bondage, whatever makes these tongues incapable of praising their true King, must be swept away, that He may be known for what He is; that His heavenly glory may not be for ever hid behind the clouds which have been drawn up from the earth. And this may reconcile us, nothing else can, to that which is the most dismal spectacle of all—the decay of faith in the Churches, which have been called out to witness of the Word of God, to testify that He is the King of kings and Lord of lords. It must be shown, by clear and manifest tokens, that the universe does not, as they have supposed, stand upon their faith, their holiness, their sacrifices; that it stands upon Him who is faithful and true, upon His all-perfect Sacrifice by which God has reconciled the world to Himself. So long as a Church, as any Church, bears witness of this truth, so long it will be doing its work, and the armies of heaven and He on the white horse will be working and fighting with it. But when one Church or another, under whatever pretext, inverts the principle of sacrifice, and puts the acts of man in place of the act of God, and denies that He has redeemed and restored mankind in His well-beloved Son, and that His mind towards men is one of Peace and not of evil; it becomes a plague and curse to the earth which it was appointed to bless, and the sharp sword which goeth out of the mouth of the Word of God will cut it asunder.

Once more, brethren, let us not be cast down, nor lose our heart and hope, for anything that we may feel within, any more than for anything that we may see around us. When the world seems most desolate of God's presence, most rushing downward by its own impulse and gravitation to a deep abyss, the Word of God who created it, is still upholding it, and directing the movements of it, let them be ever so irregular and tortuous, to His own gracious and glorious ends. When it seems most, as if all acts and all events obeyed a law of selfishness, that law is really producing nothing, accomplishing nothing; it is merely intercepting, for a little while, by its feeble, insolent, vacillating rebellions, the calm, onward march of those armies which obey the true law of the universe, the law of sacrifice. A man may ask in sadness and bitterness : ' But how can ' I ever be joined to these armies ; how can I ever yield ' to that law ? If self be but a rebellious power, yet in ' me it seems a victorious one. I try to oppose it, but ' each hour it comes upon me with fresh might. The ' trophy of yesterday is exchanged for the more shameful ' defeat of to-day. I shall be forced to yield at last, ' however I fight. I may as well yield at once.' When any man says this—as we all have said it in the misery of our hearts, in mockery of the better convictions that were working in us,—oh, let him recollect, that He, from whom those holier desires have proceeded—weak as they may seem, ineffectual as they have proved—' *hath on His vesture and on His thigh a name written,* KING OF KINGS AND LORD OF LORDS.' The secret of strength, friend and brother, of all moral purpose is to assure thyself that thou art not engaged in a battle between two portions of thy own nature. It is Christ in thee who is inviting thee, urging thee, commanding thee, to every brave, and true, and earnest effort. And in His commandment is life ; what He bids thee do, He will enable thee to do. The might of His own sacrifice is with thee. He who gave up Himself without spot to God, will enable thee to offer thyself, an acceptable and reasonable sacrifice, to do His will, to glorify His name.

And with moral purpose will come hope. When we think of Christ as a Being at a distance from us—

who has merely done a mighty work; when we eat the bread and drink the wine in remembrance of an absent Friend, not as pledges of a near and present one; the pressure of evil that crushes down our faith, and hope, and love, seems to make the past redemption wholly unavailing for our great necessity. But *Christ in us*, as St. Paul told the Colossians, is *the hope of glory*. What we want is not that, we should attain some separate and selfish bliss, but that He, who has been striving with us all our lives through, to deliver us from the separation and selfishness which have been our torment and our curse, should finally effect His own purpose; that He should be manifested to us, and to the world, as the King who has vanquished by sacrifice; that we should be His willing servants, the free children of His Father, formed into one family and body by His blessed Spirit for ever. Amen.

NOTE.

Some readers will detect a resemblance between certain passages in these Sermons and the Sermon of Archdeacon Hare, On the Law of Sacrifice. Though I have not read that Sermon recently, I may have often fallen into the train of thought which is there followed out so carefully; it is quite possible that I may have unconsciously adopted some of its expressions. Having joyfully confessed obligations to some with whom I have no natural sympathy, it must be a great satisfaction to own them in the case of a dear friend. I would observe, however, that the plagiarisms must be looked for in the ethical passages of this volume, to which, I trust, no devout reader will take exception; for whatever is offensive in the theology, I am alone responsible.

A very learned work, expressly on the theology of this subject, appeared in the course of last year. I feel that it would be an impertinence to say how far the sentiments in a book so unlearned, so merely practical as this, differ or accord with those which Mr. Thompson has put forth in his Bampton Lectures. But since no reader will suspect that our methods of thinking are similar, or that we are proposing to ourselves the same object, I hope I shall not be doing Mr. Thompson an injury, if I express the satisfaction it has caused me, as an affectionate member of the University which he adorns, to meet in a modern book of Divinity, bearing the Oxford imprimatur, such various lore, so much earnest thought, so much devout feeling, such freedom from party bias.

THE END.

CHARLES DICKENS AND EVANS, CRYSTAL PALACE PRESS.

WORKS BY THE LATE

FREDERICK DENISON MAURICE, M.A.

COLLECTED WORKS.

In Monthly Volumes from October 1892. Crown 8vo.
3s. 6d. per volume.

1. CHRISTMAS DAY AND OTHER SERMONS.
2. THEOLOGICAL ESSAYS.
3. THE PROPHETS AND KINGS OF THE OLD TESTAMENT. New Edition. This volume contains discourses on Samuel I. and II., Kings I. and II., Amos, Joel, Hosea, Isaiah, Micah, Habakkuk, Jeremiah, and Ezekiel.
4. THE PATRIARCHS AND LAWGIVERS OF THE OLD TESTAMENT. This volume contains discourses on the Pentateuch, Joshua, Judges, and the beginning of the First Book of Samuel.
5. THE GOSPEL OF THE KINGDOM OF HEAVEN.
6. THE GOSPEL OF ST. JOHN. A Series of Discourses.
7. EPISTLES OF ST. JOHN. A Series of Lectures on Christian Ethics.
8. LECTURES ON THE APOCALYPSE.
9. THE FRIENDSHIP OF BOOKS, and other Lectures.
10. SOCIAL MORALITY.
11. PRAYER-BOOK AND LORD'S PRAYER.
12. THE DOCTRINE OF SACRIFICE DEDUCED FROM THE SCRIPTURES.

LINCOLN'S INN SERMONS. In Six Volumes. Crown 8vo. 3s. 6d. each.

MORAL AND METAPHYSICAL PHILOSOPHY. Vol. I.—Ancient Philosophy and the First to the Thirteenth Centuries. Vol. II.—Fourteenth Century and the French Revolution, with a Glimpse into the Nineteenth Century. Third Edition. 2 vols. 8vo, 16s.

THE UNITY OF THE NEW TESTAMENT. A Synopsis of the First Three Gospels and of the Epistles of St. James, St. Jude, St. Peter, and St. Paul. Second Edition. 2 vols. Crown 8vo, 12s.

THE KINGDOM OF CHRIST; or, Hints to a Quaker respecting the Principle, Constitution, and Ordinances of the Catholic Church. Third Edition. 2 vols. Crown 8vo, 12s.

MACMILLAN AND CO., LONDON.

WORKS BY THE LATE
FREDERICK DENISON MAURICE, M.A.

THE RELIGIONS OF THE WORLD, AND THEIR RELATIONS TO CHRISTIANITY. Fifth Edition. Crown 8vo, 4s. 6d.

ON THE SABBATH DAY; THE CHARACTER OF THE WARRIOR; AND ON THE INTERPRETATION OF HISTORY. Fcap. 8vo, 2s. 6d.

LEARNING AND WORKING. Six Lectures on the Foundation of Colleges for Working Men. Crown 8vo, 4s. 6d.

THE LORD'S PRAYER, THE CREED, AND THE COMMANDMENTS. A Manual for Parents and Schoolmasters. To which is added the Order of the Scriptures. 18mo, 1s.

EXPOSITORY SERMONS ON THE PRAYER-BOOK, CONSIDERED ESPECIALLY IN REFERENCE TO THE ROMISH SYSTEM; AND ON THE LORD'S PRAYER. New Edition. Crown 8vo, 6s.

SERMONS PREACHED IN COUNTRY CHURCHES. Second Edition. Crown 8vo, 6s.

THE CONSCIENCE. Lectures on Casuistry delivered in the University of Cambridge. Second and Cheaper Edition. Crown 8vo, 4s. 6d.

DIALOGUES ON FAMILY WORSHIP. Crown 8vo, 4s. 6d.

THE COMMUNION SERVICE FROM THE BOOK OF COMMON PRAYER, WITH SELECT READINGS FROM THE WRITINGS OF THE REV. F. D. MAURICE. Edited by the Right Rev. J. W. COLENSO, D.D., Bishop of Natal. Sixth Edition. 16mo, 2s. 6d.

THE LIFE OF FREDERICK DENISON MAURICE, chiefly told in his own Letters. Edited by his son, FREDERICK MAURICE. With two Portraits. Two Vols. Third Edition. Demy 8vo, 36s. Popular Edition. Two Vols. Crown 8vo, 16s.

MACMILLAN AND CO., LONDON.

5.6.93.

January 1893

A Catalogue

of

Theological Works

published by

Macmillan & Co.

Bedford Street, Strand, London

The Old Testament—*continued.*

WARBURTONIAN LECTURES ON THE MINOR PROPHETS. By Rev. A. F. KIRKPATRICK, B.D. Crown 8vo. [*In the Press.*

THE PATRIARCHS AND LAWGIVERS OF THE OLD TESTAMENT. By FREDERICK DENISON MAURICE. New Edition. Crown 8vo. 3s. 6d.

THE PROPHETS AND KINGS OF THE OLD TESTAMENT. By the same. New Edition. Crown 8vo. 3s. 6d.

THE CANON OF THE OLD TESTAMENT. An Essay on the Growth and Formation of the Hebrew Canon of Scripture. By Rev. Prof. H. E. RYLE. Crown 8vo. 6s.

THE EARLY NARRATIVES OF GENESIS. By Rev. Prof. H. E. RYLE. Cr. 8vo. 3s. net.

The Pentateuch—

AN HISTORICO-CRITICAL INQUIRY INTO THE ORIGIN AND COMPOSITION OF THE HEXATEUCH (PENTATEUCH AND BOOK OF JOSHUA). By Prof. A. KUENEN. Translated by PHILIP H. WICKSTEED, M.A. 8vo. 14s.

The Psalms—

THE PSALMS CHRONOLOGICALLY ARRANGED. An Amended Version, with Historical Introductions and Explanatory Notes. By Four Friends. New Edition. Crown 8vo. 5s. net.

GOLDEN TREASURY PSALTER. The Student's Edition. Being an Edition with briefer Notes of "The Psalms Chronologically Arranged by Four Friends." 18mo. 3s. 6d.

THE PSALMS. With Introductions and Critical Notes. By A. C. JENNINGS, M.A., and W. H. LOWE, M.A. In 2 vols. 2nd Edition. Crown 8vo. 10s. 6d. each.

INTRODUCTION TO THE STUDY AND USE OF THE PSALMS. By Rev. J. F. THRUPP. 2nd Edition. 2 vols. 8vo. 21s.

Isaiah—

ISAIAH XL.—LXVI. With the Shorter Prophecies allied to it. By MATTHEW ARNOLD. With Notes. Crown 8vo. 5s.

ISAIAH OF JERUSALEM. In the Authorised English Version, with Introduction, Corrections, and Notes. By the same. Cr. 8vo. 4s. 6d.

A BIBLE-READING FOR SCHOOLS. The Great Prophecy of Israel's Restoration (Isaiah xl.-lxvi.) Arranged and Edited for Young Learners. By the same. 4th Edition. 18mo. 1s.

COMMENTARY ON THE BOOK OF ISAIAH, Critical, Historical, and Prophetical; including a Revised English Translation. By T. R. BIRKS. 2nd Edition. 8vo. 12s. 6d.

THE BOOK OF ISAIAH CHRONOLOGICALLY ARRANGED. By T. K. CHEYNE. Crown 8vo. 7s. 6d.

Zechariah—

THE HEBREW STUDENT'S COMMENTARY ON ZECHARIAH, Hebrew and LXX. By W. H. LOWE, M.A. 8vo. 10s. 6d.

THE NEW TESTAMENT

APOCRYPHAL GOSPEL OF PETER. The Greek Text of the Newly-Discovered Fragment. 8vo. Sewed. 1s.

THE NEW TESTAMENT. Essay on the Right Estimation of MS. Evidence in the Text of the New Testament. By T. R. BIRKS. Crown 8vo. 3s. 6d.

THE SOTERIOLOGY OF THE NEW TESTAMENT. By W. P. DU BOSE, M.A. Crown 8vo. 7s. 6d.

THE MESSAGES OF THE BOOKS. Being Discourses and Notes on the Books of the New Testament. By Ven. Archdeacon FARRAR. 8vo. 14s.

THE CLASSICAL ELEMENT IN THE NEW TESTAMENT. Considered as a Proof of its Genuineness, with an Appendix on the Oldest Authorities used in the Formation of the Canon. By C. H. HOOLE. 8vo. 10s. 6d.

ON A FRESH REVISION OF THE ENGLISH NEW TESTAMENT. With an Appendix on the last Petition of the Lord's Prayer. By Bishop LIGHTFOOT. Crown 8vo. 7s. 6d.

DISSERTATIONS ON THE APOSTOLIC AGE. By Bishop LIGHTFOOT. 8vo. 14s.

THE UNITY OF THE NEW TESTAMENT. By F. D. MAURICE. 2nd Edition. 2 vols. Crown 8vo. 12s.

A COMPANION TO THE GREEK TESTAMENT AND THE ENGLISH VERSION. By PHILIP SCHAFF, D.D. Cr. 8vo. 12s.

A GENERAL SURVEY OF THE HISTORY OF THE CANON OF THE NEW TESTAMENT DURING THE FIRST FOUR CENTURIES. By Right Rev. Bishop WESTCOTT. 6th Edition. Crown 8vo. 10s. 6d.

THE NEW TESTAMENT IN THE ORIGINAL GREEK. The Text revised by Bishop WESTCOTT, D.D., and Prof. F. J. A. HORT, D.D. 2 vols. Crown 8vo. 10s. 6d. each.—Vol. I. Text; II. Introduction and Appendix.

THE NEW TESTAMENT IN THE ORIGINAL GREEK, for Schools. The Text revised by Bishop WESTCOTT, D.D., and F. J. A. HORT, D.D. 12mo, cloth, 4s. 6d.; 18mo, roan, red edges, 5s. 6d.; morocco, gilt edges, 6s. 6d.

THE GOSPELS—

THE COMMON TRADITION OF THE SYNOPTIC GOSPELS, in the Text of the Revised Version. By Rev. E. A. ABBOTT and W. G. RUSHBROOKE. Crown 8vo. 3s. 6d.

SYNOPTICON: An Exposition of the Common Matter of the Synoptic Gospels. By W. G. RUSHBROOKE. Printed in Colours. In Six Parts, and Appendix. 4to.—Part I. 3s. 6d. Parts II. and III. 7s. Parts IV. V. and VI. with Indices, 10s. 6d. Appendices, 10s. 6d. Complete in 1 vol., 35s. Indispensable to a Theological Student.

INTRODUCTION TO THE STUDY OF THE FOUR GOSPELS. By Right Rev. Bishop WESTCOTT. 7th Ed. Cr. 8vo. 10s. 6d.

THE COMPOSITION OF THE FOUR GOSPELS. By Rev. ARTHUR WRIGHT. Crown 8vo. 5s.

Gospel of St. Matthew—

THE GOSPEL ACCORDING TO ST. MATTHEW. Greek Text as Revised by Bishop WESTCOTT and Dr. HORT. With Introduction and Notes by Rev. A. SLOMAN, M.A. Fcap. 8vo. 2s. 6d.

CHOICE NOTES ON ST. MATTHEW, drawn from Old and New Sources. Crown 8vo. 4s. 6d. (St. Matthew and St. Mark in 1 vol. 9s.)

Gospel of St. Mark—

SCHOOL READINGS IN THE GREEK TESTAMENT. Being the Outlines of the Life of our Lord as given by St. Mark, with additions from the Text of the other Evangelists. Edited, with Notes and Vocabulary, by Rev. A. CALVERT, M.A. Fcap. 8vo. 2s. 6d.

CHOICE NOTES ON ST. MARK, drawn from Old and New Sources. Cr. 8vo. 4s. 6d. (St. Matthew and St. Mark in 1 vol. 9s.)

Gospel of St. Luke—

THE GOSPEL ACCORDING TO ST. LUKE. The Greek Text as Revised by Bishop WESTCOTT and Dr. HORT. With Introduction and Notes by Rev. J. BOND, M.A. Fcap. 8vo. 2s. 6d.

CHOICE NOTES ON ST. LUKE, drawn from Old and New Sources. Crown 8vo. 4s. 6d.

THE GOSPEL OF THE KINGDOM OF HEAVEN. A Course of Lectures on the Gospel of St. Luke. By F. D. MAURICE. 3rd Edition. Crown 8vo. 6s.

Gospel of St. John—

THE CENTRAL TEACHING OF CHRIST. Being a Study and Exposition of St. John, Chapters XIII. to XVII. By Rev. CANON BERNARD, M.A. Crown 8vo. 7s. 6d.

THE GOSPEL OF ST. JOHN. By F. D. MAURICE. 8th Ed. Cr. 8vo. 6s.

CHOICE NOTES ON ST. JOHN, drawn from Old and New Sources. Crown 8vo. 4s. 6d.

THE ACTS OF THE APOSTLES—

THE ACTS OF THE APOSTLES. Being the Greek Text as Revised by Bishop WESTCOTT and Dr. HORT. With Explanatory Notes by T. E. PAGE, M.A. Fcap. 8vo. 3s. 6d.

THE CHURCH OF THE FIRST DAYS. THE CHURCH OF JERUSALEM. THE CHURCH OF THE GENTILES. THE CHURCH OF THE WORLD. Lectures on the Acts of the Apostles. By Very Rev. C. J. VAUGHAN. Crown 8vo. 10s. 6d.

THE EPISTLES of St. Paul—

ST. PAUL'S EPISTLE TO THE ROMANS. The Greek Text, with English Notes. By Very Rev. C. J. VAUGHAN. 7th Edition. Crown 8vo. 7s. 6d.

A COMMENTARY ON ST. PAUL'S TWO EPISTLES TO THE CORINTHIANS. Greek Text, with Commentary. By Rev. W. KAY. 8vo. 9s.

THEOLOGICAL CATALOGUE 5

Of St. Paul—*continued*.
   ST. PAUL'S EPISTLE TO THE GALATIANS. A Revised Text, with Introduction, Notes, and Dissertations. By Bishop LIGHTFOOT. 10th Edition. 8vo. 12s.
   ST. PAUL'S EPISTLE TO THE PHILIPPIANS. A Revised Text, with Introduction, Notes, and Dissertations. By the same. 9th Edition. 8vo. 12s.
   ST. PAUL'S EPISTLE TO THE PHILIPPIANS. With translation, Paraphrase, and Notes for English Readers. By Very Rev. C. J. VAUGHAN. Crown 8vo. 5s.
   ST. PAUL'S EPISTLES TO THE COLOSSIANS AND TO PHILEMON. A Revised Text, with Introductions, etc. By Bishop LIGHTFOOT. 9th Edition. 8vo. 12s.
   THE EPISTLES OF ST. PAUL TO THE EPHESIANS, THE COLOSSIANS, AND PHILEMON. With Introductions and Notes. By Rev. J. LL. DAVIES. 2nd Edition. 8vo. 7s. 6d.
   THE EPISTLES OF ST. PAUL. For English Readers. Part I. containing the First Epistle to the Thessalonians. By Very Rev. C. J. VAUGHAN. 2nd Edition. 8vo. Sewed. 1s. 6d.
   ST. PAUL'S EPISTLES TO THE THESSALONIANS, COMMENTARY ON THE GREEK TEXT. By Prof. JOHN EADIE. 8vo. 12s.

The Epistle of St. James—
   THE EPISTLE OF ST. JAMES. The Greek Text, with Introduction and Notes. By Rev. JOSEPH MAYOR, M.A. 8vo. 14s.

The Epistles of St. John—
   THE EPISTLES OF ST. JOHN. By F. D. MAURICE. 4th Edition. Crown 8vo. 6s.
   THE EPISTLES OF ST. JOHN. The Greek Text, with Notes. By Right Rev. Bishop WESTCOTT. 3rd Edition. 8vo. 12s. 6d.

The Epistle to the Hebrews—
   THE EPISTLE TO THE HEBREWS IN GREEK AND ENGLISH. With Notes. By Rev. FREDERIC RENDALL. Crown 8vo. 6s.
   THE EPISTLE TO THE HEBREWS. English Text, with Commentary. By the same. Crown 8vo. 7s. 6d.
   THE EPISTLE TO THE HEBREWS. With Notes. By Very Rev. C. J. VAUGHAN. Crown 8vo. 7s. 6d.
   THE EPISTLE TO THE HEBREWS. The Greek Text, with Notes and Essays. By Right Rev. Bishop WESTCOTT. 8vo. 14s.

REVELATION—
   LECTURES ON THE APOCALYPSE. By F. D. MAURICE. 2nd Edition. Crown 8vo. 6s.
   LECTURES ON THE APOCALYPSE. By Rev. Prof. W. MILLIGAN. Crown 8vo. 5s.
   THE REVELATION OF ST. JOHN. By Rev. Prof. W. MILLIGAN. 2nd Edition. Crown 8vo. 7s. 6d.

REVELATION—*continued.*
>LECTURES ON THE REVELATION OF ST. JOHN. By Very Rev. C. J. VAUGHAN. 5th Edition. Crown 8vo. 10s. 6d.

>THE BIBLE WORD-BOOK. By W. ALDIS WRIGHT. 2nd Edition. Crown 8vo. 7s. 6d.

Christian Church, History of the

Church (Dean).—THE OXFORD MOVEMENT. Twelve Years, 1833-45. Globe 8vo. 5s.
Cunningham (Rev. John).—THE GROWTH OF THE CHURCH IN ITS ORGANISATION AND INSTITUTIONS. 8vo. 9s.
Dale (A. W. W.)—THE SYNOD OF ELVIRA, AND CHRISTIAN LIFE IN THE FOURTH CENTURY. Cr. 8vo. 10s. 6d.
Hardwick (Archdeacon).—A HISTORY OF THE CHRISTIAN CHURCH. Middle Age. Ed. by Bishop STUBBS. Cr. 8vo. 10s. 6d.
A HISTORY OF THE CHRISTIAN CHURCH DURING THE REFORMATION. Revised by Bishop STUBBS. Cr. 8vo. 10s. 6d.
Hort (Dr. F. J. A.)—TWO DISSERTATIONS. I. On ΜΟΝΟΓΕΝΗΣ ΘΕΟΣ in Scripture and Tradition. II. On the "Constantinopolitan" Creed and other Eastern Creeds of the Fourth Century. 8vo. 7s. 6d.
Killen (W. D.)—ECCLESIASTICAL HISTORY OF IRELAND, FROM THE EARLIEST DATE TO THE PRESENT TIME. 2 vols. 8vo. 25s.
Simpson (W.)—AN EPITOME OF THE HISTORY OF THE CHRISTIAN CHURCH. Fcap. 8vo. 3s. 6d.
Vaughan (Very Rev. C. J., Dean of Llandaff).—THE CHURCH OF THE FIRST DAYS. THE CHURCH OF JERUSALEM. THE CHURCH OF THE GENTILES. THE CHURCH OF THE WORLD. Crown 8vo. 10s. 6d.
Ward (W.)—WILLIAM GEORGE WARD AND THE OXFORD MOVEMENT. Portrait. 8vo. 14s.

The Church of England

Catechism of—
>A CLASS-BOOK OF THE CATECHISM OF THE CHURCH OF ENGLAND. By Rev. Canon MACLEAR. 18mo. 1s. 6d.
>A FIRST CLASS-BOOK OF THE CATECHISM OF THE CHURCH OF ENGLAND, with Scripture Proofs for Junior Classes and Schools. By the same. 18mo. 6d.
>THE ORDER OF CONFIRMATION, with Prayers and Devotions. By the Rev. Canon MACLEAR. 32mo. 6d.

Collects—
COLLECTS OF THE CHURCH OF ENGLAND. With a Coloured Floral Design to each Collect. Crown 8vo. 12s.

Disestablishment—
DISESTABLISHMENT AND DISENDOWMENT. What are they? By Prof. E. A. FREEMAN. 4th Edition. Crown 8vo. 1s.
DISESTABLISHMENT : or, A Defence of the Principle of a National Church. By GEORGE HARWOOD. 8vo. 12s.
A DEFENCE OF THE CHURCH OF ENGLAND AGAINST DISESTABLISHMENT. By ROUNDELL, EARL OF SELBORNE. Crown 8vo. 2s. 6d.
ANCIENT FACTS & FICTIONS CONCERNING CHURCHES AND TITHES. By the same. 2nd Edition. Crown 8vo. 7s. 6d.

Dissent in its Relation to—
DISSENT IN ITS RELATION TO THE CHURCH OF ENGLAND. By Rev. G. H. CURTEIS. Bampton Lectures for 1871. Crown 8vo. 7s. 6d.

Holy Communion—
THE COMMUNION SERVICE FROM THE BOOK OF COMMON PRAYER, with Select Readings from the Writings of the Rev. F. D. MAURICE. Edited by Bishop COLENSO. 6th Edition. 16mo. 2s. 6d.
BEFORE THE TABLE : An Inquiry, Historical and Theological, into the Meaning of the Consecration Rubric in the Communion Service of the Church of England. By Very Rev. J. S. HOWSON. 8vo. 7s. 6d.
FIRST COMMUNION, with Prayers and Devotions for the newly Confirmed. By Rev. Canon MACLEAR. 32mo. 6d.
A MANUAL OF INSTRUCTION FOR CONFIRMATION AND FIRST COMMUNION, with Prayers and Devotions. By the same. 32mo. 2s.

Liturgy—
A COMPANION TO THE LECTIONARY. By Rev. W. BENHAM, B.D. Crown 8vo. 4s. 6d.
AN INTRODUCTION TO THE CREEDS. By Rev. Canon MACLEAR. 18mo. 3s. 6d.
AN INTRODUCTION TO THE THIRTY-NINE ARTICLES. By the same. 18mo. [*In the Press.*
A HISTORY OF THE BOOK OF COMMON PRAYER. By Rev. F. PROCTER. 18th Edition. Crown 8vo. 10s. 6d.
AN ELEMENTARY INTRODUCTION TO THE BOOK OF COMMON PRAYER. By Rev. F. PROCTER and Rev. Canon MACLEAR. 18mo. 2s. 6d.
TWELVE DISCOURSES ON SUBJECTS CONNECTED WITH THE LITURGY AND WORSHIP OF THE CHURCH OF ENGLAND. By Very Rev. C. J. VAUGHAN. 4th Edition. Fcap. 8vo. 6s.

Devotional Books

Brooke (S. A.).—FORM OF MORNING AND EVENING PRAYER, and for the Administration of the Lord's Supper, together with the Baptismal and Marriage Services, Bedford Chapel, Bloomsbury. Fcap. 8vo. 1s. net.

Eastlake (Lady).—FELLOWSHIP: LETTERS ADDRESSED TO MY SISTER-MOURNERS. Crown 8vo. 2s. 6d.

IMITATIO CHRISTI, LIBRI IV. Printed in Borders after Holbein, Dürer, and other old Masters, containing Dances of Death, Acts of Mercy, Emblems, etc. Crown 8vo. 7s. 6d.

Kingsley (Charles).—OUT OF THE DEEP: WORDS FOR THE SORROWFUL. From the writings of CHARLES KINGSLEY. Extra fcap. 8vo. 3s. 6d.

DAILY THOUGHTS. Selected from the Writings of CHARLES KINGSLEY. By his Wife. Crown 8vo. 6s.

FROM DEATH TO LIFE. Fragments of Teaching to a Village Congregation. With Letters on the "Life after Death." Edited by his Wife. Fcap. 8vo. 2s. 6d.

Maclear (Rev. Canon).—A MANUAL OF INSTRUCTION FOR CONFIRMATION AND FIRST COMMUNION, WITH PRAYERS AND DEVOTIONS. 32mo. 2s.

THE HOUR OF SORROW; OR, THE OFFICE FOR THE BURIAL OF THE DEAD. 32mo. 2s.

Maurice (Frederick Denison).—LESSONS OF HOPE. Readings from the Works of F. D. MAURICE. Selected by Rev. J. LL. DAVIES, M.A. Crown 8vo. 5s.

RAYS OF SUNLIGHT FOR DARK DAYS. With a Preface by Very Rev. C. J. VAUGHAN, D.D. New Edition. 18mo. 3s. 6d.

Service (Rev. John).—PRAYERS FOR PUBLIC WORSHIP. Crown 8vo. 4s. 6d.

THE WORSHIP OF GOD, AND FELLOWSHIP AMONG MEN. By FREDERICK DENISON MAURICE and others. Fcap. 8vo. 3s. 6d.

Welby-Gregory (The Hon. Lady).—LINKS AND CLUES. 2nd Edition. Crown 8vo. 6s.

Westcott (Rt. Rev. B. F., Bishop of Durham).—THOUGHTS ON REVELATION AND LIFE. Selections from the Writings of Bishop WESTCOTT. Edited by Rev. S. PHILLIPS. Crown 8vo. 6s.

Wilbraham (Frances M.)—IN THE SERE AND YELLOW LEAF: THOUGHTS AND RECOLLECTIONS FOR OLD AND YOUNG. Globe 8vo. 3s. 6d.

The Fathers

Cunningham (Rev. W.)—THE EPISTLE OF ST. BARNABAS. A Dissertation, including a Discussion of its Date and Authorship. Together with the Greek Text, the Latin Version, and a New English Translation and Commentary. Crown 8vo. 7s. 6d.

Donaldson (Prof. James).—THE APOSTOLICAL FATHERS. A Critical Account of their Genuine Writings, and of their Doctrines. 2nd Edition. Crown 8vo. 7s. 6d.

Lightfoot (Bishop).—THE APOSTOLIC FATHERS. Part I. St. Clement of Rome. Revised Texts, with Introductions, Notes, Dissertations, and Translations. 2 vols. 8vo. 32s.

THE APOSTOLIC FATHERS. Part II. St. Ignatius to St. Polycarp. Revised Texts, with Introductions, Notes, Dissertations, and Translations. 3 vols. 2nd Edition. Demy 8vo. 48s.

THE APOSTOLIC FATHERS. Abridged Edition. With Short Introductions, Greek Text, and English Translation. 8vo. 16s.

Hymnology

Brooke (S. A.)—CHRISTIAN HYMNS. Edited and arranged. Fcap. 8vo. 2s. net.

This may also be had bound up with the Form of Service at Bedford Chapel, Bloomsbury. Price complete, 3s. net.

Palgrave (Prof. F. T.)—ORIGINAL HYMNS. 18mo. 1s. 6d.

Selborne (Roundell, Earl of)—

THE BOOK OF PRAISE. From the best English Hymn Writers. 18mo. 2s. 6d. net.

A HYMNAL. Chiefly from *The Book of Praise*. In various sizes.—A. Royal 32mo. 6d.—B. Small 18mo, larger type. 1s.—C. Same Edition, fine paper. 1s. 6d.—An Edition with Music, Selected, Harmonised, and Composed by John Hullah. Square 18mo. 3s. 6d.

Woods (M. A.)—HYMNS FOR SCHOOL WORSHIP. Compiled by M. A. Woods. 18mo. 1s. 6d.

Sermons, Lectures, Addresses, and Theological Essays

(*See also* '*Bible*,' '*Church of England*,' '*Fathers*.')

Abbot (Francis)—

SCIENTIFIC THEISM. Crown 8vo. 7s. 6d.

THE WAY OUT OF AGNOSTICISM: or, The Philosophy of Free Religion. Crown 8vo. 4s. 6d.

Abbott (Rev. E. A.)—

CAMBRIDGE SERMONS. 8vo. 6s.

OXFORD SERMONS. 8vo. 7s. 6d.

PHILOMYTHUS. An Antidote against Credulity. A discussion of Cardinal Newman's Essay on Ecclesiastical Miracles. 2nd Edition. Crown 8vo. 3s. 6d.

NEWMANIANISM. A Reply. Crown 8vo. Sewed, 1s. net.

Ainger (Rev. Alfred, Canon of Bristol).—SERMONS PREACHED IN THE TEMPLE CHURCH. Extra fcap. 8vo. 6s.

Alexander (W., Bishop of Derry and Raphoe).—THE LEADING IDEAS OF THE GOSPELS. New Edition, Revised and Enlarged. Crown 8vo. 6s.

Baines (Rev. Edward).—SERMONS. With a Preface and Memoir, by A. BARRY, D.D., late Bishop of Sydney. Crown 8vo. 6s.

Bather (Archdeacon).—ON SOME MINISTERIAL DUTIES, CATECHISING, PREACHING, ETC. Edited, with a Preface, by Very Rev. C. J. VAUGHAN, D.D. Fcap. 8vo. 4s. 6d.

Binnie (Rev. William).—SERMONS. Crown 8vo. 6s.

Birks (Thomas Rawson)—
 THE DIFFICULTIES OF BELIEF IN CONNECTION WITH THE CREATION AND THE FALL, REDEMPTION, AND JUDGMENT. 2nd Edition. Crown 8vo. 5s.
 JUSTIFICATION AND IMPUTED RIGHTEOUSNESS. Being a Review of Ten Sermons on the Nature and Effects of Faith, by JAMES THOMAS O'BRIEN, D.D., late Bishop of Ossory, Ferns, and Leighlin. Crown 8vo. 6s.
 SUPERNATURAL REVELATION : or, First Principles of Moral Theology. 8vo. 8s.

Brooke (Rev. Stopford A.)—SHORT SERMONS. Cr. 8vo. 6s.

Brooks (Phillips, Bishop of Massachusetts)—
 THE CANDLE OF THE LORD, and other Sermons. Crown 8vo. 6s.
 SERMONS PREACHED IN ENGLISH CHURCHES. Crown 8vo. 6s.
 TWENTY SERMONS. Crown 8vo. 6s.
 TOLERANCE. Crown 8vo. 2s. 6d.
 THE LIGHT OF THE WORLD. Crown 8vo. 3s. 6d.

Brunton (T. Lauder).—THE BIBLE AND SCIENCE. With Illustrations. Crown 8vo. 10s. 6d.

Butler (Rev. George).—SERMONS PREACHED IN CHELTENHAM COLLEGE CHAPEL. 8vo. 7s. 6d.

Butler (W. Archer)—
 SERMONS, DOCTRINAL AND PRACTICAL. 11th Edition. 8vo. 8s.
 SECOND SERIES OF SERMONS. 8vo. 7s.

Campbell (Dr. John M'Leod)—
 THE NATURE OF THE ATONEMENT. 6th Ed. Cr. 8vo. 6s.
 REMINISCENCES AND REFLECTIONS. Edited with an Introductory Narrative, by his Son, DONALD CAMPBELL, M.A. Crown 8vo. 7s. 6d.
 THOUGHTS ON REVELATION. 2nd Edition. Crown 8vo. 5s.
 RESPONSIBILITY FOR THE GIFT OF ETERNAL LIFE. Compiled from Sermons preached at Row, in the years 1829-31. Crown 8vo. 5s.

Canterbury (Edward White, Archbishop of)—
BOY-LIFE: its Trial, its Strength, its Fulness. Sundays in Wellington College, 1859-73. 4th Edition. Crown 8vo. 6s.
THE SEVEN GIFTS. Addressed to the Diocese of Canterbury in his Primary Visitation. 2nd Edition. Crown 8vo. 6s.
CHRIST AND HIS TIMES. Addressed to the Diocese of Canterbury in his Second Visitation. Crown 8vo. 6s.

Carpenter (W. Boyd, Bishop of Ripon)—
TRUTH IN TALE. Addresses, chiefly to Children. Crown 8vo. 4s. 6d.
THE PERMANENT ELEMENTS OF RELIGION: Bampton Lectures, 1887. 2nd Edition. Crown 8vo. 6s.

Cazenove (J. Gibson).—CONCERNING THE BEING AND ATTRIBUTES OF GOD. 8vo. 5s.

Church (Dean)—
HUMAN LIFE AND ITS CONDITIONS. Crown 8vo. 6s.
THE GIFTS OF CIVILISATION, and other Sermons and Lectures. 2nd Edition. Crown 8vo. 7s. 6d.
DISCIPLINE OF THE CHRISTIAN CHARACTER, and other Sermons. Crown 8vo. 4s. 6d.
ADVENT SERMONS. 1885. Crown 8vo. 4s. 6d.
VILLAGE SERMONS. Crown 8vo. 6s.
CATHEDRAL AND UNIVERSITY SERMONS. Crown 8vo. 6s.
CLERGYMAN'S SELF-EXAMINATION CONCERNING THE APOSTLES' CREED. Extra fcap. 8vo. 1s. 6d.

Congreve (Rev. John).—HIGH HOPES AND PLEADINGS FOR A REASONABLE FAITH, NOBLER THOUGHTS, LARGER CHARITY. Crown 8vo. 5s.

Cooke (Josiah P., Jun.)—RELIGION AND CHEMISTRY. Crown 8vo. 7s. 6d.

Cotton (Bishop).—SERMONS PREACHED TO ENGLISH CONGREGATIONS IN INDIA. Crown 8vo. 7s. 6d.

Cunningham (Rev. W.)—CHRISTIAN CIVILISATION, WITH SPECIAL REFERENCE TO INDIA. Cr. 8vo. 5s.

Curteis (Rev. G. H.)—THE SCIENTIFIC OBSTACLES TO CHRISTIAN BELIEF. The Boyle Lectures, 1884. Cr. 8vo. 6s.

Davies (Rev. J. Llewelyn)—
THE GOSPEL AND MODERN LIFE. 2nd Edition, to which is added Morality according to the Sacrament of the Lord's Supper. Extra fcap. 8vo. 6s.
SOCIAL QUESTIONS FROM THE POINT OF VIEW OF CHRISTIAN THEOLOGY. 2nd Edition. Crown 8vo. 6s.
WARNINGS AGAINST SUPERSTITION. Extra fcap. 8vo. 2s. 6d.
THE CHRISTIAN CALLING. Extra fcap. 8vo. 6s.
ORDER AND GROWTH AS INVOLVED IN THE SPIRITUAL CONSTITUTION OF HUMAN SOCIETY. Crown 8vo. 3s. 6d.

Davies (Rev. J. Llewelyn)—*continued.*
   BAPTISM, CONFIRMATION, AND THE LORD'S SUPPER, as interpreted by their Outward Signs. Three Addresses. New Edition. 18mo. 1s.
Diggle (Rev. J. W.)—GODLINESS AND MANLINESS. A Miscellany of Brief Papers touching the Relation of Religion to Life. Crown 8vo. 6s.
Drummond (Prof. James).—INTRODUCTION TO THE STUDY OF THEOLOGY. Crown 8vo. 5s.
ECCE HOMO. A Survey of the Life and Work of Jesus Christ. 20th Edition. Globe 8vo. 6s.
Ellerton (Rev. John).—THE HOLIEST MANHOOD, AND ITS LESSONS FOR BUSY LIVES. Crown 8vo. 6s.
FAITH AND CONDUCT: An Essay on Verifiable Religion. Crown 8vo. 7s. 6d.
Farrar (Ven. F. W., Archdeacon of Westminster)—
   THE HISTORY OF INTERPRETATION. Being the Bampton Lectures, 1885. 8vo. 16s.
   Collected Edition of the Sermons, etc. Crown 8vo. 3s. 6d. each.
   SEEKERS AFTER GOD.
   ETERNAL HOPE. Sermons Preached in Westminster Abbey.
   THE FALL OF MAN, and other Sermons.
   THE WITNESS OF HISTORY TO CHRIST. Hulsean Lectures.
   THE SILENCE AND VOICES OF GOD.
   IN THE DAYS OF THY YOUTH. Sermons on Practical Subjects.
   SAINTLY WORKERS. Five Lenten Lectures.
   EPHPHATHA: or, The Amelioration of the World.
   MERCY AND JUDGMENT. A few last words on Christian Eschatology.
   SERMONS AND ADDRESSES delivered in America.
Fiske (John).—MAN'S DESTINY VIEWED IN THE LIGHT OF HIS ORIGIN. Crown 8vo. 3s. 6d.
Forbes (Rev. Granville).—THE VOICE OF GOD IN THE PSALMS. Crown 8vo. 6s. 6d.
Fowle (Rev. T. W.)—A NEW ANALOGY BETWEEN REVEALED RELIGION AND THE COURSE AND CONSTITUTION OF NATURE. Crown 8vo. 6s.
Fraser (Bishop).—SERMONS. Edited by Rev. JOHN W. DIGGLE. 2 vols. Crown 8vo. 6s. each.
Hamilton (John)—
   ON TRUTH AND ERROR. Crown 8vo. 5s.
   ARTHUR'S SEAT: or, The Church of the Banned. Crown 8vo. 6s.
   ABOVE AND AROUND: Thoughts on God and Man. 12mo. 2s. 6d.
Hardwick (Archdeacon).—CHRIST AND OTHER MASTERS. 6th Edition. Crown 8vo. 10s. 6d.

Hare (Julius Charles)—
THE MISSION OF THE COMFORTER. New Edition. Edited by Dean PLUMPTRE. Crown 8vo. 7s. 6d.
THE VICTORY OF FAITH. Edited by Dean PLUMPTRE, with Introductory Notices by Prof. MAURICE and Dean STANLEY. Crown 8vo. 6s. 6d.

Harper (Father Thomas, S.J.)—THE METAPHYSICS OF THE SCHOOL. In 5 vols. Vols. I. and II. 8vo. 18s. each. Vol. III. Part I. 12s.

Harris (Rev. G. C.)—SERMONS. With a Memoir by CHARLOTTE M. YONGE, and Portrait. Extra fcap. 8vo. 6s.

Hutton (R. H.)—
ESSAYS ON SOME OF THE MODERN GUIDES OF ENGLISH THOUGHT IN MATTERS OF FAITH. Globe 8vo. 6s.
THEOLOGICAL ESSAYS. Globe 8vo. 6s.

Illingworth (Rev. J. R.)—SERMONS PREACHED IN A COLLEGE CHAPEL. Crown 8vo. 5s.
UNIVERSITY AND CATHEDRAL SERMONS. Crown 8vo. [*In the Press.*

Jacob (Rev. J. A.)—BUILDING IN SILENCE, and other Sermons. Extra fcap. 8vo. 6s.

James (Rev. Herbert).—THE COUNTRY CLERGYMAN AND HIS WORK. Crown 8vo. 6s.

Jeans (Rev. G. E.)—HAILEYBURY CHAPEL, and other Sermons. Fcap. 8vo. 3s. 6d.

Jellett (Rev. Dr.)—
THE ELDER SON, and other Sermons. Crown 8vo. 6s.
THE EFFICACY OF PRAYER. 3rd Edition. Crown 8vo. 5s.

Kellogg (Rev. S. H.)—THE LIGHT OF ASIA AND THE LIGHT OF THE WORLD. Crown 8vo. 7s. 6d.
THE GENESIS AND GROWTH OF RELIGION. Cr. 8vo. 6s.

Kingsley (Charles)—
VILLAGE AND TOWN AND COUNTRY SERMONS. Crown 8vo. 3s. 6d.
THE WATER OF LIFE, and other Sermons. Crown 8vo. 3s. 6d.
SERMONS ON NATIONAL SUBJECTS, AND THE KING OF THE EARTH. Crown 8vo. 3s. 6d.
SERMONS FOR THE TIMES. Crown 8vo. 3s. 6d.
GOOD NEWS OF GOD. Crown 8vo. 3s. 6d.
THE GOSPEL OF THE PENTATEUCH, AND DAVID. Crown 8vo. 3s. 6d.
DISCIPLINE, and other Sermons. Crown 8vo. 3s. 6d.
WESTMINSTER SERMONS. Crown 8vo. 3s. 6d.
ALL SAINTS' DAY, and other Sermons. Crown 8vo. 3s. 6d.

Kirkpatrick (Prof. A. F.)—THE DIVINE LIBRARY OF THE OLD TESTAMENT. Its Origin, Preservation, Inspiration, and Permanent Value. Crown 8vo. 3s. net.

Kirkpatrick (Prof. A. F.)—*continued.*
 THE DOCTRINE OF THE PROPHETS. Warburtonian Lectures 1886-1890. Crown 8vo. 6s.

Kynaston (Rev. Herbert, D.D.)—SERMONS PREACHED IN THE COLLEGE CHAPEL, CHELTENHAM. Crown 8vo. 6s.

Lightfoot (Bishop)—
 LEADERS IN THE NORTHERN CHURCH: Sermons Preached in the Diocese of Durham. 2nd Edition. Crown 8vo. 6s.
 ORDINATION ADDRESSES AND COUNSELS TO CLERGY. Crown 8vo. 6s.
 CAMBRIDGE SERMONS. Crown 8vo. 6s.
 SERMONS PREACHED IN ST. PAUL'S CATHEDRAL. Crown 8vo. 6s.
 SERMONS PREACHED ON SPECIAL OCCASIONS. Crown 8vo. 6s.
 A CHARGE DELIVERED TO THE CLERGY OF THE DIOCESE OF DURHAM, 25th Nov. 1886. Demy 8vo. 2s.
 ESSAYS ON THE WORK ENTITLED "Supernatural Religion." 8vo. 10s. 6d.
 DISSERTATIONS ON THE APOSTOLIC AGE. 8vo. 14s.
 BIBLICAL MISCELLANIES. 8vo. [*In the Press.*

Maclaren (Rev. Alexander)—
 SERMONS PREACHED AT MANCHESTER. 11th Edition. Fcap. 8vo. 4s. 6d.
 A SECOND SERIES OF SERMONS. 7th Ed. Fcap. 8vo. 4s. 6d.
 A THIRD SERIES. 6th Edition. Fcap. 8vo. 4s. 6d.
 WEEK-DAY EVENING ADDRESSES. 4th Ed. Fcap. 8vo. 2s. 6d.
 THE SECRET OF POWER, AND OTHER SERMONS. Fcap. 8vo. 4s. 6d.

Macmillan (Rev. Hugh)—
 BIBLE TEACHINGS IN NATURE. 15th Ed. Globe 8vo. 6s.
 THE TRUE VINE; OR, THE ANALOGIES OF OUR LORD'S ALLEGORY. 5th Edition. Globe 8vo. 6s.
 THE MINISTRY OF NATURE. 8th Edition. Globe 8vo. 6s.
 THE SABBATH OF THE FIELDS. 6th Edition. Globe 8vo. 6s.
 THE MARRIAGE IN CANA. Globe 8vo. 6s.
 TWO WORLDS ARE OURS. 3rd Edition. Globe 8vo. 6s.
 THE OLIVE LEAF. Globe 8vo. 6s.
 THE GATE BEAUTIFUL AND OTHER BIBLE TEACHINGS FOR THE YOUNG. Crown 8vo. 3s. 6d.

Mahaffy (Rev. Prof.)—THE DECAY OF MODERN PREACHING: AN ESSAY. Crown 8vo. 3s. 6d.

Maturin (Rev. W.)—THE BLESSEDNESS OF THE DEAD IN CHRIST. Crown 8vo. 7s. 6d.

Maurice (Frederick Denison)—
 THE KINGDOM OF CHRIST. 3rd Ed. 2 Vols. Cr. 8vo. 12s.
 EXPOSITORY SERMONS ON THE PRAYER-BOOK; AND ON THE LORD'S PRAYER. New Edition. Crown 8vo. 6s.

THEOLOGICAL CATALOGUE 15

Maurice (Frederick Denison)—*continued*.
SERMONS PREACHED IN COUNTRY CHURCHES. 2nd Edition. Crown 8vo. 6s.
THE CONSCIENCE. Lectures on Casuistry. 3rd Ed. Cr. 8vo. 4s. 6d.
DIALOGUES ON FAMILY WORSHIP. Crown 8vo. 4s. 6d.
THE DOCTRINE OF SACRIFICE DEDUCED FROM THE SCRIPTURES. 2nd Edition. Crown 8vo. 6s.
THE RELIGIONS OF THE WORLD. 6th Edition. Cr. 8vo. 4s. 6d.
ON THE SABBATH DAY; THE CHARACTER OF THE WARRIOR; AND ON THE INTERPRETATION OF HISTORY. Fcap. 8vo. 2s. 6d.
LEARNING AND WORKING. Crown 8vo. 4s. 6d.
THE LORD'S PRAYER, THE CREED, AND THE COMMANDMENTS. 18mo. 1s.
SERMONS PREACHED IN LINCOLN'S INN CHAPEL. In Six Volumes. Crown 8vo. 3s. 6d. each.

Collected Works. Monthly Volumes from October 1892. Crown 8vo. 3s. 6d. each.
CHRISTMAS DAY AND OTHER SERMONS.
THEOLOGICAL ESSAYS.
PROPHETS AND KINGS.
PATRIARCHS AND LAWGIVERS.
THE GOSPEL OF THE KINGDOM OF HEAVEN.
GOSPEL OF ST. JOHN.
EPISTLE OF ST. JOHN.
LECTURES ON THE APOCALYPSE.
FRIENDSHIP OF BOOKS.
SOCIAL MORALITY.
PRAYER BOOK AND LORD'S PRAYER.
THE DOCTRINE OF SACRIFICE.

Milligan (Rev. Prof. W.)—THE RESURRECTION OF OUR LORD. Fourth Thousand. Crown 8vo. 5s.
THE ASCENSION AND HEAVENLY PRIESTHOOD OF OUR LORD. *Baird Lectures*, 1891. Crown 8vo. 7s. 6d.

Moorhouse (J., Bishop of Manchester)—
JACOB: Three Sermons. Extra fcap. 8vo. 3s. 6d.
THE TEACHING OF CHRIST. Its Conditions, Secret, and Results. Crown 8vo. 3s. net.

Mylne (L. G., Bishop of Bombay).—SERMONS PREACHED IN ST. THOMAS'S CATHEDRAL, BOMBAY. Crown 8vo. 6s.
NATURAL RELIGION. By the author of "Ecce Homo." 3rd Edition. Globe 8vo. 6s.

Pattison (Mark).—SERMONS. Crown 8vo. 6s.
PAUL OF TARSUS. 8vo. 10s. 6d.
PHILOCHRISTUS. Memoirs of a Disciple of the Lord. 3rd Ed. 8vo. 12s.

Plumptre (Dean). — MOVEMENTS IN RELIGIOUS THOUGHT. Fcap. 8vo. 3s. 6d.

Potter (R.)—THE RELATION OF ETHICS TO RELIGION. Crown 8vo. 2s. 6d.

REASONABLE FAITH: A Short Religious Essay for the Times. By "Three Friends." Crown 8vo. 1s.

Reichel (C. P., Bishop of Meath)—
THE LORD'S PRAYER, and other Sermons. Crown 8vo. 7s. 6d.
CATHEDRAL AND UNIVERSITY SERMONS. Crown 8vo. 6s.

Rendall (Rev. F.)—THE THEOLOGY OF THE HEBREW CHRISTIANS. Crown 8vo. 5s.

Reynolds (H. R.)—NOTES OF THE CHRISTIAN LIFE. Crown 8vo. 7s. 6d.

Robinson (Prebendary H. G.)—MAN IN THE IMAGE OF GOD, and other Sermons. Crown 8vo. 7s. 6d.

Russell (Dean).—THE LIGHT THAT LIGHTETH EVERY MAN: Sermons. With an introduction by Dean PLUMPTRE, D.D. Crown 8vo. 6s.

Salmon (Rev. Prof. George)—
NON-MIRACULOUS CHRISTIANITY, and other Sermons. 2nd Edition. Crown 8vo. 6s.
GNOSTICISM AND AGNOSTICISM, and other Sermons. Crown 8vo. 7s. 6d.

Sandford (C. W., Bishop of Gibraltar).—COUNSEL TO ENGLISH CHURCHMEN ABROAD. Crown 8vo. 6s.

SCOTCH SERMONS, 1880. By Principal CAIRD and others. 3rd Edition. 8vo. 10s. 6d.

Service (Rev. John).—SERMONS. With Portrait. Crown 8vo. 6s.

Shirley (W. N.)—ELIJAH: Four University Sermons. Fcap. 8vo. 2s. 6d.

Smith (Rev. Travers).—MAN'S KNOWLEDGE OF MAN AND OF GOD. Crown 8vo. 6s.

Smith (W. Saumarez).—THE BLOOD OF THE NEW COVENANT: A Theological Essay. Crown 8vo. 2s. 6d.

Stanley (Dean)—
THE NATIONAL THANKSGIVING. Sermons preached in Westminster Abbey. 2nd Edition. Crown 8vo. 2s. 6d.
ADDRESSES AND SERMONS delivered during a visit to the United States and Canada in 1878. Crown 8vo. 6s.

Stewart (Prof. Balfour) and **Tait** (Prof. P. G.)—THE UNSEEN UNIVERSE; OR, PHYSICAL SPECULATIONS ON A FUTURE STATE. 15th Edition. Crown 8vo. 6s.
PARADOXICAL PHILOSOPHY: A Sequel to "The Unseen Universe." Crown 8vo. 7s. 6d.

Stubbs (Rev. C. W.)—FOR CHRIST AND CITY. Sermons and Addresses. Crown 8vo. 6s.

Tait (Archbishop)—
THE PRESENT POSITION OF THE CHURCH OF ENGLAND. Being the Charge delivered at his Primary Visitation. 8vo. 3s. 6d.
DUTIES OF THE CHURCH OF ENGLAND. Being seven Addresses delivered at his Second Visitation. 8vo. 4s. 6d.
THE CHURCH OF THE FUTURE. Charges delivered at his Third Quadrennial Visitation. 2nd Edition. Crown 8vo. 3s. 6d.

Taylor (Isaac).—THE RESTORATION OF BELIEF. Crown 8vo. 8s. 6d.

Temple (Frederick, Bishop of London)—
SERMONS PREACHED IN THE CHAPEL OF RUGBY SCHOOL. SECOND SERIES. 3rd Edition. Extra fcap. 8vo. 6s.
THIRD SERIES. 4th Edition. Extra fcap. 8vo. 6s.
THE RELATIONS BETWEEN RELIGION AND SCIENCE. Bampton Lectures, 1884. 7th and Cheaper Ed. Cr. 8vo. 6s.

Trench (Archbishop).—HULSEAN LECTURES. 8vo. 7s. 6d.

Tulloch (Principal).—THE CHRIST OF THE GOSPELS AND THE CHRIST OF MODERN CRITICISM. Extra fcap. 8vo. 4s. 6d.

Vaughan (C. J., Dean of Llandaff)—
MEMORIALS OF HARROW SUNDAYS. 5th Edition. Crown 8vo. 10s. 6d.
EPIPHANY, LENT, AND EASTER. 3rd Ed. Cr. 8vo. 10s. 6d.
HEROES OF FAITH. 2nd Edition. Crown 8vo. 6s.
LIFE'S WORK AND GOD'S DISCIPLINE. 3rd Edition. Extra fcap. 8vo. 2s. 6d.
THE WHOLESOME WORDS OF JESUS CHRIST. 2nd Edition. Fcap. 8vo. 3s. 6d.
FOES OF FAITH. 2nd Edition. Fcap. 8vo. 3s. 6d.
CHRIST SATISFYING THE INSTINCTS OF HUMANITY. 2nd Edition. Extra fcap. 8vo. 3s. 6d.
COUNSELS FOR YOUNG STUDENTS. Fcap. 8vo. 2s. 6d.
THE TWO GREAT TEMPTATIONS. 2nd Ed. Fcap. 8vo. 3s. 6d.
ADDRESSES FOR YOUNG CLERGYMEN. Extra fcap. 8vo. 4s. 6d.
"MY SON, GIVE ME THINE HEART." Extra fcap. 8vo. 5s.
REST AWHILE. Addresses to Toilers in the Ministry. Extra fcap. 8vo. 5s.
TEMPLE SERMONS. Crown 8vo. 10s. 6d.
AUTHORISED OR REVISED? Sermons on some of the Texts in which the Revised Version differs from the Authorised. Crown 8vo. 7s. 6d.
LESSONS OF THE CROSS AND PASSION. WORDS FROM THE CROSS. THE REIGN OF SIN. THE LORD'S PRAYER. Four Courses of Lent Lectures. Crown 8vo. 10s. 6d.
UNIVERSITY SERMONS. NEW AND OLD. Cr. 8vo. 10s. 6d.

Vaughan (C. J., Dean of Llandaff)—*continued.*
 NOTES FOR LECTURES ON CONFIRMATION. Fcap. 8vo. 1s. 6d.
 THE PRAYERS OF JESUS CHRIST: a closing volume of Lent Lectures delivered in the Temple Church. Globe 8vo. 3s. 6d.
 DONCASTER SERMONS. Lessons of Life and Godliness, and Words from the Gospels. Cr. 8vo. 10s. 6d.
 RESTFUL THOUGHTS IN RESTLESS TIMES. Crown 8vo.
 [In the Press.

Vaughan (Rev. D. J.)—THE PRESENT TRIAL OF FAITH. Crown 8vo. 9s.

Vaughan (Rev. E. T.)—SOME REASONS OF OUR CHRISTIAN HOPE. Hulsean Lectures for 1875. Crown 8vo. 6s. 6d.

Vaughan (Rev. Robert).—STONES FROM THE QUARRY. Sermons. Crown 8vo. 5s.

Venn (Rev. John).—ON SOME CHARACTERISTICS OF BELIEF, SCIENTIFIC AND RELIGIOUS. 8vo. 6s. 6d.

Warington (G.)—THE WEEK OF CREATION. Cr. 8vo. 4s. 6d.

Welldon (Rev. J. E. C.)—THE SPIRITUAL LIFE, and other Sermons. Crown 8vo. 6s.

Westcott (B. F., Bishop of Durham)—
 ON THE RELIGIOUS OFFICE OF THE UNIVERSITIES. Sermons. Crown 8vo. 4s. 6d.
 GIFTS FOR MINISTRY. Addresses to Candidates for Ordination. Crown 8vo. 1s. 6d.
 THE VICTORY OF THE CROSS. Sermons preached during Holy Week, 1888, in Hereford Cathedral. Crown 8vo. 3s. 6d.
 FROM STRENGTH TO STRENGTH. Three Sermons (In Memoriam J. B. D.) Crown 8vo. 2s.
 THE REVELATION OF THE RISEN LORD. Cr. 8vo. 6s.
 THE HISTORIC FAITH. 3rd Edition. Crown 8vo. 6s.
 THE GOSPEL OF THE RESURRECTION. 6th Ed. Cr. 8vo. 6s.
 THE REVELATION OF THE FATHER. Crown 8vo. 6s.
 CHRISTUS CONSUMMATOR. 2nd Edition. Crown 8vo. 6s.
 SOME THOUGHTS FROM THE ORDINAL. Cr. 8vo. 1s. 6d.
 SOCIAL ASPECTS OF CHRISTIANITY. Crown 8vo. 6s.
 ESSAYS IN THE HISTORY OF RELIGIOUS THOUGHT IN THE WEST. Globe 8vo. 6s.
 THE GOSPEL OF LIFE. Cr. 8vo. 6s.

Wickham (Rev. E. C.)—WELLINGTON COLLEGE SERMONS. Crown 8vo. 6s.

Wilkins (Prof. A. S.)—THE LIGHT OF THE WORLD: an Essay. 2nd Edition. Crown 8vo. 3s. 6d.

Wilson (J. M., Archdeacon of Manchester)—
 SERMONS PREACHED IN CLIFTON COLLEGE CHAPEL. Second Series. 1888-90. Crown 8vo. 6s.
 ESSAYS AND ADDRESSES. Crown 8vo. 4s. 6d.
 SOME CONTRIBUTIONS TO THE RELIGIOUS THOUGHT OF OUR TIME. Crown 8vo. 6s.

www.ingramcontent.com/pod-product-compliance
Lightning Source LLC
Chambersburg PA
CBHW030358230426
43664CB00007BB/647